LIBERALISM AND THE SOCIAL PROBLEM

A COLLECTION OF EARLY SPEECHES AS A MEMBER OF PARLIAMENT

Winston Spencer Churchill

ARC
MANOR
Rockville, MD
2007

Originally published by Hodder & Stoughton, London, as *Liberalism and the Social Problem* by **Winston Spencer Churchill**, 1909. This edition of *Liberalism and the Social Problem: A Collection of Early Speeches as a Member of Parliament*, in its current format, copyright © Arc Manor 2007. This book, in whole or in part, may not be copied or reproduced in its current format by any means, electronic, mechanical or otherwise without the permission of the publisher.

The Original text has been reformatted for clarity and to fit this edition.

Arc Manor, Arc Manor Classic Reprints and the Arc Manor logo are trademarks or registered trademarks of Arc Manor Publishers, Rockville, Maryland. All other trademarks are properties of their respective owners.

ISBN-10: 0-9786536-4-5

ISBN-13: 978-0-9786536-4-4

Library of Congress Cataloging-in-Publication Data

Churchill, Winston, Sir, 1874-1965.
  Liberalism and the social problem : a collection of early speeches as a member of Parliament / by Winston Spencer Churchill.
     p. cm.
  "Originally published as 'Liberalism and the social problem' by Winston Spencer Churchill by Hodder & Stoughton, London, 1909."
  ISBN 978-0-9786536-4-4 (perfect bound : alk. paper)
  1. Great Britain--Politics and government--1901-1910. 2. Working class--Great Britain. 3. Taxation--Great Britain. 4. Finance, Public--Great Britain--History--1815-1918. I. Title.

  JN231.C48 2007
  361.6'10941--dc22
                              2006102313

ARC
MANOR
2007

P. O. Box 10339
Rockville, MD 20849-0339
United States of America

TABLE OF CONTENTS

PREFACE

*T*hese are the principal speeches I have made within the last four years. They have been chosen and collected with the idea of presenting a consistent and simultaneous view of the general field of British politics in an hour of fateful decision. I have exercised full freedom in compression and in verbal correction necessary to make them easier to read. Facts and figures have been, where necessary, revised, ephemeral matter eliminated, and epithets here and there reconsidered. But opinions and arguments are unaltered; they are hereby confirmed, and I press them earnestly and insistently upon the public.

We approach what is not merely a party crisis but a national climacteric. Never did a great people enter upon a period of trial and choice with more sincere and disinterested desire to know the truth and to do justice in their generation. I believe they will succeed.

WINSTON S. CHURCHILL.

33 ECCLESTON SQUARE.

OCTOBER 26, 1909.

INTRODUCTION

$\mathcal{T}$he series of speeches included in this volume ranges, in point of time, from the earlier months of Sir Henry Campbell-Bannerman's Government to the latest phase in the fortunes of Mr. Asquith's succeeding Ministry, and forms an argumentative defence of the basis of policy common to both Administrations. The addresses it contains deal with nearly all the great political topics of the last four years--with Free Trade, Colonial Preferences, the South African settlement, the latest and probably the final charter of trade unionism, the Miners' Bill, the measures for establishing Trade Boards and Labour Exchanges, the schemes of compulsory and voluntary assurance, and the Budget. They possess the further characteristic of describing and commending these proposals as "interdependent" parts of a large and fruitful plan of Liberal statesmanship. Of this scheme the Budget is at once the foundation and the most powerful and attractive feature. If it prospers, the social policy for which it provides prospers too. If it fails, the policy falls to the ground.

The material of these speeches is therefore of great importance to the future of democracy in this country. Let me say a word as to their authorship. To a friendly critic they appear to present not only rare and highly trained qualities of statement and persuasion, but a unity and sincerity of thought which give them a place above mere party dialectics. Mr. Churchill's distinguished service to Liberalism has not been long in point of years, but it opened with the first speeches he ever delivered in the House of Commons. No competent observers of political activities, and of the characters and temperaments which direct them, can have doubted from the first moment of Mr. Churchill's appearance on the stage where his moral and intellectual sympathies lay and whither they would lead him. It is a true and, indeed, an obvious comment on his career to say that

3

he began where his father left off--as a Democrat and a Free Trader, and that on these inherited instincts and tendencies he has built what both his friends and his enemies expected him to build. Mr. Churchill came to Liberalism from the same fold as Gladstone, and for the same reason--that it presented the one field of work open to a political talent of a high stamp, and to a wide and eager outlook on the future of our social order. Liberalism and Mr. Churchill have both had good reason to congratulate themselves on that choice, and the party which failed to draw him into a disastrous and reactionary change of view has no reason to resent it. Before he became a Liberal Mr. Churchill had taken the broad views of the South African problem that his father's later opinions commended to him, and he was properly chosen to expound to the House of Commons the plan of self-government that embodied them.

If, therefore, the political groundwork of these speeches is sound Liberal principle, their meaning and purpose, taken in connection with the Budget, and the industrial reforms for which it provides, signify a notable advance into places where the thinkers, the pioneers, the men in the advanced trenches, are accustomed to dwell. Let us acknowledge, with a sense of pleasure and relief, that this is new territory. New, that is to say, for this country; not new to the best organisations of industrial society that we know of. New as a clearly seen vision and a connected plan of British, statesmanship; not new as actual experiment in legislation, and as theory held by progressive thinkers of many schools, including some of the fathers of modern Liberal doctrine, and most of our economists. What is there in these pages repugnant to writers of the type of John Mill, Jevons, and Marshall? How much of them would even be repelled by Cobden? In the main they preach a gospel--that of national "efficiency"--common to all reformers, and accepted by Bismarck, the modern archetype of "Empire-makers," as necessary to the consolidation of the great German nation. An average Australian or Canadian statesman would read them through with almost complete approval of every passage, save only their defence of Free Trade. Nay more; the apology for property which they put forward--that it must be "associated in the minds of the mass of the people with ideas of justice and reason"--is that on which the friends of true conservatism build when they think of the evils of modern civilisation and the great and continuous efforts necessary to repair them. Who does not conclude, with Mr. Churchill, that "a more scientific, a more elaborate, a more comprehensive social organisation" is indispensable to our country if it is to continue its march to greatness? Back or forward we must go.

Mr. Churchill, indeed, has thought it wise to raise the specific point at which, in the process of seeking a finer use and adaptation of the human material which forms society, the progressive and reforming statesman parts company with the dogmatic Socialist. There is no need to labour a distinction which arises from the nature and the activities of the two forces. British Liberalism is both a mental habit and a method of politics. Through both these characteristics it is bound to criticise a State so long as in any degree it rests on the principles of "Penguin Island"--"respect for the rich and contempt for the poor," and to modify or repeal the rights of property where they clearly conflict with human rights. But its idealism and its practical responsibilities forbid it to accept the elimination of private enterprise and the assumption by the State of all the instruments of production and distribution. Socialism has great power of emotional and even religious appeal, of which it would be wise for Liberalism to take account, and it is, on the whole, a beneficent force in society. But as pure dogma it fits the spirit of man no more exactly than the Shorter Catechism. As Mr. Churchill well says, both the collectivist and the individualist principles have deep roots in human life, and the statesman can ignore neither.

In the main, therefore, these speeches, with all their fresh brilliancy of colouring and treatment, hold up the good old banner of social progress, which we erect against reactionist and revolutionist alike. The "old Liberal" will find the case for Free Trade, for peace, for representative government, stated as powerfully and convincingly as he could wish. Their actual newness consists in the fact that not only do they open up to Liberalism what it always wants--a wide domain of congenial thought and energy, but they offer it two propositions which it can reject only at its peril. The first is that there can and must be a deep, sharp abridgment of the sphere of industrial life which has been marked out as hopeless, or as an inevitable part of the social system.

Here the new Liberalism parts with _laissez-faire_, and those who defend it. It assumes that the State must take in hand the problems of industrial insecurity and unemployment, and must solve them. The issue is vital. Protection has already made its bid. It will assure the workman what is in his mind more than cheap food--namely, secure wages; it affects to give him all his life, or nearly all his life, a market for his labour so wide and so steady that the fear of forced idleness will almost be banished from it. The promise is false. Protection by itself has in no country annulled or seriously qualified unemployment. But the need to which it appeals is absolutely real; for the modern State it is a problem of the Sphinx, neither to be shirked nor wrongly answered. And the alternative remedy offered in these pages has already, as their author abundantly shows, succeeded even in the very partial forms in which it has been applied. The labour market can be steadied and equalised over a great industrial field. Part of its surplus can be provided for. What Mr. Churchill calls "diseased industries" can be cut off from the main body, or restored to some measure of health. The State can set up a minimum standard of health and wage, below which it will not allow its citizens to sink; it can step in and dispense employment and restorative force under strictly specified conditions, to a small body of more or less "sick" workers; it can supply security for a far greater, less dependent, and more efficient mass of labourers, in recurring crises of accident, sickness, invalidity, and unemployment, and can do so with every hope of enlisting in its service voluntary forces and individual virtues of great value.

This is not a problem of "relief," it is a method of humanity, and its aim is not merely to increase the mechanical force of the State, but to raise the average of character, of _morale_, in its citizens. Nor do these speeches represent only a batch of platform promises. The great scheme of social betterment preached in these pages is already embodied in half a dozen Acts of Parliament, with corresponding organisations in the Board of Trade and elsewhere; and if the Budget passes, the crown can be put upon them next year or the year after by measures of insurance against invalidity and unemployment.

Mr. Churchill's second proposition is the correlative of the first. How shall this imposing fabric of industrial security be reared and made safe? The answer is, by modifying, without vitally changing, the basis of taxation. The workman cannot be asked to pay for everything, as under Protection he must pay. In any case, he must pay for something. But if he is asked for too much, the sources of physical efficiency are drained, and the main purpose of the new Liberalism--the ideal of an educated, hopeful, and vigorous people--is destroyed. Now Liberalism, in ceasing to rely on indirect taxation as its main source of revenue, has opened up for contribution not merely the superfluities of society, the "accumulations of profit," as Mr. Churchill calls them, but those special forms of wealth which are "social" in origin, which depend on some monopoly of material agents, on means not of helping the community but of hindering it, not of enriching its powers and resources, but of depleting them for private advantage. In other words, the State in future will increasingly ask the taxpayer not only "What have you got?" but "How did you get it?" No one contends that such an analysis can be perfect; but, on the other hand, can a community desirous of realising what Goethe calls "practical Christianity," ignore it? And if in this process it enters the sphere of morals, as Ruskin long ago urged it to do, as well as the path of economic justice, is the step a wrong one? Has it not already been taken not only in this Budget, but in its predecessor, in which the Prime Minister made the memorable distinction between earned and unearned income? Those who answer these questions in the Liberal sense will find in these speeches a body of vigorous and persuasive reasoning on their side.

6

It is therefore the main purpose of these speeches to show that Liberalism has a message of the utmost consequence to our times. They link it afresh with the movement of life, which when it overtakes parties condemns and destroys them. They give it an immediate mission and an outlook on the wider moral domain, which belongs to no single generation. This double character is vital to a Party which must not desert the larger ways in which the spirit of man walks, while it quits at its peril the work of practical, everyday service to existing society.

A word as to the literary quality of these addresses, widely varied as they are in subject. The summit of a man's powers--his full capacity of reason, comparison, expression--are not usually reached at so early a point in his career as that which Mr. Churchill has attained. But in directness and clearness of thought, in the power to build up a political theory, and present it as an impressive and convincing argument, in the force of rhetoric and the power of sympathy, readers of these addresses will find few examples of modern English speech-making to compare with them. They revive the almost forgotten art of oratory, and they connect it with ideas born of our age, and springing from its conscience and its practical needs, and, above all, essential to its happiness.

H.W. MASSINGHAM.

I - THE RECORD OF THE GOVERNMENT

THE CONCILIATION OF SOUTH AFRICA

THE TRANSVAAL CONSTITUTION

THE ORANGE FREE STATE CONSTITUTION

LIBERALISM AND SOCIALISM

IMPERIAL PREFERENCE—I

IMPERIAL PREFERENCE—II

THE HOUSE OF LORDS

THE DUNDEE ELECTION

THE CONCILIATION OF SOUTH AFRICA
HOUSE OF COMMONS, *APRIL 5, 1906*

We have travelled a long way since this Parliament assembled, in the discussion of the Transvaal and Orange River Colony Constitutions. When the change of Government took place Mr. Lyttelton's Constitution was before us. That instrument provided for representative and not responsible government. Under that Constitution the election would have been held in March of this year, and the Assembly would have met in June, if the home Government had not changed. But just at the time that the Government changed in December two questions arose—the question of whether or not soldiers of the British Army in garrison should be allowed to vote; and the question whether it would not be better to have sixty constituencies instead of thirty; and, as both questions involved necessary alterations in the Letters Patent, the time was ripe, quite apart from any difference which the change of the men at the helm might make, for a reconsideration and review of the whole form of the government which was to be given to the two Colonies.

The objection that must most readily occur in considering Mr. Lyttelton's Constitution is that it was unworkable. It proposed that there should be from six to nine nominated Ministers in an Assembly of thirty-five, afterwards to be increased to sixty elective members. The position of a Minister is one of considerable difficulty. He often has to defend rather an awkward case. When favourable facts are wanting he has to depend upon the nimbleness of his wits, and, when these fail him, he has to fall back upon the loyalty of his supporters. But no Minister can move very far upon his road with satisfaction or success if he has not behind him either a nominated majority or an organised Party majority. Mr. Lyttelton's Ministers had neither. They would have been alone, hopelessly outnumbered in an Assembly, the greater part of which was avowedly in favour of responsible and not of representative government. These Ministers, with one exception, had no previous Parliamentary experience and no ascertained Parliamentary ability. They would have been forced to carry their Bills and their Estimates through an Assembly in the main opposed to them. All this time, while we should have given to these Ministers this serious duty, we should ourselves have had to bear the whole responsibility in this country for everything that was done under their authority; and their authority could only be exerted through an Assembly which, as things stood, they could not control.

The Committee can easily imagine the telegrams and the questions which would have been addressed from Downing Street and the House of Commons to these Ministers on native matters, on the question of the administration of the Chinese Ordinance, on all the numerous intricate questions with which we are at the present moment involved in South Africa. And what would have been the position of these Ministers, faced with these embarrassments in a hostile Assembly in which they had few friends—what possibility would they have had of maintaining themselves in such an Assembly? Is it not certain that they would have broken down under the strain to which they would have been exposed, that the Assembly would have been infuriated, that Parties differing from each other on every conceivable question, divided from each other by race and religion and language, would have united in common hatred of the interference of the outside Power and the government of bureaucrats. Then we should very speedily have got to the bottom of the hill. There would have been a swift transition. The Legislative Assembly would have converted itself into a constituent Assembly, and it would have taken by force all that the Government now have it in their power to concede with grace, distinction, and authority. On these grounds his Majesty's Government came to the conclusion that it would be right to omit the stage of representative government altogether and to go directly to the stage of responsible government.

It is the same in politics as it is in war. When one crest line has been left, it is necessary to go to the next. To halt half-way in the valley between is to court swift and certain destruction, and the moment you have abandoned the safe position of a Crown Colony government, or government with an adequate nominated majority, there is no stopping-place whatever on which you may rest the sole of your foot, until you come to a responsible Legislative Assembly with an executive obeying that Assembly. These arguments convinced his Majesty's Government that it would be necessary to annul the Letters Patent issued on March 31, 1905, and make an end of the Lyttelton Constitution. That Constitution now passes away into the never-never land, into a sort of chilly limbo that is reserved for the disowned or abortive political progeny of many distinguished men.

The Government, and those who support them, may rejoice that we have been able to take this first most important step in our South African policy with such a very general measure of agreement, with, indeed, a consensus of opinion which almost amounts to unanimity. Both races, every Party, every class, every section in South Africa have agreed in the course which his Majesty's Government have adopted in abandoning representative government and going at once to responsible government. That is already a very great thing, but it was not always so. Those who sat in the last Parliament will remember that it was not always so. We remember that Lord Milner was entirely opposed to granting responsible government. We know that Mr. Lyttelton wrote pages and pages in the Blue Book of last year proving how futile and dangerous responsible government would be; and the right hon. Member for West Birmingham, who took the Government decision as a matter of course on the first day of the present session, made a speech last session in which he indicated in terms of great gravity and force, that he thought it was wholly premature to grant responsible government to the Transvaal. But all that is abandoned now. I heard the right hon. Member for West Birmingham, in the name of the Party opposite, accept the policy of his Majesty's Government. I heard the hon. Member for Blackpool this afternoon say that he hoped that responsible government would be given to the Transvaal at the earliest possible moment. In regard to the Orange River Colony, it is quite true that the official Opposition, so far as I gather their view, think that it should be delayed, and should not be given at the same time as to the Transvaal; but that is not the view of the right hon. Member for West Birmingham. Speaking in the House of Commons on July 27, 1905, the right hon. gentleman said:

"Objection has also been taken that the same government which is now being given to the Transvaal has not been given to the Orange River Colony. I think that the experiment might have been far better tried in the Orange River Colony. It is quite true that in that Colony there is an enormous majority of the Dutch or Boer population. But they have shown by long experience that they are most capable and moderate administrators—under the admirable rule of President Brand they set an example to the whole of South Africa; and although I think there is some danger in this experiment, it is in the Orange River Colony that I myself would have been inclined, in the first instance, to take the risk."

It is true the right hon. gentleman was speaking of representative government; but it cannot be disputed that if an advance were to be made in associating the people of the conquered Colonies with the government of those Colonies, the right hon. gentleman thought that it had better be in the Orange River Colony first. But at any rate now it is incontestable that there is no Party in this country or in the Transvaal that opposes the grant of responsible government to the Transvaal. That is a great advance, and shows that we have been able to take our first step with the approbation of all concerned.

But the Opposition, having abandoned their resistance to the grant of responsible government, now contend that on no account must the basis of the Lyttelton Constitution be departed from. I am not convinced by that argument. The Government are to pursue a new purpose, but to adhere to the old framework. We are to cut off the head of the Lyttelton Constitution, but are to preserve the old trunk and graft a new head on it. I do not believe that any Government, approaching this question from a new point of view, uncompromised and unfettered, would be bound by the framework and details of the Lyttelton Constitution. It may be that that Constitution contains many excellent principles, but the Government have a right to consider things from the beginning, freshly and freely, to make their own plans in accordance with their own ideas, and to present those plans for the acceptance of the House.

The noble lord the Member for South Birmingham spoke of the principle of "one vote, one value," which was embodied in the Lyttelton Constitution. The principle of "one vote, one value" is in itself an orthodox and unimpeachable principle of democracy. It is a logical, numerical principle. If the attempt be made to discriminate between man and man because one has more children and lives in the country, it would be arguable that we should discriminate because another man has more brains or more money, or lives in the town, or for any other of the many reasons that differentiate one human being from another. The only safe principle, I think, is that for electoral purposes all men are equal, and that voting power, as far as possible, should be evenly distributed among them.

In the Transvaal the principle of "one vote, one value" can be made operative only upon a basis of voters. In nearly every other country in the world, population is the usual basis of distribution, for population is the same as electorate and electorate the same as population. On both bases the distribution of the constituencies would be the same. There is, for instance, no part of this country which is more married, or more celibate, or more prolific than any other part. It is only in the Transvaal, this country of afflicting dualities and of curious contradictions, where everything is twisted, disturbed, and abnormal, that there is a great disparity between the distribution of seats on the basis of voters and on the basis of population. The high price of provisions in the towns restricts the growth of urban population, and the dullness of the country districts appears to be favourable to the growth of large families. It is a scientific and unimpeachable fact that, if you desire to apply the principle of "one vote, one value" to the Constitution of the Transvaal, that principle can best be attained—I am not sure that it cannot only be attained—on the basis of voters, and that is the basis Mr. Lyttelton took in the Constitution he formed.

But Mr. Lyttelton's plan did not stop there. Side by side with this basis of voters, he had an artificial franchise of £100 annual value. That is a very much lower qualification in South Africa, than it would be in this country, and I do not think that the franchise which Mr. Lyttelton proposed could be called an undemocratic franchise, albeit that it was an artificial franchise, because it yielded 89,000 voters out of a population of 300,000, and that is a much more fertile franchise, even after making allowance for the abnormal conditions of a new country, than we have in this country or than is the case in some American and European States. So that I do not accuse Mr. Lyttelton of having formulated an undemocratic franchise, but taking these two points together—the unusual basis of distribution with the apparently artificial franchise—acting and reacting, as they must have done, one upon the other—there was sufficient ground to favour the suspicion, at any rate, that something was intended in the nature of a dodge, in the nature of a trick, artificially to depress the balance in one direction and to tilt it in the other.

In dealing with nationalities, nothing is more fatal than a dodge. Wrongs will be forgiven, sufferings and losses will be forgiven or forgotten, battles will be remembered only as they recall the martial virtues of the combatants; but anything like chicane, anything like a trick, will always rankle. The Government are concerned in South Africa not only to do what is fair, but to do what South Africa will accept as fair. They are concerned not merely to choose a balance which will deal evenly between the races, but one which will secure the acceptance of both races.

We meet unjust charges in good heart. The permanence and security of British sovereignty in South Africa is not a matter of indifference to his Majesty's Ministers. Surely no honourable Member believes that we could wish to cheat the British race in the Transvaal of any numerical preponderance which may properly belong to them. Equally with our political opponents we desire to see the maintenance of British supremacy in South Africa. But we seek to secure it by a different method. There is a profound difference between the schools of thought which exist upon South African politics in this House. We think that British authority in South Africa has got to stand on two legs. You have laboured for ten years to make it stand on one. We on this side know that if British dominion is to endure in South Africa it must endure with the assent of the Dutch, as well as of the British. We think that the position of the Crown in South Africa, and let me add the position of Agents and Ministers of the Crown in South Africa, should be just as much above and remote from racial feuds, as the position of the Crown in this country is above our Party politics. We do not seek to pit one race against the other in the hope of profiting from the quarrel. We hope to build upon the reconciliation and not upon the rivalry of races. We hope that it may be our fortune so to dispose of affairs that these two valiant, strong races may dwell together side by side in peace and amity under the shelter of an equal flag.

THE TRANSVAAL CONSTITUTION

HOUSE OF COMMONS, *JULY 31, 1906*

*J*t is my duty this afternoon, on behalf of the Government, to lay before the Committee the outline and character of the constitutional settlement which we have in contemplation in regard to the lately annexed Colonies in South Africa. This is, I suppose, upon the whole, the most considerable business with which this new Parliament has had to deal. But although no one will deny its importance, or undervalue the keen emotions and anxieties which it excites on both sides of the House, and the solemn memories which it revives, yet I am persuaded that there is no reason why we should be hotly, sharply, or bitterly divided on the subject; on the contrary, I think its very importance makes it incumbent on all who participate in the discussion—and I will certainly be bound by my own precept—to cultivate and observe a studious avoidance of anything likely to excite the ordinary recriminations and rejoinders of Party politics and partisanship.

After all, there is no real difference of principle between the two great historic Parties on this question. The late Government have repeatedly declared that it was their intention at the earliest possible moment—laying great stress upon that phrase—to extend representative and responsible institutions to the new Colonies; and before his Majesty's present advisers took office the only question in dispute was, When? On the debate on the Address, the right hon. Member for West Birmingham—whose absence to-day and its cause I am quite sure are equally regretted in all parts of the House—spoke on this question with his customary breadth of view and courage of thought. He said: "The responsibility for this decision lies with the Government now in power. They have more knowledge than we have; and if they consider it safe to give this large grant, and if they

17

turn out to be right, no one will be better pleased than we. I do not think that, although important, this change should be described as a change in colonial policy, but as continuity of colonial policy."

If, then, we are agreed upon the principle, I do not think that serious or vital differences can arise upon the method. Because, after all, no one can contend that it is right to extend responsible government, but not right to extend it fairly. No one can contend that it is right to grant the forms of free institutions, and yet to preserve by some device the means of control. And so I should hope that we may proceed in this debate without any acute divergences becoming revealed.

I am in a position to-day only to announce the decision to which the Government have come with respect to the Transvaal. The case of the Transvaal is urgent. It is the nerve-centre of South Africa. It is the arena in which all questions of South African politics—social, moral, racial, and economic—are fought out; and this new country, so lately reclaimed from the wilderness, with a white population of less than 300,000 souls, already reproduces in perfect miniature all those dark, tangled, and conflicting problems usually to be found in populous and old-established European States. The case of the Transvaal differs fundamentally from the case of the Orange River Colony. The latter has been in the past, and will be again in the future, a tranquil agricultural State, pursuing under a wise and tolerant Government a happy destiny of its own. All I have to say about the Orange River Colony this afternoon is this—that there will be no unnecessary delay in the granting of a Constitution; and that in the granting of that Constitution we shall be animated only by a desire to secure a fair representation of all classes of inhabitants in the country, and to give effective expression to the will of the majority.

When we came into office, we found a Constitution already prepared for the Transvaal by the right hon. Member for St. George's, Hanover Square.[1] That Constitution is no more. I hope the right hon. gentleman will not suspect me of any malevolence towards his offspring. I would have nourished and fostered it with a tender care; but life was already extinct. It had ceased to breathe even before it was born; but I trust the right hon. gentleman will console himself by remembering that there are many possibilities of constitutional settlements lying before him in the future. After all, the Abbé Sieyès, when the Constitution of 1791 was broken into pieces, was very little younger than the right hon. gentleman, and he had time to make and survive two new Constitutions.

Frankly, what I may, for brevity's sake, call the Lyttelton Constitution was utterly unworkable. It surrendered the machinery of power; it preserved the whole burden of responsibility and administration. Nine official gentlemen, nearly all without Parliamentary experience, and

---

[1]   Mr. Lyttelton had meanwhile been elected for that Constituency.

I daresay without Parliamentary aptitudes, without the support of that nominated majority which I am quite convinced that the right hon. Member for West Birmingham had always contemplated in any scheme of representative government, and without the support of an organised party, were to be placed in a Chamber of thirty-five elected members who possessed the power of the purse. The Boers would either have abstained altogether from participating in that Constitution, or they would have gone in only for the purpose of wrecking it. The British party was split into two sections, and one section, the Responsibles, made public declarations of their intention to bring about a constitutional deadlock by obstruction and refusing supplies, and all the other apparatus of Parliamentary discontent. In fact, the Constitution of the right hon. gentleman seemed bound inevitably to conjure up that nightmare of all modern politicians, government resting on consent, and consent not forthcoming.

As I told the House in May, his Majesty's Government thought it their duty to review the whole question. We thought it our duty and our right to start fair, free, and untrammelled, and we have treated the Lyttelton Constitution as if it had never been. One guiding principle has animated his Majesty's Government in their policy—to make no difference in this grant of responsible government between Boer and Briton in South Africa. We propose to extend to both races the fullest privileges and rights of British citizenship; and we intend to make no discrimination in the grant of that great boon, between the men who have fought most loyally for us and those who have resisted the British arms with the most desperate courage. By the Treaty of Vereeniging, in which the peace between the Dutch and British races was declared for ever, by Article 1 of that treaty the flower of the Boer nation and its most renowned leaders recognised the lawful authority of his Majesty King Edward VII, and henceforth, from that moment, British supremacy in South Africa stood on the sure foundations of military honour and warlike achievement.

This decision in favour of even-handed dealing arises from no ingratitude on our part towards those who have nobly sustained the British cause in years gone by. It involves no injustice to the British population of the Transvaal. We have been careful at each point of this constitutional settlement to secure for the British every advantage that they may justly claim. But the future of South Africa, and, I will add, its permanent inclusion in the British Empire, demand that the King should be equally Sovereign of both races, and that both races should learn to look upon this country as their friend.

When I last spoke in this House on the question of the South African Constitution, I took occasion to affirm the excellence of the general principle, one vote one value. I pointed out that it was a logical and unimpeachable principle to act upon; that the only safe rule for doing justice electorally between man and man was to assume—a large assumption in some cases—that all men are equal and that all discriminations between them are unhealthy and undemocratic. Now the principle of one vote one value can be applied and realised in this country, either upon the basis of population, or upon the basis of voters. It makes no difference which is selected; for there is no part of this country which is more married, or more prolific than another, and exactly the same distribution and exactly the same number of members would result whether the voters or the population basis were taken in a Redistribution Bill. But in South Africa the disparity of conditions between the new population and the old makes a very great difference between the urban and the rural populations, and it is undoubtedly true that if it be desired to preserve the principle of one vote one value, it is the voters' basis and not the population basis that must be taken in the Transvaal—and that is the basis which his Majesty's Government have determined to adopt.

The right hon. gentleman the Member for St. George's, Hanover Square, had proposed to establish a franchise qualification of £100 annual value. That is not nearly such a high property-qualification as it would be in this country. I do not quarrel with the right hon. gentleman's Constitution on the ground that his franchise was not perfectly fair, or not a perfectly *bonâ fide* and generous measure of representation. But it is undoubtedly true that a property-qualification of £100 annual value told more severely against the Boers than against the British, because living in the towns is so expensive that almost everybody who lives in the towns, and who is not utterly destitute, has a property-qualification of £100 annual value. But in the country districts there are numbers of men, very poor but perfectly respectable and worthy citizens—day labourers, farmers' sons, and others—who would not have that qualification, and who consequently would have been excluded by the property-qualification, low as it is having regard to the conditions in South Africa. Quite apart from South African questions and affairs, his Majesty's Government profess a strong preference for the principle of manhood suffrage as against any property-qualification, and we have therefore determined that manhood suffrage shall be the basis on which votes are distributed.

It is true that in the prolonged negotiations and discussions which have taken place upon this question manhood suffrage has been demanded by one party and the voters' basis by the other, and there has been a tacit, though quite informal agreement that the one principle should balance the other. But that is not the position of his Majesty's Government in regard to either of these propositions. We defend both on their merits. We defend "one vote, one value," and we defend manhood suffrage, strictly on their merits as just and equitable principles between man and man throughout the Transvaal. We have therefore decided that all adult males of twenty-one years of age, who have resided in the Transvaal for six months, who do not belong to the British garrison—should be permitted to vote under the secrecy of the ballot for the election of Members of Parliament.

Now there is one subject to which I must refer incidentally. The question of female suffrage has been brought to the notice of various members of the Government on various occasions and in various ways. We have very carefully considered that matter, and we have come to the conclusion that it would not be right for us to subject a young Colony, unable to speak for itself, to the hazards of an experiment which we have not had the gallantry to undergo ourselves; and we shall leave that question to the new Legislature to determine.

I come now to the question of electoral divisions. There are two alternatives before us on this branch of the subject—equal electoral areas or the old magisterial districts. When I say "old," I mean old in the sense that they are existing magisterial districts. There are arguments for both of these courses. Equal electoral areas have the advantage of being symmetrical and are capable of more strict and mathematical distribution. But the Boers have expressed a very strong desire to have the old magisterial districts preserved. I think it is rather a sentimental view on their part, because upon the whole I think the wastage of Boer votes will, owing to excessive plurality in certain divisions, be slightly greater in the old magisterial districts than in equal electoral areas. The Boers have, however, been very anxious that the old areas of their former Constitution, of their local life, should be interfered with as little as possible, and that is a matter of serious concern to his Majesty's Government. Further, there is a great saving of precious time and expense in avoiding the extra work of new delimitation which would be necessary if the country were to be cut up into equal mathematical electoral areas.

The decision to adopt the old magisterial areas, which divide the Transvaal into sixteen electoral divisions, of which the Witwatersrand is only one, involves another question. How are you to subdivide these magisterial districts for the purpose of allocating members? Some will have two, some three, some a number of members; and on what system will you allocate the members to these divisions? We have considered the question of proportional representation. It is the only perfect way in which minorities of every shade and view and interest can receive effective representation. And Lord Elgin was careful to instruct the Committee as a special point to inquire into the possibility of adopting the system of proportional representation. The Committee examined many witnesses, and went most thoroughly into this question. They, however, advise us that there is absolutely no support for such a proposal in the Transvaal, and that its adoption—I will not say its imposition—would be unpopular and incomprehensible throughout the country. If a scientific or proportional representation cannot be adopted, then I say unhesitatingly that the next best way of protecting minorities is to go straight for single-member seats. Some of us have experience of double-barrelled seats in this country; there used to be several three-barrelled seats. But I am convinced that if either of those two systems had been applied to the electoral divisions of the Transvaal, it would only have led to the swamping of one or two local minorities which with single-member divisions would have returned just that very class of moderate, independent, Dutch or British Members whom we particularly desire to see represented in the new Assembly. Therefore, with the desire of not extinguishing these local minorities, his Majesty's Government have decided that single-member constituencies, or man against man, shall be the rule in the Transvaal. But I should add that the subdivision of these electoral districts into their respective constituencies will not proceed upon hard mathematical lines, but that they will be grouped together in accordance with the existing field cornetcies of which they are composed, as that will involve as little change as possible in the ideas of the rural population and in the existing boundaries.

The Committee will realise that this is a question with an elusive climax. It is like going up a mountain. Each successive peak appears in turn the summit, and yet there is always another pinnacle beyond. We have now settled that the Members are to be allotted to single-member constituencies based on the old magisterial districts according to the adult male residents there. But how are we to apply that principle? How are we to find out how many adult males there are in each of the districts of the country, and so to find the quota of electors or proper number of Members for each division? The proverbial three alternatives present themselves. We might take the Lyttelton voters' list revised and supplemented. We might make a new voters' list, or we might take the census of 1904.

Lord Selborne has pointed out to us that it might take just as long a time to revise the Lyttelton voters' list as to make a new voters' list, which would occupy seven months. So that, with the necessary interval for the arrangements for election, ten months would elapse before the Transvaal would be able to possess responsible institutions. I think we shall have the assent of all South African parties in our desire to avoid that delay. I am sorry that so much delay has already taken place. It was necessary that the Cabinet should secure complete information. But to keep a country seething on the verge of an exciting general election is very prejudicial to trade. It increases agitation and impedes the healthy process of development. We are bound to terminate the uncertainty at the earliest possible moment; and we have therefore determined to adopt the census of 1904.

Let me ask the Committee now to examine the sixteen magisterial districts. I think it is necessary to do so before allocating the Members amongst them. In all the discussions in South Africa these have been divided into three areas—the Witwatersrand, Pretoria, and the "Rest of the Transvaal." Pretoria is the metropolis of the Transvaal. It has a very independent public opinion of its own; it is strongly British, and it is rapidly increasing. It is believed that Pretoria will return three, four, or five Members of the Responsible Party, which is the moderate British Party, and is independent of and detached from the Progressive Association. The "Rest of the Transvaal" consists of the old constituencies who sent Boer Members to the old Legislature. There will, however, be one or two seats which may be won by Progressive or Responsible British candidates, but in general "The rest of the country" will return a compact body of members of Het Volk.

Having said that, I now come to the Rand. We must consider the Rand without any bias or prejudice whatever. The Rand is not a town or city, but a mining district covering 1,600 square miles, whose population of adult males practically balances the whole of the rest of the country. The Rand population is not, as some people imagine, a foreign population. The great majority of it is British, and a very large portion of it consists of as good, honest, hard-working men as are to be found in any constituency in this country. But there are also on the Rand a considerable proportion of Dutch. Krugersdorp Rural is Dutch, and has always been excluded from the Rand in the discussions that have taken place in South Africa, and included in the "Rest of the Transvaal." But in addition to that there are the towns of Fordsburgh, which is half Dutch, and two other suburbs which also have a Dutch population; and it is believed that these will afford seats for members of the Responsible British Party with the support of Het Volk. I must say further that the British community upon the Rand is divided into four main political parties. There is the Transvaal Progressive Association, a great and powerful association which arises out of the mining interest. There is the Responsible Government Association; there is the Transvaal Political Association—a moderate body standing between the Responsibles and the Progressives—and there are the labour associations, which are numerous. There are three main labour associations, or really four—the Independent Labour Party, the Transvaal Labour League, the Trade and Labour Council of the Witwatersrand, and the Trade and Labour Council of Pretoria. Why do I bring these facts before the Committee? I do so because I feel it necessary to show how impossible it is to try to dismiss the problems of this complicated community with a gesture or to solve their difficulties with a phrase, and how unfair it would be to deprive such a community, in which there are at work all the counter-checks and rival forces that we see here in our own political life, of its proper share of representation.

Applying the adult male list in the census of 1904 to the three areas I have spoken of, I should allot thirty-two Members to the Rand, six to Pretoria, and thirty to the rest of the country; or, if you include Krugersdorp Rural in the Rand, it would read thirty-three to the Rand, six to Pretoria, and twenty-nine to the rest of the country. Arrived at that point, the Committee in South Africa had good hopes, not merely of arriving at a just settlement, but of arriving at an agreement between all the parties. I am not going to afflict the House with a chronicle of the negotiations which took place. They were fruitless. It is enough to say that there were good hopes that if the Progressive complaint, that the adoption of the census of 1904 did not allow for the increase in the population which has taken place since the census was taken, could be met, a general agreement could be reached. The Boers, whose belief that we were going to treat them fairly and justly has been a pleasant feature in the whole of these negotiations, and will, believe me, be an inestimable factor of value in the future history of South Africa—the Boers with reluctance and under pressure, but guided by the Committee, with whom they were on friendly terms, were willing to agree to a distribution which allotted one more seat to meet this increase of the population in the Witwatersrand area, and the proposal then became 33, 6, and 30, or, including Krugersdorp Rural, 34, 6, 29. The Responsible Party agreed to that. The Progressives hesitated. The great majority of them certainly wished to come in and come to a general agreement on those terms. Certain leaders, however, stood out for one or two or three seats more, and, although Lord Selborne expressed the opinion that the arrangement proposed, namely, 33, 6, 30, excluding Krugersdorp Rural, was a perfectly fair one to the British vote in the Transvaal, those leaders still remained unconvinced and obdurate, and all hopes of a definite agreement fell through.

The Committee returned to this country, bringing with them the recommendation that the Government on their own responsibility should fix the allocation of seats at that very point where the agreement of one Party was still preserved and where the agreement of the other was so very nearly won. And that is what we have decided to do. We have decided to allocate thirty-four seats, including Krugersdorp Rural, to the Rand, six to Pretoria, and twenty-nine to the rest of the country. Lord Selborne wishes it to be known that he concurs in this arrangement. Now I am quite ready to admit that every Constitution ought to rest either upon symmetry or upon acceptance. Our Transvaal Constitution does not rest upon either symmetry or acceptance, but it is very near symmetry and very near acceptance, and in so far as it has departed from symmetry it has moved towards acceptance, and is furthermore sustained throughout by fair dealing, for I am honestly convinced that the addition of an extra member to the Witwatersrand areas which has been made is justified by the increase of the population which has taken place since the census.

On such a basis as this the Transvaal Assembly will be created. It will consist of sixty-nine members, who will receive for their services adequate payment. They will be elected for five years. The Speaker will vacate his seat after being elected. The reason for that provision is that the majority in this Parliament, as in the Cape Parliament, with which the government is carried on, is likely to be very small, and it would be a great hardship if the Party in power were to deprive itself of one of the two or three votes which, when Parties are evenly balanced, are necessary for carrying on the government. It would be a great disaster if we had in the Transvaal a succession of weak Ministries going out upon a single vote, one way or the other. And it is found that when Parties have a very small majority and are forced to part with one of their Members for the purpose of filling the chair, they do not always select the Member who is best suited to that high office, but the Member who can best be spared.

Now let me come to the question of language. Under the Constitution of the right hon. gentleman the Member for St. George's, Hanover Square, the Members of the Assembly would have been permitted to speak Dutch if they asked permission and obtained permission from the Speaker. We are not able to lend ourselves to that condition. We are of opinion that such a discrimination would be invidious. The recognition of their language is precious to a small people. I have never been able to work myself into a passion because there are in parts of South Africa Dutch people who wish to have Dutch teachers to teach Dutch children Dutch. I have not so poor an opinion of the English language, with its priceless literary treasures and its world-wide business connections, as not to believe that it can safely be exposed to the open competition of a dialect like the *taal*. We believe that the only sure way to preserve in the years that are to come such a language as the *taal* would be to make it a proscribed language, which would be spoken by the people with deliberation and with malice, as a protest against what they regarded, and would rightly regard, as an act of intolerance. Therefore we have decided to follow the Cape practice and allow the members of the Transvaal Parliament to address that Assembly indifferently in Dutch or English.

I shall be asked what will be the result of the arrangement that we have made. I decline to speculate or prophesy on that point. It would be indecent and improper. I cannot even tell in this country at the next election how large the Liberal majority will be. Still less would I recommend hon. gentlemen here to forecast the results of contests in which they will not be candidates. I cannot tell how the British in the Transvaal will vote. There are a great many new questions, social and

25

economic, which are beginning to apply a salutary counter-irritant to old racial sores. The division between the two races, thank God, is not quite so clear-cut as it used to be. But this I know—that as there are undoubtedly more British voters in the Transvaal than there are Dutch, and as these British voters have not at any point in the Constitutional Settlement been treated unfairly, it will be easily within their power to obtain a British majority, if they all combine to obtain it. I nourish the hope that the Government that will be called into life by these elections will be a coalition Government with some moderate leader acceptable to both parties, and a Government which embraces in its Party members of both races. Such a solution would be a godsend to South Africa. But whatever may be the outcome, his Majesty's Government are confident that the Ministers who may be summoned, from whatever Party they may be drawn, to whatever race they may belong, will in no circumstances fail in their duty to the Crown.

I should like to say also that this Parliament will be of a high representative authority, and it will be the duty of whoever may be called upon to represent Colonial business in this House to stand between that Parliament and all unjustifiable interference from whatever quarters of the House it may come.

I now approach the question of the Second Chamber. That is not a very attractive subject. We on this side of the House are not particularly enamoured of Second Chambers, and I do not know that our love for these institutions will grow sweeter as the years pass by. But we have to be governed by colonial practice; and there is no colony in the Empire that has not a Second Chamber. The greater number of these Second Chambers are nominated; and I think that the quality of nominated Second Chambers, and their use in practice, have not been found to be inferior to those of the elective bodies. His Majesty's Government desire to secure, if they can, some special protection for native interests which is not likely to be afforded by any electoral arrangement, I am sorry to say. We are unable however to countenance the creation in a permanent form of a nominated Second Chamber. But in view of the position of native affairs, in view of the disadvantage of complicating the elections, to which all classes in the Transvaal have been so long looking forward, and most particularly because of the extra delays that would be involved in the creation of a new elective body, the Cabinet have resolved for this Parliament only, and as a purely provisional arrangement, to institute a nominated Legislative Council of fifteen members. They will be nominated by the Crown, that is to say at home, and vacancies, if any, by death or resignation, will be filled by the High Commissioner, on the advice of the responsible Ministers. During the course of the first Parliament in the Transvaal arrangements will be completed for the establishment of an elective Second Chamber, and if necessary further Letters Patent will be issued to constitute it.

Under the Treaty of Vereeniging we undertook that no franchise should be extended to natives before the grant of self-government. I am not going to plunge into the argument as to what word the "native" means, in its legal or technical character, because in regard to such a treaty, upon which we are relying for such grave issues, we must be bound very largely by the interpretation which the other party places upon it; and it is undoubted that the Boers would regard it as a breach of that treaty, if the franchise were in the first instance extended to any persons who are not white men. We may regret that decision. We may regret that there is no willingness in the Transvaal and Orange River Colony to make arrangements which have been found not altogether harmful in Cape Colony. But we are bound by this treaty. Meanwhile we make certain reservations. Any legislation which imposes disabilities on natives which are not imposed on Europeans will be reserved to the Secretary of State, and the Governor will not give his assent before receiving the Secretary of State's decision. Legislation that will effect the alienation of native lands will also be reserved. It is customary to make some provision in money for native interests, such as education, by reserving a certain sum for administration by the High Commissioner or some other political or Imperial official. We propose to reserve Swaziland to the direct administration of the High Commissioner, with the limiting provision that no settlement he may make is to be less advantageous to the natives than the existing arrangement.

On November 30, 1906, the arrangement for recruiting Chinese in China will cease and determine. Our consuls will withdraw the powers they have delegated to the mining agents, and I earnestly trust that no British Government will ever renew them. A clause in the Constitution will provide for the abrogation of the existing Chinese Labour Ordinance after a reasonable interval. I am not yet in a position to say what will be a reasonable interval, but time must be given to the new Assembly to take stock of the position and to consider the labour question as a whole. I said just now there would be a clause with regard to differential legislation as between white persons and others, and to this clause will be added the words: "No law will be assented to which sanctions any condition of service or residence of a servile character." We have been invited to use the word "slavery" or the words "semblance of slavery," but such expressions would be needlessly wounding, and the words we have chosen are much more effective, because much more precise and much more restrained, and they point an accurate forefinger at the very evil we desire to prevent.

I have now finished laying before the House the constitutional settlement, and I should like to say that our proposals are interdependent. They must be considered as a whole; they must be accepted or rejected as a whole. I say this in no spirit of disrespect to the Committee, because evidently it is a matter which the Executive Government should decide on its own responsibility; and if the policy which we declare were changed, new men would have to be found to carry out another plan. We are prepared to make this settlement in the name of the Liberal Party. That is sufficient authority for us; but there is a higher authority which we should earnestly desire to obtain. I make no appeal, but I address myself particularly to the right hon. gentlemen who sit opposite, who are long versed in public affairs, and who will not be able all their lives to escape from a heavy South African responsibility. They are the accepted guides of a Party which, though in a minority in this House, nevertheless embodies nearly half the nation. I will ask them seriously whether they will not pause before they commit themselves to violent or rash denunciations of this great arrangement. I will ask them, further, whether they cannot join with us to invest the grant of a free Constitution to the Transvaal with something of a national sanction. With all our majority we can only make it the gift of a Party; they can make it the gift of England. And if that were so, I am quite sure that all those inestimable blessings which we confidently hope will flow from this decision, will be gained more surely and much more speedily; and the first real step will have been taken to withdraw South African affairs from the arena of British party politics, in which they have inflicted injury on both political parties and in which they have suffered grievous injury themselves. I ask that that may be considered; but in any case we are prepared to go forward alone, and Letters Patent will be issued in strict conformity with the settlement I have explained this afternoon if we should continue to enjoy the support of a Parliamentary majority.

THE ORANGE FREE STATE CONSTITUTION

HOUSE OF COMMONS, *DECEMBER 17, 1906*

*L*etters Patent have been issued during the last week conferring a Constitution upon the Transvaal Colony. These instruments have now been for some days at the disposal of the House, and this afternoon affords an occasion for their discussion. Other Letters Patent conferring a Constitution upon the Orange River Colony are in an advanced state of preparation, and I think it would be generally convenient if I were to make a statement as to the character and scope of that Constitution. With that view I have, by the direction of the Prime Minister, placed upon the Paper a Resolution which I now move, permitting a general discussion upon the constitutional arrangements which we are making both in the Transvaal and in the Orange River Colony. Now, Sir, by the Treaty of Vereeniging, Great Britain promised full self-government to the peoples of the two Boer Republics which had been conquered and annexed as the result of the war. This intention of giving responsible government did not arise out of the terms of peace, although it is, of course, solemnly expressed in them. It has always been the settled and successful colonial policy of this country during the last fifty years to allow great liberties of self-government to distant communities under the Crown, and no responsible statesman, and no British Cabinet, so far as I know, ever contemplated any other solution of the South African problem but that of full self-government. The idea which I have seen put forward in some quarters, that, in order to get full satisfaction for the expense and the exertions to which we were put in the war, we are bound to continue governing those peoples according to our pleasure and against their will, and that that is, as it were, an agreeable exercise which is to be some compensation for our labours, is an idea which no doubt finds expression in the columns of certain newspapers, but to which I do not think any serious person ever gave any countenance. No, Sir, the ultimate object, namely, the bestowal of full self-government, was not lost sight of even in the height of the war; and as all parties were agreed that some interval for reconstruction must necessarily intervene, the only questions at issue between us have been questions of manner and questions of time.

How much difference is there between Parties in this House as to time? It is now more than three years since Lord Milner, speaking in the Inter-colonial Council, bore emphatic testimony to the faithfulness with which the Boers—those who had been fighting against us—had observed their side of the terms of peace. Lord Milner said:

"It is perfectly true that the Boer population, the men who signed the terms of peace at Vereeniging, have loyally observed those terms and have carried them out faithfully. They profess to-day, and I absolutely believe them, that no idea of an armed rising or unlawful action is in their minds. I may say I am in constant, perhaps I should say frequent communication with the men who in the war fought us so manfully and then made manful terms. We differ on many points, no doubt, and I do not expect them to rejoice with us in what has happened, or to feel affection for a man who, like myself, has been instrumental in bringing about the great change which has come over the Constitution of the country. But I firmly believe their word when they come forward and meet us, and, without professing to agree in all respects with the policy of the Government, declare that they desire to co-operate in all questions affecting the prosperity of the country and the maintenance of public order. I accept the assurance they give in that respect, and I think it is practically impossible to put your hands on anything done by myself or any member of the Government which can be regarded as a manifestation of distrust of the men who have shown themselves, and do show themselves, men of honour. Let me say, then, I am perfectly satisfied that so great is the influence of their leaders over the minds of the main section of the Boer population that so long as those leaders maintain that attitude a general rising is out of the question."

Those are the words which Lord Milner used three years ago, and I think they are words which do justice to the subject and to the speaker. But more than two years have passed since the representations were made to the right hon. gentleman the Member for St. George's, Hanover Square, which induced him to confer a measure of self-government on the Transvaal. Those representations laid stress on the fact that the desire for self-government was not put forward only by the Boers, but that both sections of the community in the Transvaal desired to take the control of affairs into their own hands. The right hon. gentleman published a Constitution. That Constitution conferred very great and wide powers.

It conferred upon an overwhelming elected majority the absolute power of the purse and control over legislation. But it has always been my submission to the House that that Constitution had about it no element of permanence, that it could not possibly have been maintained as an enduring, or even a workable settlement; and I am bound to say—I do not wish to be controversial this afternoon if I can avoid it—that, when I read the statement that this representative government stage would have been a convenient educative stage in the transition to full self-government, the whole experience of British colonial policy does not justify such an assumption. The system of representative government without responsible Ministers, without responsible powers, has led to endless friction and inconvenience wherever and whenever it has been employed. It has failed in Canada, it has failed in Natal and Cape Colony. It has been condemned by almost every high colonial authority who has studied this question. I do not think I need quote any more conclusive authority upon that subject than that of Lord Durham. Lord Durham, in his celebrated Report, says of this particular system:

"It is difficult to understand how any English statesmen could have imagined that representative and irresponsible government could be successfully combined. There seems, indeed, to be an idea that the character of representative institutions ought to be thus modified in Colonies; that it is an incident of colonial dependence that the officers of government should be nominated by the Crown without any reference to the wishes of the community whose interests are entrusted to their keeping. It has never been very clearly explained what are the Imperial interests which require this complete nullification of representative government. But if there is such a necessity it is quite clear that a representative Government in a Colony must be a mockery and a source of confusion, for those who support this system have never yet been able to devise or exhibit in the practical working of colonial government any means for making so complete an abrogation of political influence palatable to the representative body."

I contend that the right hon. gentleman's Constitution would have broken down in its first session, and that we should have then been forced to concede grudgingly and in a hurry the full measure of responsible government which, with all due formality, and without any precipitancy, the Letters Patent issued last week have now conferred. But even the right hon. gentleman himself did not intend his Constitution to be a permanent settlement. He intended it to be a transition, and a brief transition; and in the correspondence which passed on this subject two or three years is sometimes named as the period for which such a Constitution might conveniently have endured—two or three years, of which, let me point out to the House, nearly two years have already gone. Seeing how little difference there is between us upon that question, I dispense with further argument as to the grant of a Transvaal Constitution, as I see the course we have adopted does commend itself to the good sense of all Parties in this country and is sustained at almost every point by almost every person conversant with South African affairs.

It is said, however, we have heard it often said, "It may be wise to grant responsible government to the Transvaal, but it is not wise to give it to the Orange River Colony. Why should you give it to the Orange River Colony too?" I say, "Why not?" Let us make it quite clear that the burden of proof always rests with those who deny or restrict the issue of full Parliamentary liberties. They have to make their case good from month to month, and from day to day. What are the reasons which have been advanced against the issue of a Constitution to the Orange River Colony? Various reasons have been put forward. We have been told, first, that the Colony is not ripe for self-government. When you have very small communities of white men in distant and immense territories, and when those communities are emerging from a wild into a more settled condition, then it is very necessary and very desirable that the growth of self-governing institutions should be gradual. But that is not the situation in the Orange River Colony. The Orange Free State was the model small republic of the world. The honourable traditions of the Free State are not challenged by any who take the trouble to study its history, either in the distant past, or in the years immediately preceding the South African war. The right hon. gentleman the Member for West Birmingham himself, speaking in this House on December 7, 1900, used language which, I think, should go far to dissipate the idle fears which we hear expressed in various quarters upon the grant of self-government to the Orange River Colony:

"We do not propose," said the right hon. gentleman, "that the Constitution of the Orange River Colony should necessarily be the same as the Constitution of the Transvaal Colony, either at starting or in the immediate future. It will be dealt with upon its own merits, dealt with separately, and we think it possible"—I ask the House to mark this— "from the circumstances with which every one is familiar, that an earlier beginning to greater political liberty may be made in the Orange River Colony than in the Transvaal. That is due to the fact that the Government of the Orange River Colony previous to the war was by common consent a very good Government, and consequently, speaking generally, of course, and not of individuals, we shall find there probably the means to creating a satisfactory administration more quickly than we can do in the case of the Transvaal Colony."

Then we have been told that responsible government presupposes Party government, and that in the Orange River Colony there are not the elements of political parties, that there is not that diversity of interests which we see in the Transvaal, that there are not the same sharp differences between town and country, or the same astonishing contrasts between wealth and poverty which prevail in the Transvaal. And we are told that, in order that responsible government should work properly, and Party government should be a success, there must be the essential elements of Party conflict. I suppose we are, as a majority in this House, admirers of the Party system of government; but I do not think that we should any of us carry our admiration of that system so far as to say that the nation is unfit to enjoy the privilege of managing its own affairs unless it can find some one to quarrel with and plenty of things to quarrel about.

Then we are told that—"The country is prospering as it is. Why change now? The land is tranquil, people are regaining the prosperity which was lost in the war. It is a pity to make a change now; now is not the moment." I admit the premise, but I draw exactly the opposite conclusion. It is just for that reason that we should now step forward and, taking occasion by the hand, make an advance in the system of government. How often in the history of nations has the golden opportunity been allowed to slip away! How often have rulers and Governments been forced to make in foul weather the very journey which they have refused to make prosperously in fair weather!

Then we are told that Imperial interests will be endangered by this grant. I do not believe that that is so. The Boer mind moves by definite steps from one political conception to another. I believe they have definitely abandoned their old ambition of creating in South Africa a United States independent of the British Crown, and have accepted that other political ideal which is represented by the Dominion of Canada and the Commonwealth of Australia. At any rate, no people have a greater right to claim respect on the ground of their loyal adherence to treaty engagements than the people of the Orange River Colony; for every one knows that it was with a most faithful adherence to their engagements, with almost Quixotic loyalty, that they followed—many of them knowing where their fortune was going to lead them, knowing full well what would be the result of their action—their sister State into the disastrous struggle of the South African war.

It is quite true that there is in existence at the present time—and I think Lord Milner has pointed it out—no bond of love between the men who fought us in that war and this country. I was reading the other day a speech by Mr. Steyn. Mr. Steyn is, of course, one of the most clearly avowed opponents of the British power. But Mr. Steyn is quite clear upon this point. He says there is no bond of love, and it would be untruthful and dishonest on their part to say that such a bond existed. But, he says, there is another bond; there is such a thing as a man's word of honour. "We gave our word of honour at Vereeniging, and it is our intention to abide strictly by that." I state my opinion as to the safety of the step we propose to take, but I cannot expect the Members opposite to set much store by that, although it is an honest and sincere opinion. But I will quote them an authority which I am sure they will not dismiss without respect. As soon as the right hon. Member for West Birmingham returned from South Africa, while his experiences in that country were fresh in his mind, while he had but newly been conversing with men of all parties there on the spot, the scene of the struggle, he made a speech in this House which really ought not to be overlooked by persons dealing with this question.

"Great importance," said the right hon. gentleman, "seems to be attached to the view that in the interests of the two Colonies it is desirable that a certain time, not a long time in the history of a nation, but still a certain time should elapse before full self-government is accorded. Whether a long time will elapse I really cannot say. One thing is clear: if the population of the Transvaal and Orange River Colony, both Boer and Briton, by a large majority, desire this self-government, even although it might seem to us to be premature, I should think it unwise to refuse it. I do not myself believe there is any such danger connected with Imperial interests that we should hesitate to accord it on that ground. The ground on which I should desire that it might be delayed is really the interest of the two Colonies themselves, and not any Imperial interest."

The peace and order of the Orange River Colony establish this case on its merits. It is a State bound to moderation by the circumstance of its geographical position. In all its history in South Africa it has been largely dependent on the goodwill of its neighbours—goodwill and friendly relations maintained with Natal and the Transvaal, on the one hand, and with the Cape Colony on the other. It is inconceivable that a State so situated in regard to its railways and its economic position generally should be a disturbing influence from the point of view of the different States of South Africa. But there is another fact which justifies this grant, and that is the extraordinary crimelessness in a political sense of the whole of that country. Let the House remember that there had been three years' war, of which two years were fierce guerilla fighting, and that on all sides there were to be found desperate men who had been for a long period holding their lives in their hands and engaged on every wild and adventurous foray. Peace is agreed on, and what happens? Absolute order exists and prevails throughout the whole country from that moment. There has not been a single case of violent crime except, I believe, one murder committed by a lunatic—hardly a case of sedition—and not a single case of prosecution for treason of any kind. I say without hesitation that in order to find a similar instance of swift transition from violent warfare to law-abiding peace you have got to look back to the days when the army of the Parliament was reviewed and disbanded at the Restoration.

I submit to the House that a case for conferring responsible government on the Orange River Colony is established on its merits. But that is not the whole question before us this afternoon. We have not merely to decide whether we will give a Constitution to the Orange River Colony, but whether, having given a Constitution to the Transvaal, we will deliberately withhold one from the Orange River Colony; and that is an argument which multiplies the others which I have used. On what ground could we refuse that equal treatment of the Orange River Colony? There is only one ground which we could assign for such a refusal, and that is that in the Orange River Colony there is sure to be a Dutch majority. I cannot conceive any more fatal assertion that could be made on the part of the Imperial Government than that on this specific racial ground they were forced to refuse liberties which otherwise they would concede. I say such a refusal would be an insult to the hundreds and thousands of loyal Dutch subjects the King has in all parts of South Africa, I say that this invidious treatment of the Orange River Colony would be the greatest blunder, a fitting pendant to all that long concatenation of fatal mistakes which has marked our policy in South Africa for so many years; and I say it would be a breach of the spirit of the terms of peace, because we could not say, "We promised you self-government by the terms of peace, but what we meant by that was that before you were to have self-government, enough persons of British origin should have arrived in the country to make quite sure you would be out-voted."

If we were to adopt such a course we should be false to that agreement, which is the great foundation of our policy in South Africa. I hope the House will earnestly sustain the importance of that Vereeniging agreement. For the first time in many years the two white races dwelling together in South Africa have found a common foundation on which they can both build, a foundation much better than Boomplaats, or the Sand River Convention, or the Conventions of 1880 and 1884, far better than Majuba Hill or the Jameson Raid. They have found a foundation which they can both look to without any feeling of shame—on the contrary, with feelings of equal honour, and I trust also with feelings of mutual forgiveness.

On those grounds, therefore, we have decided to give to the Orange River Colony full responsible government. We eschew altogether the idea of treating them differently from the Transvaal, or interposing any state of limited self-government between them and the full enjoyment of their right. There is to be a Legislature which will consist of two Chambers, as in the Transvaal. The First Chamber will be elected upon a voters' basis and by manhood suffrage. The residential qualification will be the same as in the Transvaal, six months. The distribution of seats has been settled by general consent. The Committee which we sent to South

Africa, and which was so very successful in arriving at an adjustment between the parties in the Transvaal, has made similar investigations in the Orange River Colony, and I think we may accept with confidence their recommendation. They recommend that the number of members should be thirty-eight. The old Volksraad had sixty members, but it was found to be much too large for the needs of the country, and on several occasions efforts were made to reduce the representation. Those efforts were not successful, from the fact, which we can all appreciate, that it is very difficult indeed to get a representative body to pass a self-denying ordinance of that character which involves the extinction of its own members. There will be separate representation of towns in the Orange River Colony. In the Volksraad there was such a representation: there were forty-two rural members and eighteen urban members. Out of the thirty-eight we propose that there shall be twenty-seven rural members and eleven urban members; rather less than a third of the representation will be that of the small towns. That is a proportion which is justified by the precedent of the old Constitution, and also by the latest census.

There will be a Second Chamber, and, as in the Transvaal, it will be nominated, for the first Parliament only, by the Governor, under instructions from the Secretary of State. It is not an hereditary Chamber; and it may be, therefore, assumed that the distribution of Parties in that Chamber will be attended by some measure of impartiality, and that there will be some general attempt to select only those persons who are really fit to exercise the important functions entrusted to them. But even so protected, the Government feel that in the ultimate issue in a conflict between the two Chambers, the first and representative Chamber must prevail. The other body may review and may suspend, but for the case of measures sent up in successive sessions from the representative Chamber on which no agreement can be reached, we have introduced the machinery which appears in the Constitution of the Australian Commonwealth, that both Chambers shall sit together, debate together, vote together, and the majority shall decide. The whole success of that operation depends upon the numerical proportion observed between the two Chambers. In the Australian Commonwealth the proportion of the First Chamber is rather more than two to one; in the Transvaal the proportion will be more than four to one, namely, sixty-five to fifteen; and in the Orange River Colony it will be thirty-eight to eleven.

The other provisions of the Constitution will mainly follow the lines of the Transvaal Constitution. The Constitution of the Orange River Colony will become effective as soon as possible; and I should think that the new Parliament might assemble in Bloemfontein some time during the autumn of next year. When that work has been completed, and the new

Parliament has assembled, the main direction of South African affairs in these Colonies will have passed from our hands.

Sir, it is the earnest desire of the Government to steer colonial affairs out of English Party politics, not only in the interest of the proper conduct of those affairs, but in order to clear the arena at home for the introduction of measures which affect the masses of the people. We have tried in South Africa to deal fairly between man and man, to adjust conflicting interests and overlapping claims. We have tried so far as possible to effect a broad-bottomed settlement of the question which should command the assent of people even beyond the great party groupings which support us.

Other liberties besides their own will be enshrined in these new Parliaments. The people of South Africa, and, in a special measure, the Boers, will become the trustees of freedom all over the world. We have tried to act with fairness and good feeling. If by any chance our counsels of reconciliation should come to nothing, if our policy should end in mocking disaster, then the resulting evil would not be confined to South Africa. Our unfortunate experience would be trumpeted forth all over the world wherever despotism wanted a good argument for bayonets, whenever an arbitrary Government wished to deny or curtail the liberties of imprisoned nationalities. But if, on the other hand, as we hope and profoundly believe, better days are in store for South Africa, if the words of President Brand, "All shall come right," are at length to be fulfilled, and if the near future should unfold to our eves a tranquil, prosperous, consolidated Afrikander nation under the protecting ægis of the British Crown, then, the good also will not be confined to South Africa; then the cause of the poor and the weak all over the world will have been sustained; and everywhere small peoples will get more room to breathe, and everywhere great empires will be encouraged by our example to step forward—and it only needs a step—into the sunshine of a more gentle and a more generous age.

LIBERALISM AND SOCIALISM
ST. ANDREW'S HALL, GLASGOW, *OCTOBER II, 1906*

(Originally published in *The Dundee Advertiser*)

*T*he first indispensable condition of democratic progress must be the maintenance of European peace. War is fatal to Liberalism. Liberalism is the world-wide antagonist of war. We have every reason to congratulate ourselves upon the general aspect of the European situation. The friendship which has grown up between Great Britain and France is a source of profound satisfaction to every serious and thinking man. The first duty of a nation is to make friends with its nearest neighbour. Six years ago France was agitated in the throes of the Dreyfus case, and Great Britain was plunged in the worst and most painful period of the South African war; and both nations—conscious as we are of one another's infirmities—were inclined to express their opinion about the conduct of the other in unmeasured terms, and keen antagonism resulted. What a contrast to-day! Ever since the King, whose services in the cause of international peace are regarded with affection in every quarter of his dominions, ever since by an act of prescience and of courage his Majesty went to Paris, the relations between Great Britain and France have steadily and progressively improved, and to-day we witness the inspiring spectacle of these two great peoples, the two most genuinely Liberal nations in the whole world, locked together in a league of friendship under standards of dispassionate justice and international goodwill. But it is absurd to suppose that the friendship which we have established with France should be in any degree a menace to any other European Power, or to the great Power of Germany.

If the prospects on the European continent are bright and tranquil, I think we have reason to feel also contentment at the course of Colonial affairs. We have had unusual difficulties in the Colonies; but in spite of every effort to excite Colonial apprehension for Party purposes against a Liberal Ministry through the instrumentality of a powerful press, the great States of the Empire have felt, and with more assurance every day, that a Liberal Administration in Downing Street will respect their rights and cherish their interests.

But I am drawn to South Africa by the memory that to-night, the 11th of October, is the anniversary of the declaration of war; and I think it is in South Africa that we have especial reason to be satisfied with the course which events have taken, since we have been in any degree responsible for their direction. One great advantage we have had—a good foundation to build on. We have had the Treaty of Vereeniging, by which peace was established between the Dutch and British races in South Africa upon terms honourable to both. We have had that treaty as our foundation— and what a mercy it is, looking back on the past, to think that the nation followed Lord Rosebery's advice at Chesterfield to terminate the war by a regular peace and a regular settlement, and were not lured away, as Lord Milner would have advised them, when he said that the war in a certain sense would never be over, into a harsh policy of unconditional surrender and pitiless subjugation.

The work of giving these free Constitutions to the two Colonies in South Africa, so lately independent Republics, is in harmony with the most sagacious instincts, and the most honoured traditions of the Liberal Party. But I notice that Lord Milner, who, as we remember, was once a Liberal candidate,—and who now appears before us sometimes in the guise of a silent and suffering public servant, sometimes in the aspect of an active, and even an acrid, political partisan, haranguing his supporters and attacking his Majesty's Ministers,—Lord Milner describes all this improving outlook as "the dreary days of reaction." Progress and reaction are no doubt relative terms. What one man calls progress another will call reaction. If you have been rapidly descending the road to ruin and you suddenly check yourself, stop, turn back, and retrace your steps, that is reaction, and no doubt your former guide will have every reason to reproach you with inconsistency. And it seems to me not at all unnatural that to one who regards three years' desolating civil war as a period of healthy and inspiring progress, a good deal of what his Majesty's Government have lately done in South Africa must appear very dreary and reactionary indeed.

But I would recommend you to leave this disconsolate proconsul alone. I do not agree with him when he says that South Africa is passing through a time of trial. South Africa is emerging from her time of trial. The darkest period is behind her. Brighter prospects lie before her. The improvement upon which we are counting is not the hectic flush of a market boom, but the steady revival and accumulation of agricultural and industrial productiveness. Soberly and solemnly men of all parties and of both races in South Africa are joining together to revive and to develop the prosperity of their own country. Grave difficulties, many dangers, long exertions lie before them; but the star of South Africa is already in the ascendant, and I look confidently forward to the time when it will take its place, united, federated, free, beside Canada and Australia, in the shining constellation of the British Empire.

When we have dealt with subjects which lie outside our own island, let us concentrate our attention on what lies within it, because the gravest problems lie at home. I shall venture to-night to make a few general observations upon those larger trendings of events which govern the incidents and the accidents of the hour. The fortunes and the interests of Liberalism and Labour are inseparably interwoven; they rise by the same forces, and in spite of similar obstacles, they face the same enemies, they are affected by the same dangers, and the history of the last thirty years shows quite clearly that their power of influencing public affairs and of commanding national attention fluctuate together. Together they are elevated, together they are depressed, and any Tory reaction which swept the Liberal Party out of power would assuredly work at least proportionate havoc in the ranks of Labour. That may not be a very palatable truth, but it is a truth none the less.

Labour! It is a great word. It moves the world, it comprises the millions, it combines many men in many lands in the sympathy of a common burden. Who has the right to speak for Labour? A good many people arrogate to themselves the right to speak for Labour. How many political Flibbertigibbets are there not running up and down the land calling themselves the people of Great Britain, and the social democracy, and the masses of the nation! But I am inclined to think, so far as any body of organised opinion can claim the right to speak for this immense portion of the human race, it is the trade unions that more than any other organisation must be considered the responsible and deputed representatives of Labour. They are the most highly organised part of Labour; they are the most responsible part; they are from day to day in contact with reality. They are not mere visionaries or dreamers weaving airy Utopias out of tobacco smoke. They are not political adventurers who are eager to remodel the world by rule-of-thumb, who are proposing to make the infinite complexities of scientific civilisation and the multitudinous phenomena of great cities conform to a few barbarous formulas which any moderately intelligent parrot could repeat in a fortnight.

The fortunes of the trade unions are interwoven with the industries they serve. The more highly organised trade unions are, the more clearly they recognise their responsibilities; the larger their membership, the greater their knowledge, the wider their outlook. Of course, trade unions will make mistakes, like everybody else, will do foolish things, and wrong things, and want more than they are likely to get, just like everybody else. But the fact remains that for thirty years trade unions have had a charter from Parliament which up to within a few years ago protected their funds, and gave them effective power to conduct a strike; and no one can say that these thirty years were bad years of British industry, that during these thirty years it was impossible to develop great businesses and carry on large manufacturing operations, because, as everybody knows perfectly well, those were good and expanding years of British trade and national enrichment.

A few years ago a series of judicial decisions utterly changed the whole character of the law regarding trade unions. It became difficult and obscure. The most skilful lawyers were unable to define it. No counsel knew what advice to tender to those who sought his guidance. Meanwhile if, in the conduct of a strike, any act of an agent, however unauthorised, transgressed the shadowy and uncertain border-line between what was legal and what was not, an action for damages might be instituted against the trade union, and if the action was successful, trade union funds, accumulated penny by penny, year by year, with which were inseparably intermingled friendly and benefit moneys, might in a moment have been swept away. That was the state of the law when his Majesty's present advisers were returned to power. We have determined to give back that charter to the trade unions. The Bill is even now passing through the House of Commons.

We are often told that there can be no progress for democracy until the Liberal Party has been destroyed. Let us examine that. Labour in this country exercises a great influence upon the Government. That is not so everywhere. It is not so, for instance, in Germany, and yet in Germany there is no Liberal Party worth speaking of. Labour there is very highly organised, and the Liberal Party there has been destroyed. In Germany there exists exactly the condition of affairs, in a Party sense, that Mr. Keir Hardie and his friends are so anxious to introduce here. A great social democratic party on the one hand, are bluntly and squarely face to face with a capitalist and military confederation on the other. That is the issue, as it presents itself in Germany; that is the issue, as I devoutly hope it may never present itself here. And what is the result? In spite of the great numbers of the Socialist Party in Germany, in spite of the high ability of its leaders, it has hardly any influence whatever upon the course of public affairs. It has to submit to food taxes and to conscription; and I observe that Herr Bebel, the distinguished leader of that Party, at Mannheim the other day was forced to admit, and admitted with great candour, that there was no other country in Europe so effectively organised as Germany to put down anything in the nature of a violent Socialist movement. That is rather a disquieting result to working men of having destroyed the Liberal Party.

But we are told to wait a bit; the Socialist Party in Germany is only three millions. How many will there be in ten years' time? That is a fair argument. I should like to say this. A great many men can jump four feet, but very few can jump six feet. After a certain distance the difficulty increases progressively. It is so with the horse-power required to drive great ships across the ocean; it is so with the lifting power required to raise balloons in the air. A balloon goes up quite easily for a certain distance, but after a certain distance it refuses to go up any farther, because the air is too rarefied to float it and sustain it. And, therefore, I would say let us examine the concrete facts.

In France, before the Revolution, property was divided among a very few people. A few thousand nobles and priests and merchants had all the wealth in the country; twenty-five million peasants had nothing. But in modern States, such as we see around us in the world to-day, property is very widely divided. I do not say it is evenly divided. I do not say it is fairly divided, but it is very widely divided. Especially is that true in Great Britain. Nowhere else in the world, except, perhaps, in France and the United States, are there such vast numbers of persons who are holders of interest-bearing, profit-bearing, rent-earning property, and the whole tendency of civilisation and of free institutions is to an ever-increasing volume of production and an increasingly wide diffusion of profit. And therein lies the essential stability of modern States. There are millions of persons who would certainly lose by anything like a general overturn, and they are everywhere the strongest and best organised millions. And I have no hesitation in saying that any violent movement would infallibly encounter an overwhelming resistance, and that any movement which was inspired by mere class prejudice, or by a desire to gain a selfish advantage, would encounter from the selfish power of the "haves" an effective resistance which would bring it to sterility and to destruction.

And here is the conclusion to which I lead you. Something more is needed if we are to get forward. There lies the function of the Liberal Party. Liberalism supplies at once the higher impulse and the practicable path; it appeals to persons by sentiments of generosity and humanity; it proceeds by courses of moderation. By gradual steps, by steady effort from day to day, from year to year, Liberalism enlists hundreds of thousands upon the side of progress and popular democratic reform whom militant Socialism would drive into violent Tory reaction. That is why the Tory Party hate us. That is why they, too, direct their attacks upon the great organisation of the Liberal Party, because they know it is through the agency of Liberalism that society will be able in the course of time to slide forward, almost painlessly—for the world is changing very fast—on to a more even and a more equal foundation. That is the mission that lies before Liberalism. The cause of the Liberal Party is the cause of the left-out millions; and because we believe that there is in all the world no other instrument of equal potency and efficacy available at the present time for the purposes of social amelioration, we are bound in duty and in honour to guard it from all attacks, whether they arise from violence or from reaction.

There is no necessity to-night to plunge into a discussion of the philosophical divergencies between Socialism and Liberalism. It is not possible to draw a hard-and-fast line between individualism and collectivism. You cannot draw it either in theory or in practice. That is where the Socialist makes a mistake. Let us not imitate that mistake. No man can be a collectivist alone or an individualist alone. He must be both an individualist and a collectivist. The nature of man is a dual nature. The character of the organisation of human society is dual. Man is at once a unique being and a gregarious animal. For some purposes he must be collectivist, for others he is, and he will for all time remain, an individualist. Collectively we have an Army and a Navy and a Civil Service; collectively we have a Post Office, and a police, and a Government; collectively we light our streets and supply ourselves with water; collectively we indulge increasingly in all the necessities of communication. But we do not make love collectively, and the ladies do not marry us collectively, and we do not eat collectively, and we do not die collectively, and it is not collectively that we face the sorrows and the hopes, the winnings and the losings of this world of accident and storm.

No view of society can possibly be complete which does not comprise within its scope both collective organisation and individual incentive. The whole tendency of civilisation is, however, towards the multiplication of the collective functions of society. The ever-growing complications of civilisation create for us new services which have to be undertaken by the State, and create for us an expansion of the existing services. There is a growing feeling, which I entirely share, against allowing those services which are in the nature of monopolies to pass into private hands. There is a pretty steady determination, which I am convinced will become effective in the present Parliament, to intercept all future unearned increment which may arise from the increase in the speculative value of the land. There will be an ever-widening area of municipal enterprise. I go farther; I should like to see the State embark on various novel and adventurous experiments, I am delighted to see that Mr. Burns is now interesting himself in afforestation. I am of opinion that the State should increasingly assume the position of the reserve employer of labour. I am very sorry we have not got the railways of this country in our hands. We

43

may do something better with the canals, and we are all agreed, every one in this hall who belongs to the Progressive Party, that the State must increasingly and earnestly concern itself with the care of the sick and the aged, and, above all, of the children.

I look forward to the universal establishment of minimum standards of life and labour, and their progressive elevation as the increasing energies of production may permit. I do not think that Liberalism in any circumstances can cut itself off from this fertile field of social effort, and I would recommend you not to be scared in discussing any of these proposals, just because some old woman comes along and tells you they are Socialistic. If you take my advice, you will judge each case on its merits. Where you find that State enterprise is likely to be ineffective, then utilise private enterprises, and do not grudge them their profits.

The existing organisation of society is driven by one mainspring—competitive selection. It may be a very imperfect organisation of society, but it is all we have got between us and barbarism. It is all we have been able to create through unnumbered centuries of effort and sacrifice. It is the whole treasure which past generations have been able to secure, and which they have been able to bequeath; and great and numerous as are the evils of the existing condition of society in this country, the advantages and achievements of the social system are greater still. Moreover, that system is one which offers an almost indefinite capacity for improvement. We may progressively eliminate the evils; we may progressively augment the goods which it contains. I do not want to see impaired the vigour of competition, but we can do much to mitigate the consequences of failure. We want to draw a line below which we will not allow persons to live and labour, yet above which they may compete with all the strength of their manhood. We want to have free competition upwards; we decline to allow free competition to run downwards. We do not want to pull down the structures of science and civilisation: but to spread a net over the abyss; and I am sure that if the vision of a fair Utopia which cheers the hearts and lights the imagination of the toiling multitudes, should ever break into reality, it will be by developments through, and modifications in, and by improvements out of, the existing competitive organisation of society; and I believe that Liberalism mobilised, and active as it is to-day, will be a principal and indispensable factor in that noble evolution.

I have been for nearly six years, in rather a short life, trained as a soldier, and I will use a military metaphor. There is no operation in war more dangerous or more important than the conduct of a rear-guard action and the extrication of a rear-guard from difficult and broken ground. In the long war which humanity wages with the elements of nature the main body of the army has won its victory. It has moved out into the open plain, into a pleasant camping ground by the water springs and in the sunshine, amid fair cities and fertile fields. But the rear-guard is entangled in the defiles, the rear-guard is still struggling in mountainous country, attacked and assailed on every side by the onslaughts of a pitiless enemy. The rear-guard is encumbered with wounded, obstructed by all the broken vehicles that have fallen back from the main line of the march, with all the stragglers and weaklings that have fallen by the way and can struggle forward no farther. It is to the rear-guard of the army that attention should be directed. There is the place for the bravest soldiers and the most trusted generals. It is there that all the resources of military science and its heaviest artillery should be employed to extricate the rear-guard—not to bring the main army back from good positions which it occupies, not to throw away the victory which it has won over the brute forces of nature—but to bring the rear-guard in, to bring them into the level plain, so that they too may dwell in a land of peace and plenty.

That is the aim of the Liberal Party, and if we work together we will do something for its definite accomplishment.

IMPERIAL PREFERENCE - I

IMPERIAL CONFERENCE,[1] DOWNING STREET, *MAY 7, 1907*

*T*he economic aspect of Imperial Preference, both from the point of view of trade and of finance, has already been dealt with very fully by the Chancellor of the Exchequer and the President of the Board of Trade, and I desire in the few observations with which I shall venture to trespass upon the indulgence of the Conference to refer very little to the economic aspect, and rather to examine one or two points about this question of a political, of a Parliamentary, and almost of a diplomatic character. I want to consider for a moment what would be the effect of a system of preferences upon the course of Parliamentary business. The course of Colonial affairs in the House of Commons is not always very smooth or very simple, and I am bound to say that, having for eighteen months been responsible for the statements on behalf of this Department which are made to the House of Commons, I feel that enormous difficulties would be added to the discharge of Colonial business in the House of Commons, if we were to involve ourselves in a system of reciprocal preferences. Every one will agree, from whatever part of the King's dominions he comes, or to whatever Party he belongs, that Colonial affairs suffer very much when brought into the arena of British Party politics. Sometimes it is one Party and sometimes it is another which is constrained to interfere in the course of purely Colonial affairs, and such interferences are nearly always fraught with vexation and inconvenience to the Dominions affected.

1   The following, among others, were present at the Conference: The Earl of Elgin, Secretary of State for the Colonies; Sir Wilfrid Laurier, Prime Minister of Canada; Sir F.W. Borden, Minister of Militia and Defence (Canada); Mr. L.P. Brodeur, Minister of Marine and Fisheries (Canada); Mr. Deakin, Prime Minister of the Commonwealth of Australia; Sir W. Lyne, Minister of Trade and Customs (Australia); Sir Joseph Ward, Prime Minister of New Zealand; Dr. L.S. Jameson, Prime Minister of Cape Colony; Dr. Smartt, Commissioner of Public Works (Cape Colony); Sir Robert Bond, Prime Minister of Newfoundland; Mr. F.R. Moor, Prime Minister of Natal; General Botha, Prime Minister of the Transvaal; Sir J.L. Mackay, on behalf of the India Office.

Now, the system of Imperial preference inevitably brings Colonial affairs into the Parliamentary and the Party arena; and, if I may say so, it brings them into the most unpleasant part of Parliamentary and political work—that part which is concerned with raising the taxation for each year. It is very easy to talk about preference in the abstract and in general terms, and very many pleasant things can be said about mutual profits and the good feeling which accrues from commercial intercourse. But in regard to preference, as in regard to all other tariff questions, the discussion cannot possibly be practical, unless the propositions are formulated in precise, exact, and substantial detail. Many people will avow themselves in favour of the principle of preference who would recoil when the schedule of taxes was presented to their inspection.

I, therefore, leave generalities about preference on one side. I leave also proposals which have been discussed that we should give a preference on existing duties. It is quite clear that no preference given upon existing duties could possibly be complete or satisfactory. It could at the very best only be a beginning, and Dr. Jameson and Dr. Smartt, when they urged us with so much force to make a beginning by giving a preference on South African tobacco, have clearly recognised and frankly stated, that that preference would in itself be of small value, but that it would be welcomed by them as conceding "the larger principle." Therefore, we are entitled to say, that before us at this Conference is not any question of making a small or tentative beginning on this or that particular duty, but we have to make up our minds upon the general principle of the application of a reciprocal preference to the trade relations of the British Empire.

If that be so, surely the representatives of the self-governing Dominions who ask us to embark on such a system, ought to state squarely and abruptly the duties which in their opinion would be necessary to give effect to such a proposal. The question whether raw material is to be taxed is absolutely vital to any consideration of Imperial preference. Although it is no doubt a very good answer, when the direct question is raised,—What are your notions? to say that the Colonies would leave that to the Mother Country, those who urge upon us a system of reciprocal preference are bound to face the conclusions of their own policy, and are bound to recognise that that request, if it is to be given effect to in any symmetrical, logical, complete, satisfactory, or even fair and just manner, must involve new taxes to us on seven or eight staple articles of consumption in this country. I lay it down, without hesitation, that no fair system of Imperial preference can be established which does not include taxes on bread, on meat, on that group of food-stuffs classified under the head of dairy produce, on wool and leather, and on other necessaries of industry.

If that be so, seven or eight new taxes would have to be imposed to give effect to this principle you have brought before us. Those taxes would have to figure every year in our annual Budget. They would have to figure in the Budget resolutions of every successive year in the House of Commons. There will be two opinions about each of these taxes; there will be those who like them and favour the principle, and who will applaud the policy, and there will be those who dislike them. There will be the powerful interests which will be favoured and the interests which will be hurt by their adoption. So you will have, as each of those taxes comes up for the year, a steady volume of Parliamentary criticism directed at it.

Now that criticism will, I imagine, flow through every channel by which those taxes may be assailed. It will seek to examine the value, necessarily in a canvassing spirit, of the Colonial Preferences as a return for which these taxes are imposed. It will seek to dwell upon the hardship to the consumers in this country of the taxes themselves. It will stray farther, I think, and it will examine the contributions which the self-governing Dominions make to the general cost of Imperial defence; and will contrast those contributions with a severe and an almost harsh exactitude with the great charges borne by the Mother Country.

There has just been a debate upon that subject in the House of Commons; but the manner in which that question when raised was received by the whole House, ought, I think, to give great satisfaction to the representatives of the self-governing Dominions. We then refused to embark upon a policy of casting-up balances as between the Colonies and the Mother Country, and, speaking on behalf of the Colonial Office, I said that the British Empire existed on the principles of a family and not on those of a syndicate. But the introduction of those seven or eight taxes into the Budget of every year will force a casting-up of balances every year from a severe financial point of view. It has been said, and will be generally admitted, that there is no such thing in this country as an anti-Colonial party. It does not exist. Even parties, like the Irish Party, not reconciled to the British Government, who take no part in our public ceremonial, are glad to take opportunities of showing the representatives of the self-governing Dominions that they welcome them here, and desire to receive them with warmth and with cordiality. But I cannot conceive any process better calculated to manufacture an anti-Colonial party, than this process of subjecting to the scrutiny of the House of Commons year by year, through the agency of taxation, the profit and loss account, in its narrow, financial aspect, of the relations of Great Britain and her Dominions and dependencies.

Then this system of reciprocal preference, at its very outset, must involve conflict with the principle of self-government, which is the root of all our Colonial and Imperial policy. The whole procedure of our Parliament arises primarily from the consideration of finance, and finance is the peg on which nearly all our discussions are hung, and from which many of them arise. That is the historic origin of a great portion of the House of Commons procedure, and there is no more deeply rooted maxim than the maxim of "grievances before supply." Now, let me suppose a system of preference in operation. When the taxes came up to be voted each year, members would use those occasions for debating Colonial questions. I can imagine that they would say: We refuse to vote the preference tax to this or that self-governing Dominion, unless or until our views, say, on native policy or some other question of internal importance to the Dominion affected have been met and have been accepted. At present, it is open to the Colony affected to reply: These matters are matters which concern us; they are within the scope of responsible, self-governing functions, and you are not called upon to interfere. It is open for the Dominion concerned to say that. It is also open for the representative of the Colonial Office in the House of Commons to say that, too, on their behalf.

But it will no longer be open, I think, for any such defence to be offered when sums of money, or what would be regarded as equivalent to sums of money, have actually to be voted in the House of Commons through the agency of these taxes for the purpose of according preference to the different Dominions of the Crown, and I think members will say, "If you complain of our interference, why do you force us to interfere? You have forced us to consider now whether we will or will not grant a preference to this or that particular Dominion for this year. We say we are not prepared to do so unless or until our views upon this or that particular internal question in that Dominion have been met and agreed to." I see a fertile, frequent, and almost inexhaustible source of friction and vexation arising from such causes alone.

There is a more serious infringement, as it seems to me, upon the principle of self-government. The preferences which have hitherto been accorded to the Mother Country by the self-governing States of the British Empire are free preferences. They are preferences which have been conceded by those States, in their own interests and also in our interests. They are freely given, and, if they gall them, can as freely be withdrawn; but the moment reciprocity is established and an agreement has been entered into to which both sides are parties, the moment the preferences become reciprocal, and there is a British preference against the Australian or Canadian preferences, they become not free preferences, but what I venture to call locked preferences, and they cannot be removed except by agreement, which is not likely to be swiftly or easily attained.

Now I must trench for one moment upon the economic aspect. What does preference mean? It can only mean one thing. It can only mean better prices. It can only mean better prices for Colonial goods. I assert, without reserve, that preference can only operate through the agency of price. All that we are told about improving and developing the cultivation of tobacco in South Africa, and calling great new areas for wheat cultivation into existence in Australia, depends upon the stimulation of the production of those commodities, through securing to the producers larger opportunities for profit. I say that unless preference means better prices it will be ineffective in achieving the objects for the sake of which it is urged. But the operation of preference consists, so far as we are concerned, in putting a penal tax upon foreign goods, and the object of putting that penal tax on foreign goods is to enable the Colonial supply to rise to the level of the foreign goods plus the tax, and by so conferring upon the Colonial producer a greater reward, to stimulate him more abundantly to cater for the supply of this particular market. I say, therefore, without hesitation, that the only manner in which a trade preference can operate is through the agency of price. If preference does not mean better prices it seems to me a great fraud on those who are asked to make sacrifices to obtain it; and by "better" prices I mean higher prices—that is to say, higher prices than the goods are worth, if sold freely in the markets of the world.

I am quite ready to admit that the fact that you make a particular branch of trade more profitable, induces more people to engage in that branch of trade. That is what I call stimulating Colonial production through the agency of price. I am quite prepared to admit that a very small tax on staple articles would affect prices in a very small manner. Reference has been made to the imposition of a shilling duty on corn, and I think it was Mr. Moor[1] who said, yesterday, that when the shilling duty was imposed prices fell, and when it was taken off prices rose. That may be quite true. I do not know that it is true, but it may be. The imposition of such a small duty as a shilling on a commodity produced in such vast abundance as wheat, might quite easily be swamped or concealed by the operation of other more powerful factors. A week of unusual sunshine, or a night of late frost, or a ring in the freights, or violent speculation, might easily swamp and cover the operation of such a small duty; but it is the opinion of those whose economic views I share—I cannot put it higher than that—that whatever circumstances may apparently conceal the effect of the duty on prices, the effect is there all the same, and that any duty that is imposed upon a commodity becomes a factor in the price of that commodity. I should have thought that was an almost incontestable proposition.

Here you have the two different sides of the bargain, the sellers and the buyers, the sellers trying to get all they can, and the buyers trying to give as little as they can. An elaborate process of what is called "the higgling of the market" goes on all over the world between exchanges linked up by telegraph, whose prices vary to a sixteenth and a thirty-second. We are invited to believe that with all that subtle process of calculation made from almost minute to minute throughout the year, the imposition of a duty or

---

[1]   The Prime Minister of Natal.

demand for £1,000,000 or £2,000,000 for this or that Government, placed suddenly upon the commodity in question as a tax, makes no difference whatever to the cost to the consumer; that it is borne either by the buyer or by the seller, or provided in some magical manner. As a matter of fact, the seller endeavours to transmit the burden to the purchaser, and the purchaser places it upon the consumer as opportunity may occur in relation to the general market situation all over the world.

That is by way of digression, only to show that we believe that a tax on a commodity is a factor in its price, which I thought was a tolerably simple proposition. What a dangerous thing it will be, year after year, to associate the idea of Empire, of our kith and kin beyond the seas, of these great, young, self-governing Dominions in which our people at present take so much pride, with an enhancement, however small, in the price of the necessary commodities of the life and the industry of Britain! It seems to me that, quite apart from the Parliamentary difficulty to which I have referred, which I think would tend to organise and create anti-Colonial sentiment, you would, by the imposition of duties upon the necessaries of life and of industry, breed steadily year by year, and accumulate at the end of a decade a deep feeling of sullen hatred of the Colonies, and of Colonial affairs among those poorer people in this country to whom Mr. Lloyd George referred so eloquently yesterday, and whose case, when stated, appeals to the sympathy of every one round this table. That would be a great disaster.

But there is another point which occurs to me, and which I would submit respectfully to the Conference in this connection. Great fluctuations occur in the price of all commodities which are subject to climatic influences. We have seen enormous fluctuations in meat and cereals and in food-stuffs generally from time to time in the world's markets. Although we buy in the markets of the whole world we observe how much the price of one year varies from that of another year. These fluctuations are due to causes beyond our control. We cannot control the causes which make the earth refuse her fruits at a certain season, nor can we, unfortunately, at present, control the speculation which always arises when an unusual stringency is discovered. Compared to these forces, the taxes which you suggest should be imposed upon food and raw materials might, I admit, be small, but they would be the only factor in price which would be absolutely in our control.

If, from circumstances which we may easily imagine, any of the great staple articles which were the subject of preference should be driven up in price to an unusual height, there would be a demand—and I think an irresistible demand—in this country that the tax should be removed. The tax would bear all the unpopularity. People would say: "This, at any rate, we can take off, and relieve the burden which is pressing so heavily upon us." But now see the difficulty in which we should then be involved. At present all our taxes are under our own control. An unpopular tax can be removed; if the Government will not remove it they can be turned out and another Government to remove the tax can be got from the people by election. It can be done at once. The Chancellor of the Exchequer can come down to the House and the tax can be repealed if there is a sufficiently fierce demand for it.

But these food taxes by which you seek to bind the Empire together—these curious links of Empire which you are asking us to forge laboriously now—would be irremovable, and upon them would descend the whole weight and burden of popular anger in time of suffering. They would be irremovable, because fixed by treaty with self-governing Dominions scattered about all over the world, and in return for those duties we should have received concessions in Colonial tariffs on the basis of which their industries would have grown up tier upon tier through a long period of time.

Although, no doubt, another Conference hastily assembled might be able to break the shackle which would fasten us—to break that fiscal bond which would join us together and release us from the obligation—that might take a great deal of time. Many Parliaments and Governments would have to be consulted, and all the difficulties of distance would intervene to prevent a speedy relief from that deadlock. If the day comes in this country when you have a stern demand—and an overwhelming demand of a Parliament, backed by a vast population suffering acutely from high food-prices—that the taxes should be removed, and on the other hand the Minister in charge has to get up and say that he will bring the matter before the next Colonial Conference two years hence, or that he will address the representatives of the Australian or Canadian Governments through the agency of the Colonial Office, and that in the meanwhile nothing can be done—when you have produced that situation, then, indeed, you will have exposed the fabric of the British Empire to a wrench and a shock which it has never before received, and which any one who cares about it, cannot fail to hope that it may never sustain.

Such a deadlock could not be relieved merely by goodwill on either side. When you begin to deflect the course of trade, you deflect it in all directions and for all time in both countries which are parties to the bargain. Your industries in your respective Colonies would have exposed themselves to a more severe competition from British goods in their markets, and would have adjusted themselves on a different basis, in consequence. Some Colonial producers would have made sacrifices in that respect for the sake of certain advantages which were to be gained by other producers in their country through a favoured entry into our market. That one side of the bargain could be suddenly removed, without inflicting injustice on the other party to the bargain, appears to me an impossibility.

I submit that preferences, even if economically desirable, would prove an element of strain and discord in the structure and system of the British Empire. Why, even in this Conference, what has been the one subject on which we have differed sharply? It has been this question of preference. It has been the one apple of discord which has been thrown into the arena of our discussions. It is quite true we meet here with a great fund of goodwill on everybody's part, on the part of the Mother Country and on the part of the representatives of the self-governing Dominions—a great fund of goodwill which has been accumulated over a long period of time when each party to this great confederation has been free to pursue its own line of development unchecked and untrammelled by interference from the other.

We have that to start upon, and consequently have been able to discuss in a very frank and friendly manner all sorts of questions. We have witnessed the spectacle of the British Minister in charge of the trade of this country defending at length and in detail the fiscal system—the purely domestic, internal fiscal system of this country—from very severe, though perfectly friendly and courteous criticism on the part of the other self-governing communities. If that fund of goodwill to which I have referred had been lacking, if ever a Conference had been called together when there was an actual anti-colonial party in existence, when there was really a deep hatred in the minds of a large portion of the people of this country against the Colonies and against taxation which was imposed at the request or desire of the Colonies, then I think it is quite possible that a Conference such as this would not pass off in the smooth and friendly manner in which this has passed off.

You would hear recrimination and reproaches exchanged across the table; you would hear assertions made that the representatives of the different States who were parties to the Conference were not really representatives of the true opinion of their respective populations, that the trend of opinion in the country which they professed to represent was opposed to their policy and would shortly effect a change in the views which they put forward. You would find all these undemocratic assertions that representatives duly elected do not really speak in the name of their people, and you would, of course, find appeals made over the heads of the respective Governments to the party organisations which supported them or opposed them in the respective countries from which they came. That appears to me to open up possibilities of very grave and serious dangers in the structure and fabric of the British Empire, from which I think we ought to labour to shield it.

My right honourable friend the Chancellor of the Exchequer has told the Conference with perfect truth—in fact it may have been even an under-estimate—that if he were to propose the principle of preference in the present House of Commons, it would be rejected by a majority of three to one. But even if the present Government could command a majority for the system, they would have no intention whatever of proposing it. It is not because we are not ready to run electoral risks that we decline to be parties to a system of preference; still less is it because the present Government is unwilling to make sacrifices, in money or otherwise, in order to weave the Empire more closely together. I think a very hopeful deflection has been given to our discussion when it is suggested that we may find a more convenient line of advance by improving communications, rather than by erecting tariffs—by making roads, as it were, across the Empire, rather than by building walls. It is because we believe the principle of preference is positively injurious to the British Empire, and would create, not union, but discord, that we have resisted the proposal.

It has been a source of regret to all of us that on this subject we cannot come to an agreement. A fundamental difference of opinion on economics, no doubt, makes agreement impossible; but although we regret that, I do not doubt that in the future, when Imperial unification has been carried to a stage which it has not now reached, and will not, perhaps, in our time attain, people in that more fortunate age will look back to the Conference of 1907 as a date in the history of the British Empire when one grand wrong turn was successfully avoided.

IMPERIAL PREFERENCE - II

HOUSE OF COMMONS, *JULY 15, 1907*

*M*r. Lyttelton had moved the following vote of censure:
"That this House regrets that his Majesty's Government have declined the invitation unanimously preferred by the Prime Ministers of the self-governing Colonies, to consider favourably any form of Colonial Preference or any measures for closer commercial union of the Empire on a preferential basis." (Mr. Lyttelton.)

This was met on behalf of the Government by the following Amendment:

"To leave out all after the word 'that' and add the words 'In the opinion of this House, the permanent unity of the British Empire will not be secured through a system of preferential duties based upon the protective taxation of food.'" (Mr. Soares)

The vote of censure was rejected, and the Amendment carried by 404 to 111.

A vote of censure is a very serious thing. When it is moved with great formality on behalf of the official Opposition, it is intended always to raise a plain and decisive issue. I must, however, observe that of all the votes of censure which have been proposed in recent times in this House, the one we are now discussing is surely the most curious. The last Government was broken up three years ago on this very question of Imperial preference. After the Government had been broken up, a continuous debate proceeded in the country for two years and a half, and it was terminated by the general election. This Parliament is the result of that election, and there is not a single gentleman on this Ministerial Bench who is not pledged, in the most specific terms, not to grant a preferential tariff to the Colonies. Now, because we have kept that promise, because we are opposed to preferential tariffs, because we have declined to grant preferential tariffs, and because we have done what all along we declared we were going to do, and were returned to do, we are made the object of this vote of censure.

It may be said, "We do not blame you for keeping your promise, but for making the pledge." But what did the Leader of the Opposition promise? He promised most emphatically before the election that if he were in power as Prime Minister when this Colonial Conference took place, he would not grant preference to the Colonies. On many occasions the right hon. gentleman said that not one, but two elections would be necessary before he would be entitled to take that tremendous step. I have the right hon. gentleman's words here. Speaking at Manchester in January 1905, the right hon. gentleman said: "If that scheme were carried out, I do not see that we could be called on to decide the colonial aspect of this question until not only one, but two elections have passed." Yet the right hon. gentleman is prepared, I presume, to join in a vote of censure on his Majesty's Government for not granting that preference which he himself was prohibited from granting by the most precise and particular engagement.

Is it a vote of censure on the Government at all? Is it not really a vote of censure on the general election? Is it not a cry of petulant vexation at the natural, ordinary, long-expected sequence of events?

The right hon. gentleman[1] who moved the Resolution made a very mild and conciliatory speech. But he confined himself to generalities. He avoided anything like a statement of concrete proposals which he thinks the Government ought to adopt. Those who take part in this controversy nowadays avoid any statement of the concrete proposals that would follow if their view were adopted. We are told what a splendid thing preference is, what noble results it would achieve, what inexpressible happiness and joy it would bring to all parts of the Empire and to all parts of the earth, what wealth would be created, how the Exchequer would gain, and how the food of the people would cheapen in price. But, though the Government is blamed for not acting on these suggestions, we are never told what is the schedule of taxes which it is proposed to introduce to give effect to these splendid and glittering aspirations.

It is perfectly impossible to discuss colonial preference apart from the schedule of duties on which it is to be based. It is idle to attempt to discuss it without a definite proposal as to the subjects of taxation and as to the degree to which those different subjects are to be taxed. And the right hon. gentleman the Member for West Birmingham, when he dealt with this question, felt that in common fairness he must be precise and definite.

[1]   Mr Lyttelton.

We know what he proposed in the way of taxation on corn, meat, fruit, and dairy produce. What we want to know is this. Is that tariff before us now? Do the Opposition stand by the right hon. Member for West Birmingham, or do they abandon him? That is what the House and the Government want to know—and that is what the Colonies want to know. It is indispensable to the discussion of this question that there should be a clear statement from the Leader of the Opposition whether or not we are to regard the Glasgow preferential tariff of the right hon. Member for West Birmingham as still current as a practical policy.

Then the House has been told that the Government might have given a preference on dutiable articles. Such a preference would introduce into our fiscal system an entirely new, and, as the Government think, the wholly vicious feature of discriminating between one class of producers and another. The whole basis of our financial and fiscal policy is, that it draws no distinction whatever between different classes of producers, whether they reside here or abroad, whether they live in foreign countries or in our Colonies. I am quite prepared to state that proposition in its simplest form. That is the fundamental principle of our fiscal system, and there is no discrimination. We have but one measure to give to those who trade with us—the just measure of equality, and there can be no better measure than that.

We are charged with pedantry in dealing with the Colonial Conference, through not making some concession upon existing dutiable articles. The Colonial representatives, when they asked for a preference on wine and tobacco, did not ask for it because it was of value to them by itself. They knew well that the operation of such a preference must be unfair and unequal. They knew well that Canada, which has the most solid claims upon us for a preferential recognition, would receive no benefit from such a preference. But the Colonial representatives of South Africa asked for a preference on wine and tobacco in order that, as they avowed with candour, we should "concede the principle." That is a perfectly proper proceeding on their part; it is the natural way of advancing the views which they hold, because it would lead up to the larger principle and the larger policy.

But the Government are opposed in this case to "the larger policy." The Government sit now on these Benches because they are opposed to it as a Government and as a Party. It is one of the fundamental conditions of our existence that we are opposed to such a policy. How, then, by any process of argument, can the Government be censured for not making an exception which must inevitably have led to and would avowedly have been used for the breaking of the great rule to which they have committed themselves?

It is a dangerous thing in this controversy, with the ugly rush of vested interests always lying in the wake of the Protectionist movement to be considered, to make even verbal concessions. Some time ago I made a speech in which I said that there was no objection to the extension of inter-colonial preference. By this I meant the reduction of duties between Colonies which have already a discriminating tariff; and it seemed to me in such a case that there is a net reduction of duty to the good. I do not see any objection to that, because under the most-favoured-nation principle we gain any advantage which is gained by either party to the transaction. In any case, the sums involved in inter-colonial preference at the present time are extremely small, and, however that might be, the matter is one which is wholly outside our control, because we have no authority over the Colonies in this respect, and we may just as well look pleasant about it and accord a sympathetic attitude to such a process.

Yes; but let those who reproach us with pedantry and with not showing a sympathetic desire to meet the Colonies listen to this: When such a statement is made by a Minister, is it accepted as a desire on the part of the Government to extend sympathetic treatment to the Colonies? Not at all. It is taken as an admission, and used for the purpose of trying to pretend that the Government have abandoned the principle of their opposition to the larger question of Imperial preference. If, although we think them unsatisfactory, we were, out of complaisance, to accord the small preferences suggested upon dutiable articles, we should be told in a minute that we had given up every logical foothold against preference, and that nothing prevented us imposing a tax on bread and meat except our inability to follow the drift of our own arguments.

I have referred to preference, but there is another proposal. The right hon. gentleman the Member for St. George's, Hanover Square, put forward a proposal earlier in the year, and it was renewed in a slightly different form by Mr. Deakin[1] at the Conference. The proposal was to impose a 1 per cent. *ad valorem* surtax on all foreign merchandise coming into the ports of the British Empire. That is the proposal which has been put forward as the least objectionable form of the preferential proposals, and it has been said of it that it was the least objectionable because it gave no loophole for the corruption which may spring up in the wake of the other proposals.

Let me ask the House to examine this proposal for a moment. Has any serious, civilised Government—I ask for information—ever been to the pains and trouble of erecting round their coasts a tariff, with all its complications, with the need of exacting certificates of origin on every class of goods, with the need of demanding strict assessment of all commodities brought to their shores—has any nation ever erected the

[1]   Prime Minister of the Australian Commonwealth.

vast and complicated network which would be involved in such a duty, simply for the paltry purpose of imposing a duty of 1 per cent.? I say there is no argument and no reason for such a course, and the only argument which could justify it is the argument used by Dr. Smartt at the Colonial Conference when he said (page 514 of the Blue Book), "The foreigner pays, and we do not." Mr. Deakin felt the force of the objection which would be entertained in this country to introducing such a tariff as the right hon. gentleman has proposed, simply for fiscal purposes, and he proceeded to say that Great Britain, if she was a party to such a bargain, should be permitted to raise the money in her own way, and to contribute her proportion to the common fund. That was a great concession to the self-government of the Mother Country.

There is no doubt a great difference between subventions and preferences. A subvention may be raised by a perfectly orthodox fiscal process. No more money is taken from the taxpayer than is required. The whole yield of the tax by which the subvention may be raised certainly goes to the Exchequer, and when the subvention is paid to the foreign or Colonial Government, it does not go, as a preference would go, to benefit particular interests in the Colony, but it goes to the Government of the Colony for the general purposes of State, and not for private advantage on either side. Therefore it seems to me that the method of subvention is on all grounds to be preferred to the method of preference.

It is of course necessary, however, in examining a question of subvention to look at it on its merits. This proposal of 1 per cent. put forward by Mr. Deakin carried the support of the official spokesman of the Opposition. Let us look at it on its merits. Look first at the proportions on which this new fund was to be subscribed. Canada was "to dedicate"—that was the expression used by Mr. Deakin—£400,000, New Zealand £20,000, Newfoundland £6,000, Cape Colony £40,000, Natal £26,000, Great Britain £4,500,000, and Australia—the proposing body—what was she to "dedicate" to this fund? No more than £100,000 a year, or one forty-fifth part of the contribution which was to be made by this country. And for what object was this fund to be accumulated? It is hard enough for the Chancellor of the Exchequer to raise the money to carry on so great an establishment as this country is forced necessarily to maintain. But here is a proposal to raise no less than £4,500,000 of extra taxation. For what objects? For objects not specified, for objects not yet discovered, for objects which could not be stated by those who made the proposal. The right hon. gentleman said that there was to be a meeting of the representatives of the different Colonies in the different great cities of the Empire—one different great city each year for seven years, excluding London, where there was to be no meeting, and they were to search for a method of spending this money. Such plans have only to be stated to fall to pieces.

The House will see that the real essential fallacy of the protectionist proposal is the idea that taxation is a good thing in itself, that it should be imposed for the fun of the thing, and then, having done it for amusement, we should go round afterwards and look for attractive methods of expenditure in order to give support to the project. These are the actual proposals made to us at the Colonial Conference. These are the sort of proposals in respect of which we are, forsooth, to be censured because we have not found it possible in the name of the Government of this country to give our assent to them.

I will submit a proposition to the House as a broad, general rule. I daresay the Leader of the Opposition may rake up some ingenious, hard case in conflict with it; but as a broad, general rule I believe it will be found true to say that there is no power in a Government to impose indirect taxation outside the limits of its territorial sovereignty. Although I am quite ready to admit that, by sudden and unexpected alterations of the tariff, temporary advantage might be gained, and some share of the wealth of other people and other countries might be netted for this or that set of traders within your own border, in the long run the whole yield of any tax, export or import, will come home to the people of that country by whom it is imposed. It will come home plus the whole cost of collecting the tax, and plus, further, the inconvenience and burden of the network of taxation which is needed. It will come home to them, if they be consumers, in the quantity, quality, or price of the articles they consume, and, if exporters, in the profit, convenience, or reserve power of the business which they conduct.

There is no parity between the sacrifices demanded of the Mother Country and the proposals of preference made by the various Colonies. To them it is merely a fresh application of their existing fiscal system. To us it is a fiscal revolution. To them it is a mere rewriting of their schedules to give an increased measure of protection to their home producers. To us it is a tax on food, and, as I assert again and again, upon raw material, and thus upon all the industries of these islands. If the Conference has established one thing clearly it is this, that none of the great self-governing Colonies of the British Empire are prepared to give us effective access to their own markets in competition with their home producers. That was established with absolute clearness; and even if they were prepared to give us effective access to their home markets, I submit to the House that, having regard to the great preponderance of our foreign trade as against our Colonial trade, it would not be worth our while to purchase the concession which they would then offer at the cost of disturbing and dislocating the whole area of our trade. Therefore, we propose to adhere, and are prepared if necessary to be censured for adhering to our general financial system, which is governed by the rule that there should be no taxation except for revenue, and based on the commercial principle of the equal treatment of all nations, and the most-favoured-nation treatment from those nations in return.

Important as are the economical arguments against a preferential policy, they are in my opinion less grave than the political disadvantages. On other occasions I have addressed the House on the grave danger and detriment to the working of our Colonial system which must follow the intermingling of the affairs of the British Empire in the party politics and financial politics of this country. To establish a preferential system with the Colonies involving differential duties upon food is to make the bond of Imperial unity dependent year after year upon the weather and the crops.

And there is even a more unstable foundation for Imperial unity. Does it never occur to right hon. gentlemen opposite that this solution which they offer of the problem of Imperial unity places the Empire not on a national, but on a purely party basis, and upon a basis repudiated by at least half the nation? Some day it may be that they will return triumphant from a general election. As party politicians they may rejoice, yet I think a wise statesman would try to win for the British Empire, our Colonial relations, the same sort of position, high above the struggle of Parties, which is now so happily occupied by the Crown and the Courts of Justice, which in less degree, though in an increasing degree, is coming to be occupied by the fighting Services. Whatever advantages from a Party point of view, or from the point of view of gratifying Colonial opinion, may be gained by food preferences, they would be very small compared with the enormous boon of keeping the field of Colonial politics separate from the social and economic issues on which Parties in this country are so fiercely divided.

It is possible to take a still wider view of this question. If I quote the right hon. gentleman the Member for West Birmingham, let me assure the House that I do not do so for the purpose of making any petty charge of inconsistency, but because the words which I am going to read are wise and true words, and stand the test of time. When the right hon. gentleman spoke at Manchester in 1897, not in the distant days before the great Home Rule split, but when he was already a Minister in the Unionist Government, and had been Secretary of State for the Colonies for nearly two years, he used these words, of the highest wisdom: "Anything in the direction of an Imperial Commercial League would weaken the Empire internally and excite the permanent hostility of the whole world. It would check the free imports of the food of the people. It is impracticable; but if it were practicable, and done in the name of the Empire, it would make the Empire odious to the working people, it would combine the whole world against us, and it would be a cause of irritation and menace. Our free commerce makes for the peace of the world."

Let us then seek to impress year after year upon the British Empire an inclusive and not an exclusive character. We who sit on this side of the House, who look forward to larger brotherhoods and more exact standards of social justice, value and cherish the British Empire because it represents more than any other similar organisation has ever represented, the peaceful co-operation of all sorts of men in all sorts of countries, and because we think it is, in that respect at least, a model of what we hope the whole world will some day become. The House has to-night a considerable and important opportunity. If in rejecting this vote of censure, which is so ill-conceived and so little deserved, we choose to adopt the Amendment, we shall have written upon the records of Parliament a profound political truth, which will not, I think, soon be challenged, and which, I believe, will never be overthrown.

THE HOUSE OF LORDS

HOUSE OF COMMONS, *JUNE 29, 1907*

*O*n June 24, Sir Henry Campbell-Bannerman had moved:
    "That, in order to give effect to the will of the people as expressed by their elected representatives, it is necessary that the power of the other House to alter or reject Bills passed by this House should be so restricted by law as to secure that within the limits of a single Parliament the final decision of the Commons shall prevail."

This was carried after three days' debate by 315 to 100.

I will not venture at any length into an abstract constitutional discussion upon this Motion, because, after all, we have an extremely practical issue before us. It seems to me that this great question must be looked at from three points of view. There is the issue between the two Houses; there is the issue between the two political Parties; and then there is the national issue. The quarrel which is now open between the House of Lords and the House of Commons arises from two events—the general election of 1906, and the rejection of the measures of the new Liberal Government, culminating in the destruction of the Education Bill by the House of Lords at the end of that year. Either of these events is memorable in itself, but placed in juxtaposition and considered together they have a multiplied significance. The general election of 1906 was the most vehement expression of public opinion which this generation has known; and that expression of public will was countered in the December of the same year by the most arbitrary and uncompromising assertion of aristocratic privilege upon record.

Let the House think of it. The process of the election of Members of Parliament is extremely elaborate. The candidates go about the country for two or three weeks saying all they have to say for themselves in the different constituencies which they are contesting; at the end of that exhaustive discussion there is an elaborate process of voting; the returns are counted with the most scrupulous care; and as the result 670 Members, representing 6,000,000 of voters and many more who take a deep interest in public affairs but have no votes, are returned to the House of Commons in the name of the people of Great Britain and Ireland. The new Parliament assembles. Scarcely any question at the election had been more a test question, so far as the supporters of the Government are concerned, than the question of the amendment of the education system of the country. A Bill dealing with education is brought forward as the principal measure of the first session of the new Parliament. Weeks are occupied in its discussion. It represents the fulfilment of the election pledges of every Member who supported it. The Bill is passed by perhaps the largest majority that ever sent a Bill from this House to another place.

Nor was it a revolutionary Bill, to turn the world upside down and inside out; on the contrary, it was a Bill which, if vitiated in any respect, was vitiated by the element of compromise. Immense concessions were made in it, and rightly, I think, to conscientious and agitated minorities. It was a Bill which so moderate and consistent a statesman as the Duke of Devonshire, of whose ill-health the House learns with grave concern, urged the House of Lords to pass into law.

Sir, the Leader of the Opposition told us the other day that it was the habit of his Majesty's Government to introduce Bills which they did not mean to pass. No one—not even the right hon. gentleman himself—can say that the Government have not earnestly desired to pass the Education Bill. Every concession that could be conceived was made, but to what purpose? After the House of Commons had humbled itself before the House of Lords, after we had gone to the extreme limit of concession which self-respect, which a proper sense of the dignity of this House, and a due observance of the pledges of the Liberal Party permitted, the House of Lords curtly, bluntly, uncharitably, and harshly flung the Bill out in our faces mutilated and destroyed. I do not wish to import an element of heat into this discussion, but I respectfully submit to the Conservative Party that that act on the part of the House of Lords places them in a new position—a new position in the sense that never before had their old position been taken up so nakedly, so brazenly, and so uncompromisingly.

It is true that we have an excuse put before us with much suavity of language in these debates—we are told that the House of Lords seeks to interpret the will of the people, and it is explained that by "the will of the people," what is meant is the persistent, sub-conscious will, as opposed to any articulate expression of it. The right hon. gentleman who leads the Opposition told us that what he meant by the persistent will was the will of the people expressed continuously over a period of thirty years. That is what he called "democracy properly understood."

Having regard to that part of the question which concerns the issue between the two Houses, we repudiate emphatically the claim of the other House to what the French call *faire l'ange*—to "play the angel," to know better than the people themselves what the people want, to have a greater authority to speak in the name of the people than their representatives sent to Parliament by the elaborate process I have described. To dispute the authority of a newly elected Parliament is something very like an incitement to violence on the part of the other House. The noble Lord[1] laughs; but we are anxious to convince him and his friends that we are in earnest. We go through all the processes which the Constitution prescribes, we produce an enormous majority, and we express the opinion of that majority, but still the noble Lord and other noble Lords, less intelligent, but more remote, tell us that they are not convinced. What steps do they suggest that we should take in order to bring home to them the earnestness of our plea? What steps do they suggest that the people should take in order to assert their wishes? I hold entirely by what I said that to dispute the authority of an elected body fresh from its constituents is a deliberate incitement to the adoption of lawless and unconstitutional methods. The assertion which the House of Lords made at the end of last year is an intolerable assertion. I believe the country is altogether unprepared for it; and I wonder it was thought worth while to risk an institution which has lasted so many centuries, in the very skirmish line of Party warfare.

I am aware there is a special reason for the temerity of the House of Lords. It is not a very complimentary reason to the Members or the leaders of the late Government, but it is argued that the Conservative Party cannot be worse than they are. No matter what they do, nor how they are hated or reprobated by the country, the Conservative Party cannot possibly occupy a more humiliating and unpleasant position than they did after the last two years of the late Administration. Consequently, having reached the low-water mark of political fortune, they think they can afford to be a little reckless, and that at the very worst they will be returned in their present numerical proportions.

That is a very natural explanation of their action; but if we for our part were to accept the assertion lately made by the House of Lords—an assertion which is the furthest point to which aristocratic privilege has attained in modern times—that assertion itself would become only the starting-point for a whole new series of precedents and of constitutional

---

[1]   Lord Robert Cecil.

retrogressions; and worse than that, if by any chance, having raised this issue, we were to be defeated upon it—if having placed this Resolution on the records of the House we were to fail to give effect to it, or were to suffer an electoral reverse as the conclusion of it—then good-bye to the power of the House of Commons. All that long process of advance in democratic institutions which has accompanied the growth of the power of the House of Commons, and which has also been attended by an expansion of the circles of comfort and culture among the people of this country—all that long process which has gone steadily onward for 200 years, and which has almost exclusively occupied the politics of the nineteenth century—will have reached its culmination. It will have come in contact with that barrier of which we have heard so much in this debate. The tide will have turned, and in the recoil of the waters they will gradually leave exposed again, altered no doubt by the conditions of the age, all the old assertions of aristocratic and plutocratic domination which we had fondly hoped had been engulfed for ever.

Hon. gentlemen opposite would be well advised to treat this Resolution seriously. This Parliament is still young, but there are some things at which they have laughed which have already become accomplished facts, I could not have during the past eighteen months listened to their taunts about the permanence of Chinese labour without reflecting now with satisfaction that Chinese labour is going. Yes, and other people may follow. We are only at the beginning of this struggle. We are not necessarily committed to every detail of the proposal; we are opening the first lines for a great siege, we have to sap up to the advanced parallels, to establish our batteries, and at no distant date open our bombardment. It may be many months before we shall be able to discern where there is a practicable breach; but the assault will come in due time.

The right hon. gentleman opposite[1] said he welcomed this contest with great confidence. I wonder if the Conservative Party realise, to use an expressive vulgarism, what they are "letting themselves in for" when this question comes to be fought out on every platform in every constituency in the country? They will not have to defend an ideal Second Chamber; they will not be able to confine themselves to airy generalities about a bicameral system and its advantages; they will have to defend *this* Second Chamber as it is—one-sided, hereditary, unpurged, unrepresentative, irresponsible, absentee. They will have to defend it with all its anomalies, all its absurdities, and all its personal bias—with all its achievements that have darkened the pages of the history of England. And let me say that weighty constitutional authorities have not considered that the policy on which we have embarked in moving this Resolution is unreasonable. Mr. Bagehot says of the House of Lords:

---

[1]   Mr. Balfour.

"It may lose its veto as the Crown has lost its veto. If most of its members neglect their duties, if all its members continue to be of one class, and that not quite the best; if its doors are shut against genius that cannot found a family, and ability which has not £5,000 a year, its power will be less year by year, and at last be gone, as so much kingly power is gone—no one knows how."

What is the position of the Conservative Party when they attempt to defend the House of Lords? They are always telling us to imitate the Colonies; they are always telling us that we ought to adopt the fiscal systems and other methods employed in the self-governing Colonies; but what is their unprejudiced view of the relations which are held between the two Chambers under the bicameral system in the Colonies and as established by their own Australian Commonwealth Act in the last Parliament? By that Act they have given power to the Lower Chamber to over-ride the Upper Chamber in certain circumstances. The Commonwealth Act says that when the Chambers differ they shall meet together, and that the majority shall decide, measures being taken, however, that the numbers of the Upper Chamber shall not be such as to swamp the opinion of the Lower Chamber. Imitating them, and following in their footsteps, we have adopted such a plan in the Transvaal and Orange River Colony Constitutions.

The Leader of the Opposition asked us yesterday whether the people are not often wrong, and he proceeded characteristically to suggest that he always considered them wrong when they voted against him. I am not prepared to take such a rough-and-ready test of the opinion and of the mental processes of the British democracy as that. I should hesitate to say that when the people pronounce against a particular measure or Party they have not pretty good reasons for doing so. I am not at all convinced that in 1900 the electors were wrong in saying that the war should be finished—by those who made it. Even in the last election I could, I daresay, find some few reasons to justify the decision which the people then took; and if we should be so unfortunate in the future as to lose that measure of public confidence now abundantly given to us, then I shall not be too sure that it will not be our own fault. Certain am I that we could not take any step more likely to forfeit the confidence of the people of England, than to continue in office after we have lost the power to pass effective legislation.

I will retort the question of the Leader of the Opposition by another question. Has the House of Lords ever been right? Has it ever been right in any of the great settled controversies which are now beyond the reach of Party argument? Was it right in delaying Catholic emancipation and the removal of Jewish disabilities? Was it right in driving this country to the verge of revolution in its effort to defeat the passage of reform? Was it right in resisting the Ballot Bill? Was it right in the almost innumerable efforts it made to prevent this House dealing with the purity of its own electoral machinery? Was it right in endeavouring to prevent the abolition of purchase in the Army? Was it right in 1880, when it rejected the Compensation for Disturbance Bill? I defy the Party opposite to produce a single instance of a settled controversy in which the House of Lords was right.

[An honourable Member: What about Home Rule?]

I expected that interruption. That is not a settled controversy. It is a matter which lies in the future. The cases I have mentioned are cases where we have carried the law into effect and have seen the results, and found that they have been good.

Let me remind the House that, but for a lucky accident, but for the fact that Letters Patent can be issued by the Crown and do not require the statutory assent of Parliament, it would very likely have been impossible for this Government to have made the constitutional settlement in the Transvaal and in the Orange River Colony, because the Constitutions would probably have been mutilated or cast out by the House of Lords, and the Executive Government would have found itself responsible for carrying out the government of Colonies on lines of which it wholly disapproved, and after their own policy had been rejected.

I proceed to inquire on what principle the House of Lords deals with Liberal measures. The right hon. Member for Dover[1] by an imaginative effort assures us that they occupy the position of the umpire. Are they even a sieve, a strainer, to stop legislation if it should reveal an undue or undesirable degree of Radicalism or Socialism? Are they the complementary critic—the critic who sees all the things which the ordinary man does not see? No one can maintain it. The attitude which the House of Lords adopts towards Liberal measures is purely tactical. When they returned to their "gilded Chamber" after the general election they found on the Woolsack and on the Treasury Bench a Lord Chancellor and a Government with which they were not familiar. When their eyes fell upon those objects, there was a light in them which meant one thing— murder; murder tempered, no doubt, by those prudential considerations which always restrain persons from acts which are contrary to the general feeling of the society in which they live. But their attitude towards the present Government has from the beginning been to select the best and most convenient opportunity of humiliating and discrediting them, and finally of banishing them from power.

Examine, in contrast with that of the Education Bill, their treatment of the Trades Disputes Bill. Lord Halsbury described that Bill as outrageous and tyrannous, and said it contained a section more disgraceful than

[1]   Mr. Wyndham.

any that appeared in any English Statute. On what ground then did they pass that Bill, if it was not the ground of political opportunism and partisanship? What safeguard can such a Second Chamber be to the commercial interests of this country? Is it not clear that they are prepared to sacrifice, if necessary, what they consider to be the true interests of the country in order to secure an advantage for the political Party whose obedient henchmen they are? The Trades Disputes Bill was a very inconvenient measure for the Conservative Party to leave open, because so long as it was left open a great mass of democratic opinion was directed against them. And so it was passed. On the other hand, the Education Bill was very inconvenient for the Liberal Party to leave open, because they are supported by Catholics and Nonconformists, and to bring in an Education Bill to satisfy those two extremes is not to solve a problem, but to solve a double acrostic. So that Bill was not passed. Upon a measure which it would be inconvenient to the Liberal Party to leave open the House of Lords rejected all compromise. Upon a measure which it would be inconvenient for the Conservative Party to leave open, they submitted at once—their action being irrespective of merits in either case. That, I suppose, is what the Leader of the Opposition called "an averaging machinery."

I press these points in order to justify me in making this statement, that the House of Lords, as it at present exists and acts, is not a national institution, but a Party dodge, an apparatus and instrument at the disposal of one political faction; and it is used in the most unscrupulous manner to injure and humiliate the opposite faction. When Conservative Members go about the country defending a Second Chamber, let them remember that this is the kind of Second Chamber they have to defend, and when they defend the veto let them remember that it is a veto used, not for national purposes, but for the grossest purposes of unscrupulous political partisanship.

I have dealt with the issues between Houses, and I come to that between Parties. Great changes in a community are very often unperceived; the focus of reality moves from one institution in the State to another, and almost imperceptibly. Sometimes the forms of institutions remain almost the same in all ceremonial aspects, and yet there will be one institution which under pretentious forms is only the husk of reality, and another which under a humble name is in fact the operative pivot of the social system. Constitutional writers have much to say about the estates of the realm, and a great deal to say about their relation to each other, and to the Sovereign. All that is found to be treated upon at length. But they say very little about the Party system. And, after all, the Party system is the dominant fact in our experience. Nothing is more striking in the last twenty-five years than the growth and expansion of Party organisation, and the way in which millions of people and their votes have been woven into its scope.

There are two great characteristics about the Party institutions of this country: the equipoise between them, and their almost incredible durability. We have only to look at the general elections of 1900 and 1906. I do not suppose any circumstances could be more depressing for a political Party than the circumstances in which the Liberal Party fought the election in 1900, except the circumstances in which the Conservative Party fought the election of 1906. At those two elections, what was the salient fact? The great mass of the voters of each political Party stood firm by the standard of their Party, and although there was an immense movement of public opinion, that movement was actually effected by the actual transference of a comparatively small number of votes.

When Parties are thus evenly balanced, to place such a weapon as the House of Lords in the hands of one of the Parties is to doom the other to destruction. I do not speak only from the Party point of view, although it explains the earnestness with which we approach this question. It is a matter of life and death to Liberalism and Radicalism. It is a question of our life or the abolition of the veto of the House of Lords. But look at it from a national point of view. Think of its injury to the smooth working of a Liberal Government. At the present time a Liberal Government, however powerful, cannot look far ahead, cannot impart design into its operations, because it knows that if at any moment its vigour falls below a certain point another body, over which it has no control, is ready to strike it a blow to its most serious injury.

It comes to this, that no matter how great the majority by which a Liberal Government is supported, it is unable to pass any legislation unless it can procure the agreement of its political opponents. Observe the position in which the present Executive Government is consequently placed. Take only the question of passive resistance. The action of the House of Lords at the present time forces the Executive Government to lock up in prison men with whose action they entirely sympathise and whose grievance they have faithfully promised to redress. Such a position is intolerable. Indeed, I am sure that if right hon. gentlemen opposite would only utilise that valuable gift of putting themselves in imagination in the position of others, they would see that no self-respecting men could continue to occupy such a position except with the object of putting an end to it for ever.

Much might be said for and against the two-Party system. But no one can doubt that it adds to the stability and cohesion of the State. The alternation of Parties in power, like the rotation of crops, has beneficial results. Each of the two Parties has services to render in the development of the national life; and the succession of new and different points of view is a real benefit to the country. A choice between responsible Ministries is a great strength to the Crown. The advantage of such a system cannot be denied. Would not the ending of such a system involve a much greater disturbance than to amend the functions of the House of Lords? Is there not a much greater cataclysm involved in the breakdown of the constitutional organisation of democracy—for that is the issue which is placed before us—than would be involved in the mere curtailment of the legislative veto which has been given to another place?

I ask the House what does such a safeguard as the House of Lords mean? Is it a safeguard at all? Enormous powers are already possessed by the House of Commons. It has finance under its control, it has the Executive Government; the control of foreign affairs and the great patronage of the State are all in the power of the House of Commons at the present time. And if you are to proceed on the basis that the people of this country will elect a mad House of Commons, and that the mad House of Commons will be represented by a mad Executive, the House of Lords is no guarantee against any excesses which such a House of Commons or such an Executive might have in contemplation. Whatever you may wish or desire, you will be forced to trust the people in all those vital and fundamental elements of government which in every State have always been held to involve the practical stability of the community.

Is the House of Lords even a security for property? Why, the greatest weapon which a democracy possesses against property is the power of taxation, and the power of taxation is wholly under the control of this House. If this House chooses, for instance, to suspend payment to the Sinking Fund, and to utilise the money for any public purpose or for any social purpose, the House of Lords could not interfere. If the House of Commons chose to double taxation on the wealthy classes, the House of Lords could not interfere in any respect. Understand I am not advocating these measures; what I am endeavouring to show to the House is that there is no real safeguard in the House of Lords even in regard to a movement against property.

But surely there are other securities upon which the stability of society depends. In the ever-increasing complexities of social problems, in the restrictions which are imposed from day to day with increasing force on the action of individuals, above all, in the dissemination of property among many classes of the population, lie the real elements of stability on which our modern society depends. There are to-day, unlike in former ages, actually millions of people who possess not merely inert property, but who possess rent-earning, profit-bearing property; and the danger with which we are confronted now is not at all whether we shall go too fast. No, the danger is that about three-fourths of the people of this country should move on in a comfortable manner into an easy life, which, with all its ups and downs, is not uncheered by fortune, while the remainder of the people shall be left to rot and fester in the slums of our cities, or wither in the deserted and abandoned hamlets of our rural districts.

That is the danger with which we are confronted at the present moment, and it invests with a deep and real significance the issue which is drawn between the two Parties to-night. It is quite true that there are rich Members of the Liberal Party, and there are poor men who are supporters of the Conservative Party; but in the main the lines of difference between the two Parties are social and economic—in the main the lines of difference are increasingly becoming the lines of cleavage between the rich and the poor. Let that reflection be with us in the struggle which we are now undertaking, and in which we shall without pause press forward, confident of this, that, if we persevere, we shall wrest from the hands of privilege and wealth the evil, ugly, and sinister weapon of the Peers' veto, which they have used so ill so long.

THE DUNDEE ELECTION

KINNAIRD HALL, DUNDEE, *MAY 14, 1908*

A new Government has come into being under a Prime Minister who, like his predecessor, is tied to Scotland by strong and intimate bonds. Give him a fair chance. Give the Government which he has brought into being the opportunity of handling the great machinery of State. Be assured that, if you do, they will employ it for the greatest good of the greatest number. I am well satisfied at what has taken place since I have been in Dundee. I see a great concentration of forces throughout the constituency. I see the opportunity of retrieving, and more than retrieving, the injury which has been done to the cause of progress and reform by elections in other parts of our island.

Ah, but, a very sad thing has happened; an awful thing has happened— the Liberal Party has gone in for Home Rule. *The Scotsman* is shocked, *The Times* is speechless, and takes three columns to express its speechlessness; *The Spectator*, that staid old weekly, has wobbled back to where it never should have wobbled from; the Ulster Unionists declare that the Government has forfeited all the confidence that they never had in it, and thousands of people who never under any circumstances voted Liberal before are saying that under no circumstances will they ever vote Liberal again. And I am supposed to be responsible for this revolution in our policy.

Why, the statements I have made on the Irish question are the logical and inevitable consequence of the Resolution which was passed by the House of Commons, in which every member of the Government voted, which was carried by an enormous majority—more than 200—a month ago[1]—a Resolution which, after explaining the plain and lamentable evils

---

[1]   March 30, 1908.

73

which can be traced to the existing system of government in Ireland, affirmed that the remedy for those evils would be found in a representative body with an Executive responsible to it, subject to the supreme authority of the Imperial Parliament.

The Irish question at the present time occupies a vastly different position to what it did in the year 1886. Ever since 1880 the attention of Parliament has been devoted constantly to Ireland, and the attention of Parliament, when devoted constantly to one object, is rarely fruitless. The twenty-five years that have passed have seen great changes in Ireland. We have seen a great scheme of local government, which Lord Salisbury said would be more disastrous than Home Rule itself, actually put into force. We have seen the scheme of land purchase, which in the year 1886 did more to injure the Home Rule Bill than anything else, actually carried, not indeed to a complete conclusion, but carried into practical effect by a Unionist Administration. These are great events; and their consequences, I think, ought to encourage us to move forward, and not to move back. They have produced results in Ireland which are beneficent, and the Irish question no longer presents itself in the tragic guise of the early eighties. They have produced an effect on Great Britain too. All over our country people have seen Bills which they were told beforehand would be ruinous to the unity and integrity of the United Kingdom—Land Bills and Local Government Bills—passed into law; and so far from the dire consequences which were apprehended from these measures, they have found—you here have found—that great good has resulted from that legislation. Many people are encouraged by what has taken place to make a step forward in the future; and I think if we need to look for any further encouragement, we should find it in the great and undisputed triumph which, under the mercy of Heaven, has attended our policy in South Africa, and has resulted in bringing into the circle of the British Empire a strong and martial race, which might easily have been estranged for ever.

The Irish polity finds its fellow nowhere in the world. It is a Government responsible neither to King nor people. It is not a democratic Government, nor an autocratic Government, nor even an oligarchical Government. It is a Government hag-ridden by forty-one administrative Boards, whose functions overlap one another and sometimes conflict with one another. Some are fed with money from the Consolidated Fund, some are supplied by vote of the House of Commons, some are supplied from savings from the Irish Development grant. Some of these Boards are under the Viceroy, some under the Chief Secretary, some under Treasury control, and some are under no control at all. The administration resulting from that system is costly, inefficient, unhandy beyond all description: a mighty staff of officials and police; a people desperately poor; taxation which rises automatically with every increase in the expenditure of this vast and wealthy island; and a population which dwindles tragically year by year. Add to all this a loyalist caste, capable and well-organised, who are taught generation after generation to look for support not to their own countrymen, but to external force derived from across the sea. There exists in effect in Ireland at the present time almost exactly the same situation which would have grown up in South Africa, if we had not had the wit and the nerve to prevent it. Take the whole of this situation as I have described it, thrust it into the arena of British politics to be the centre of contending factions, and the panorama of Irish government is complete.

With these facts before us, upon the authority of men like Lord Dunraven, Sir Joseph West-Ridgeway, Sir Antony MacDonnell, Lord Dudley, and others who have served the Crown in Ireland—is it wonderful that we should refuse to turn our eyes away from the vision of that other Ireland, free to control her own destiny in all that properly concerns herself, free to devote the native genius of her people to the purposes of her own self-culture—the vision of that other Ireland which Mr. Gladstone had reserved as the culminating achievement of his long and glorious career? Is it wonderful that we should refuse to turn our eyes away from that? No; I say that the desire and the aim of making a national settlement with Ireland on lines which would enable the people of that country to manage their own purely local affairs, is not an aim that can be separated from the general march of the Liberal army. If I come forward on your platform here at Dundee it is on the clear understanding that I do not preclude myself from trying to reconcile Ireland to England on a basis of freedom and justice.

I said just now that this was an important election. Yes, the effect upon his Majesty's Government and upon the Liberal Party for good or ill from this election cannot fail to be far-reaching. There are strong forces against us. Do not underrate the growing strength of the Tory reaction now in progress in many of the constituencies in England. I say it earnestly to those who are members of the Labour Party here to-day—do not underrate the storm which is gathering over your heads as well as ours. I am not afraid of the forces which are against us. With your support we shall overwhelm them—with your support we shall bear them down. Ah, but we must have that support.

It is not the enemy in front that I fear, but the division which too often makes itself manifest in progressive ranks—it is that division, that dispersion of forces, that internecine struggle in the moments of great emergency, in the moments when the issue hangs in the balance—it is that which, I fear, may weaken our efforts and may perhaps deprive us of success otherwise within our grasp.

There are cross-currents in this election. You cannot be unconscious of that. They flow this way and that way, and they disturb the clear issue which we should like to establish between the general body of those whose desire it is to move forward, and those who wish to revert to the old and barbarous prejudices and contentions of the past—to the fiscal systems and to the methods of government and administration, and to the Jingo foreign policies across the seas, from which we hoped we had shaken ourselves clear.

I want to-night to speak about these cross-currents; and let me first say a word about Socialism. There are a great many Socialists whose characters and whose views I have much respect for—men some of whom I know well, and whose friendship I enjoy. A good many of those gentlemen who have delightful, rosy views of a noble and brilliant future for the world, are so remote from hard facts of daily life and of ordinary politics that I am not very sure that they will bring any useful or effective influence to bear upon the immediate course of events. To the revolutionary Socialist, whether dreamer or politician, I do not appeal as the Liberal candidate for Dundee. I recognise that they are perfectly right in voting against me and voting against the Liberals, because Liberalism is not Socialism, and never will be. There is a great gulf fixed. It is not only a gulf of method, it is a gulf of principle. There are many steps we have to take which our Socialist opponents or friends, whichever they like to call themselves, will have to take with us; but there are immense differences of principle and of political philosophy between our views and their views.

Liberalism has its own history and its own tradition. Socialism has its own formulas and aims. Socialism seeks to pull down wealth; Liberalism seeks to raise up poverty. Socialism would destroy private interests; Liberalism would preserve private interests in the only way in which they can be safely and justly preserved, namely, by reconciling them with public right. Socialism would kill enterprise; Liberalism would rescue enterprise from the trammels of privilege and preference. Socialism assails the pre-eminence of the individual; Liberalism seeks, and shall seek more in the future, to build up a minimum standard for the mass. Socialism exalts the rule; Liberalism exalts the man. Socialism attacks capital; Liberalism attacks monopoly.

These are the great distinctions which I draw, and which, I think, you will agree I am right in drawing at this election between our respective policies and moods. Don't think that Liberalism is a faith that is played out; that it is a creed to which there is no expanding future. As long as the world rolls round, Liberalism will have its part to play—grand, beneficent, and ameliorating—in relation to men and States.

The truth lies in these matters, as it always lies in difficult matters, midway between extreme formulas. It is in the nice adjustment of the respective ideas of collectivism and individualism that the problem of the world and the solution of that problem lie in the years to come. But I have no hesitation in saying that I am on the side of those who think that a greater collective element should be introduced into the State and municipalities. I should like to see the State undertaking new functions, stepping forward into new spheres of activity, particularly in services which are in the nature of monopolies. There I see a wide field for State enterprise. But when we are told to exalt and admire a philosophy which destroys individualism and seeks to replace it absolutely by collectivism, I say that is a monstrous and imbecile conception, which can find no real acceptance in the brains and hearts—and the hearts are as trustworthy as the brains—in the hearts of sensible people.

Now I pass over the revolutionary Socialists, who, I admit, if they feel inclined, are justified in throwing away their votes on Saturday next, and I come to the Labour and to the Trade Union element in our midst. There I have one or two words to say of rather a straight character, if you don't object, and which, I hope, will be taken in good part, and will be studied and examined seriously. Labour in Britain is not Socialism. It is quite true that the Socialistic element has imposed a complexion on Labour, rather against its will, and is now supported in its action by funds almost entirely supplied by Trade Unions. But Trade Unions are not Socialistic. They are undoubtedly individualist organisations, more in the character of the old Guilds, and lean much more in the direction of the culture of the individual than in that of the smooth and bloodless uniformity of the mass. Now, the Trade Unions are the most respectable and the most powerful element in the labour world. They are the social bulwarks of our industrial system. They are the necessary guard-rails of a highly competitive machine, and I have the right, as a member of his Majesty's Government, to speak with good confidence to Trade Unionists, because we have done more for Trade Unionists than any other Government that has ever been.

How stands the case of the Trade Unionists? Do they really believe, I put this question to them fairly—do they really believe that there is no difference whatever between a Tory and a Liberal Government? Do Trade Unionists desire the downfall of the existing Liberal Government? Would they really like to send a message of encouragement to the House of Lords—for that is what it comes to—to reject and mutilate Liberal and Radical legislation—and Labour legislation now before Parliament? Would they send such a message of encouragement to the House of Lords as this—"House of Lords, you were right in your estimate of public opinion when you denied the extension of the Provision of Meals to School Children Bill to Scotland, when you threw out the Scottish Land Valuation Bill, when you threw out the Scottish Small Holders Bill—when you did all this you were right." Do you wish to send that message to the House of Lords? But that will be the consequence of every vote subtracted from the Liberal majority.

Why, gentlemen, let me return to the general current of events. What is the Government doing at present, and what has it done in its brief existence? Within the limits under which it works, and under the present authority of the House of Lords, what has it done and what is it doing for Trade Unionists? It has passed the Trades Disputes Act. The Workmen's Compensation Act has extended the benefits of compensation to six million persons not affected by previous legislation. The qualification of Justices of the Peace—the citizens' Privy Councillorship, as I call it—has been reduced so as to make it more easy for persons not possessed of this world's goods to qualify to take their place on the civic Bench. You know the land legislation for England, which is designed to secure that the suitable man who wants a small parcel of land to cultivate for his own profit and advantage shall not be prevented from obtaining it by feudal legislation, by old legal formalities or class prejudice. And is the Licensing Bill not well worth a good blow struck, and struck now, while the iron is hot? Then there is the Miners' Eight Hours Bill, a measure that has been advocated by the miners for twenty years, and justified by the highest medical testimony on humanitarian and hygienic grounds. It is costing us votes and supporters. It is costing us by-elections, yet it is being driven through. Have we not a right to claim the support of the Trade Unionists who are associated with the miners? Don't they feel that this measure is hanging in the balance, not in the House of Commons, but in the balance in the House of Lords, which attaches to by-elections an importance which, in their arrogant assertion, entitles them to mutilate or reject legislation, even although it comes to them by the majority of a Parliament newly elected on a suffrage of six millions. Then there is the question of old-age pensions, a question that has been much misused and mishandled in the past.

That was a pledge given by our opponents to win the election of 1895, and after the lapse of thirteen years of toil and stress, the Liberal Party is able to take it up, and will implement it in an effective fashion. Now, is there one of all these subjects which does not command the support of Trade Unionists and responsible Labour leaders? The Government is fighting for these measures. The Government is risking its life and power for these and similar objects. The Tory Party is opposing it on every point. The Tory Party is gaining popularity from the resistance of the interests which are affected by the passing of such measures of social reform. The House of Lords is the weapon of the Tory Party. With that weapon they can make a Liberal Government ridiculous. Are the Labour leaders, are Trade Unionists, confronted at this moment with the menace of reaction, deliberately going to throw in their lot with the House of Lords? I don't think they will. The record in Labour legislation under the existence of the present Government is a record which deserves, and will, I believe, command, the support of the great mass of the labouring classes of our country.

But I say, in all seriousness, that if the Liberal Government is on the one hand confronted by the House of Lords, fortified by sporadic by-elections, and on the other hand is attacked, abused, derided, by a section of those for whom it is fighting, then that Government, whatever its hopes, whatever its energies, whatever its strength, will be weakened, will perhaps succumb, and will be replaced by another Government. And by what other Government will it be replaced? There can be no other result from such a division of progressive forces than to instal a Tory and Protectionist Government in power. That will not be fatal to us. Liberalism will not be killed. Liberalism is a quickening spirit—it is immortal. It will live on through all the days, be they good days or be they evil days. No! I believe it will even burn stronger and brighter and more helpful in evil days than in good—just like your harbour-lights, which shine out across the sea, and which on a calm night gleam with soft refulgence, but through the storm flash a message of life to those who toil on the rough waters.

But it takes a great party to govern Great Britain—no clique, no faction, no cabal, can govern the forty millions of people who live in this island. It takes a vast concentration of forces to make a governing instrument. You have now got a Radical and democratic governing instrument, and if this Administration is broken, that instrument will be shattered. It has been recreated painfully and laboriously after twenty years by courage and fidelity. It has come into being—it is here. It is now at work, and by legislation and by the influence which it can exercise throughout the whole world, it is making even our opponents talk our language, making all parties in the State think of social reform, and concern themselves with social and domestic affairs. Beware how you injure that great instrument, as Mr. Gladstone called it—or weaken it at a moment when the masses of this country have need of it. Why, what would happen, if this present Government were to perish? On its tomb would be written: "Beware of social reform. The labouring classes will not support a Government engaged in social reform. Every social reform will cost you votes. Beware of social reform. 'Learn to think Imperially.'"

An inconclusive verdict from Dundee, the home of Scottish Radicalism—an inconclusive, or, still more, a disastrous verdict—would carry a message of despair to every one in all parts of our island and in our sister island who is working for the essential influences and truths of Liberalism and progress. Down, down, down would fall the high hopes of the social reformer. The constructive plans now forming in so many brains would melt into air. The old régime would be reinstated, reinstalled. Like the Bourbons, they will have learned nothing and will have forgotten nothing. We shall step out of the period of adventurous hope in which we have lived for a brief spell; we shall step back to the period of obstinate and prejudiced negations. For Ireland—ten years of resolute government; for England—dear food and cheaper gin; and for Scotland—the superior wisdom of the House of Lords! Is that the work you want to do, men of Dundee? Is that the work to which you will put your precious franchises—your votes, which have been won for you by so much struggle in the past? No; I am confident that this city, which has of its own free will plunged into the very centre of national politics, will grasp the opportunity now presented; that its command will not be back, but forward; that its counsel will be not timidity, but courage, and that it will aim not at dividing, but at rallying the progressive forces, not at dissipating, but at combining the energies of reform. That will be the message which you will send in tones which no man can mistake—so that a keen, strong, northern air shall sweep across our land to nerve and brace the hearts of men, to encourage the weak, to fortify the strong, to uplift the generous, to correct the proud.

In time of war, when an action has been joined for a long time, and the lines are locked in fierce conflict, and stragglers are coming in and the wounded drifting away, when the reserves begin to waver here and there, it is on such an occasion that Scottish regiments have so often won distinction; it is on these occasions that you have seen some valiant brigade march straight forward into the battle smoke, into the confusion of the field, right into the heart of the fight. That is what you have to do at this moment. "Scotland for ever!"

Now I turn my argument to the other side of the field, to the other quarter, from which we are subject to attack; I turn in my appeal from Trade Unionists, from the Labour men, who ought in all fairness to recognise the work this Government is doing and back them in their sore struggle; I turn to the rich and the powerful, to Unionist and Conservative elements, who, nevertheless, upon Free Trade, upon temperance, and upon other questions of moral enlightenment, feel a considerable sympathy with the Liberal Party; I turn to those who say, "We like Free Trade and we are Liberals at heart, but this Government is too Radical: we don't like its Radical measures. Why can't they let well alone? What do they mean by introducing all these measures, all these Bills, which," so they say, "disturb credit and trade, and interfere with the course of business, and cause so many class-struggles in the country?" I turn to those who complain we are too Radical in this and in that, and that we are moving too quickly, and I say to them: "Look at this political situation, not as party men, but as Britons; look at it in the light of history; look at it in the light of philosophy; and look at it in the light of broad-minded, Christian charity."

Why is it that life and property are more secure in Britain than in any other country in the world? Why is it that our credit is so high and that our commerce stretches so far? Is it because of the repressive laws which we impose? Why, gentlemen, there are laws far more severe than any prevailing in this country, or that have prevailed here for many years, now in force in great States in Europe, and yet there is no complete security of life and property notwithstanding all these repressive laws. Is it because of the House of Lords, that life and property are secure? Why, orders of aristocracy more powerful, much more homogeneous, of greater privileges, acting with much greater energy than our aristocracy, have been swept away in other countries until not a vestige, or scarce a vestige, of their existence remains. Is it because of the British Constitution that life and property are secure? Why, the British Constitution is mainly British common sense. There never were forty millions of people dwelling together who had less of an arbitrary and rigid Constitution than we have here. The Constitution of France, the Constitution of Germany, the Constitution of the United States are far more rigid, far better fortified against popular movement, than the Constitution under which we in these islands have moved steadily forward abreast of the centuries on the whole to a better state than any other country.

I will tell those wealthy and powerful people what the secret of the security of life and property in Britain is. The security arises from the continuation of that very class-struggle which they lament and of which they complain, which goes on ceaselessly in our country, which goes on tirelessly, with perpetual friction, a struggle between class and class which never sinks into lethargy, and never breaks into violence, but which from year to year makes possible a steady and constant advance. It is on the nature of that class-struggle in Britain that the security of life and property is fundamentally reposed. We are always changing; like nature, we change a great deal, although we change very slowly. We are always reaching a higher level after each change, but yet with the harmony of our life unbroken and unimpaired. And I say also to those persons here, to whom I now make my appeal: wealthy men, men of light and leading have never been all on one side in our country. There have always been men of power and position who have sacrificed and exerted themselves in the popular cause; and that is why there is so little class-hatred here, in spite of all the squalor and misery which we see around us. There, gentlemen, lies the true evolution of democracy. That is how we have preserved the golden thread of historical continuity, when so many other nations have lost it for ever. That is the only way in which your island life as you know it, and love it, can be preserved in all its grace and in all its freedom—can be elevated, expanded, and illumined for those who will occupy our places when our share in the world's work is done.

And I appeal to the leaders of industry and of learning in this city to range themselves on the side of a policy which will vigilantly seek the welfare of the masses, and which will strictly refuse to profit through their detriment; and, in spite of the violence of extremists, in spite of the harshness of controversy which hard conditions produce, in spite of many forces which may seem to those gentlemen ungrateful, I ask them to pursue and persevere in their crusade—for it is a crusade—of social progress and advance.

Cologne Cathedral took 600 years to build. Generations of architects and builders lived and died while the work was in progress. Still the work went on. Sometimes a generation built wrongly, and the next generation had to unbuild, and the next generation had to build again. Still the work went on through all the centuries, till at last there stood forth to the world a mighty monument of beauty and of truth to command the admiration and inspire the reverence of mankind. So let it be with the British Commonwealth. Let us build wisely, let us build surely, let us build faithfully, let us build, not for the moment, but for future years, seeking to establish here below what we hope to find above—a house of many mansions, where there shall be room for all.

The result of the election was declared as follows

Churchill (Liberal)	7,079
Baxter (Conservative)	4,370
Stuart (Socialist)	4,014
Scrymgeour (Prohibitionist)	655
Liberal majority	**2,709**

II - SOCIAL ORGANISATION

THE SECOND READING OF THE MINES (EIGHT HOURS) BILL

UNEMPLOYMENT

THE SOCIAL FIELD

THE APPROACHING CONFLICT

THE SECOND READING OF THE ANTI-SWEATING BILL

LABOUR EXCHANGES AND UNEMPLOYMENT INSURANCE

THE SECOND READING OF THE MINES
(EIGHT HOURS) BILL

HOUSE OF COMMONS, *JULY 6, 1908*

*W*hatever arguments may be urged against this measure, no one can say that the Government have acted with precipitation in bringing it before the House and the country. It has been debated for twenty years. Parliaments, Tory and Liberal, have affirmed the principle, and I do not suppose there ever was a similar reform put forward in this House upon a greater volume of scientific and accurate information, or after more prolonged, careful, and sustained scrutiny. If the debate on the Second Reading has thrown very little new light on this question, it is because it has been fully and thoroughly explored on former occasions; and not only has it been fully explored, but it is now illuminated by the admirable Report which has been presented by the Departmental Committee appointed last session.

This Report, while exciting approval on all sides, gives no complete satisfaction to any. It balances, and weighs, but it does not finally pronounce. It aims less at deciding this controversy, than at defining the limits within which its economic aspect may be said to lie. I think any one who reads the Report with attention will feel, after careful study, that the limits of the economic controversy are moderately restricted. We have to consider on the one hand the gross reduction of one-tenth in the hours of labour of underground workmen, taking the average over all classes of men and all sorts of mines. And on the other hand we have as a set-off against that gross reduction certain very important mitigations which are enumerated in the Report, to which I shall briefly refer.

The first economic question which the House has to settle is, whether these mitigations which are enumerated will have the effect of overtaking the reduction which is to follow the curtailment of hours, or, if not, how far they will fall short in overtaking that reduction.

I do not suppose that any hon. gentleman is likely to change his opinion on a question of such complexity at this late stage of the debate, and therefore I shall only refer by name to these mitigations, bearing in mind how important they are. There are those which depend on the arrangements of employers, and those which depend on the volition of the workers. With regard to the employers, there is improved organisation by methods of haulage and winding, and other means specified in the Report. There is the more extensive application of coal-cutting machinery, and the sinking of new pits with modern appliances, which is progressing in many parts of the country.

There is the system of double and multiple shifts. The extension of the system will not be so difficult as has sometimes been supposed. At the present moment, taking the statistics of 1906, a quarter only of the workers below ground are employed in mines in which there is only one coal-getting shift, and in all the mines in which there are two or more coal-getting shifts the first shift preponderates in number greatly over the second, and, therefore, in applying this system of double or multiple shifts, in so far as it is necessary to apply it, we shall not have to face the difficulty of a complete transformation in the methods of working a great many of the mines, but it will be a mere extension of the system which at present exists over a great portion of the coal-getting area.

From the side of labour, the mitigations which may be expected as off-sets to the original reduction are not less important. There is the increased efficiency, of which we have instances actually on record in this Report, which has followed from the reduction of hours. There is the power of the worker, if he chooses, to increase his earnings on a short day. There is "absenteeism," which has always been affected by a reduction of hours, and which amounts to 6.6 per cent. of the working time of the mines, and there is the margin of stoppages through slack trade and other circumstances, which at present aggregates 7 per cent. of the working time of the mines. Taking these last two alone, they aggregate 13 per cent., or considerably more, as a margin, than the reduction of working time which will be caused by the operation of this Bill, even when the full operation is reached.

First of all then, let the House consider carefully whether from these sources it is possible to overtake the 10 per cent. reduction which, in the first instance, the Bill imposes. It is a question nicely balanced; it offers matter for fair argument this way and that, but, taking all the means of mitigation together, not only singly but collectively, it is surely very difficult to believe that masters and men, organised as they are, and working together with good will, and with ample time to accommodate themselves to new arrangements, will not be able from all sources to overtake the comparatively small reduction in hours the Bill will effect.

I am inclined to an opinion that good use will be made of these margins, but even if we assume, for the sake of the argument, that there will be a net reduction in consequence of the passage of this Bill in the output of coal, that reduction must be temporary and transient in its character. For fifty years there have been continuous changes in the conditions of coal-mining in this country. The hours have been reduced, the conditions of boy labour have been restricted, wages have been raised, compensation has been provided, and precautions against accidents have been multiplied. All these changes, the wisdom of which nobody disputes, may from a purely and crudely economic standpoint be said to militate against production. We have heard many prophecies, but what has been the history of the coal trade? There has been a steady, unbroken expansion of output during the last fifty years. In the period of ten years ending in 1874, 76,000,000 tons were produced; in the next ten years 112,000,000; in the next ten years 145,000,000; in the next ten years 172,000,000; and in the last period of ten years 214,000,000—a figure which has been greatly exceeded since.

If it be admitted that there may be a certain reduction in output as a consequence of this Bill, that reduction must be considered, not by itself, not in isolation, but in relation to the steady and persistent movement of coal production for the last fifty years. To me it seems certain that the small temporary restriction will be lost in the general tendency to expansion, as the eddy is carried forward by the stream and the recoiling wave is lost in the advancing tide.

But these arguments would be wholly vitiated if it could be shown that the restriction of hours was so violent in its character, so sudden in its application, so rigid in its methods as, not merely to cause a certain shrinkage in the volume of the output, but to upset the economy of the coal-mining industry. In that case there would be not merely a curtailment which might be mitigated, but we should have injured and possibly disorganised the industry; and it is at this point that it is proper for the House to consider the safeguards introduced by the Government into the Bill. These safeguards are of the greatest importance.

There is the safeguard of overtime. Sixty hours a year are permitted. In districts where men work ten days a fortnight, twelve weeks may be one hour longer than the usual time allowed by the Bill; and where the days laboured are only four in the week, fifteen weeks of extended time will be possible through the provision of overtime. There are provisions with regard to the labour of certain persons permitted to remain below ground beyond the legal hours for special purposes, and there is a power which relaxes the Bill altogether in an emergency which is likely to delay or arrest the general work of the mine, and, of course, in any case where there is accident or danger. Finally, if there should be risk of a corner or an unexpected rise in price, the Government have power by Order in Council to suspend the whole operation of the law in order to prevent anything like a serious crisis arising in the coal trade.

I cannot bring myself to believe that with all these safeguards it will not be possible for the coal industry, if given time, to accommodate itself to the new conditions. It is only two years ago that I was invited from the benches opposite to contemplate the approaching ruin of the gold mines of the Rand through the change introduced in the methods of working. That change has been enforced, with the result that working expenses have been reduced, and the standard of production has increased. In making that transition, if time had not been allowed to tide over the period of change, then, indeed, you might have had that disaster which hon. gentlemen opposite have always been ready to apprehend. But there is here to be a gradual process of adaptation, for which not less than five years is permitted.

We are told that positive reasons, and not negative reasons, ought to be given in support of a measure which regulates the hours of adult labour— that you ought to show, not that it will do no harm, but that good will come from it. There are, of course, such reasons in support of this Bill, but they are so obvious that they have not been dwelt upon as much as they might have been. The reasons are social reasons. We believe that the well-being of the mining population, numbering some 900,000 persons, will be sensibly advanced in respect of health, industrial efficiency, habits of temperance, education, culture, and the general standard of life. We have seen that in the past the shortening of hours has produced beneficial effects in these respects, and we notice that in those parts of the country where the hours of coal-mining are shortest, the University Extension lecturers find that the miners take an intelligent interest in their lectures— and it is among the miners of Fifeshire that a considerable development in gardening and also of saving to enable them to own their own houses, has followed on a longer period of leisure.

But the general march of industrial democracy is not towards inadequate hours of work, but towards sufficient hours of leisure. That is the movement among the working people all over the country. They are not content that their lives should remain mere alternations between bed and the factory. They demand time to look about them, time to see their homes by daylight, to see their children, time to think and read and cultivate their gardens—time, in short, to live. That is very strange, perhaps, but that is the request they have made and are making with increasing force and reason as years pass by.

No one is to be pitied for having to work hard, for nature has contrived a special reward for the man who works hard. It gives him an extra relish, which enables him to gather in a brief space from simple pleasures a satisfaction in search of which the social idler wanders vainly through the twenty-four hours. But this reward, so precious in itself, is snatched away from the man who has won it, if the hours of his labour are too long or the conditions of his labour too severe to leave any time for him to enjoy what he has won.

Professor Marshall, in his "Principles of Economics," says:

"The influence which the standard of hours of work exerts on economic activities is partially obscured by the fact that the earnings of a human being are commonly counted gross; no special reckoning being made for his wear-and-tear, of which he is himself rather careless. Further, very little account is taken of the evil effects of the overwork of men on the well-being of the next generation.... When the hours and the general conditions of labour are such as to cause great wear-and-tear of body or mind or both, and to lead to a low standard of living; when there has been a want of that leisure, rest, and repose which are among the necessaries for efficiency, then the labour has been extravagant from the point of view of society at large.... And, since material wealth exists for the sake of man, and not man for the sake of material wealth, the replacement of inefficient and stunted human lives by more efficient and fuller lives would be a gain of a higher order than any temporary material loss that might have been occasioned on the way."

If it be said that these arguments are general, is it not true that special circumstances differentiate the case of coal-miners from that of many other industries in this country? Others have spoken of the heat of the mine, the danger of fire-damp, of the cramped position, of the muscular exertions of the miner, at work in moist galleries perhaps a mile under the ground. I select the single fact of deprivation of natural light. That alone is enough to justify Parliament in directing upon the industry of coal-mining a specially severe scrutiny and introducing regulations of a different character from those elsewhere.

The hon. Member for Windsor[1] who moved the rejection of this Bill described it as a reckless and foolhardy experiment. I see the miner emerging from the pit after eight hours' work with the assertion on his lips that he, at any rate, has paid his daily debt to his fellow men. Is the House of Commons now going to say to him, "You have no right to be here. You have only worked eight hours. Your appearance on the surface of the earth after eight hours' work is, to quote the hon. Member, 'a reckless and

[1]   Mr. J.F. Mason.

89

foolhardy experiment'"? I do not wonder at the miners' demand. I cannot find it in my heart to feel the slightest surprise, or indignation, or mental disturbance at it. My capacity for wonder is entirely absorbed, not by the miners' demand, but by the gentleman in the silk hat and white waistcoat who has the composure and the complacency to deny that demand and dispute it with him.

The hon. Member for Dulwich[1]—himself a convinced protectionist, with a tariff with 1,200 articles in its schedules in his coat-tail pocket—has given us a delightful lecture on the importance of cheapness of production. Think of the poor consumer! Think of the importance to our industries of cheapness of production! We on this side are great admirers of cheapness of production. We have reminded the hon. gentleman of it often; but why should cheapness of production always be achieved at the expense of the human factor? The hon. gentleman spoke with anxiety of the possibility of a rise in miners' wages as a consequence of this Bill. Has he considered the relation of miners' wages to the selling prices of coal? At the pit's mouth the underground-workers' wages are only 60 per cent. of the selling price of coal. Free on board on the Tyne, the proportion is only 38 per cent. As coal is sold here in the south of England the proportion of wages is less than one-fifth of the whole price. Is it not clear that there are other factors at least which require consideration before you decide to deal with the human factor, which first attracts the attention of the hon. gentleman?

What about mining royalties? In all this talk about the importance of cheap coal to our industries and to the poor consumer we have had no mention of mining royalties. No. We never mention that. Yet, will the House believe it, it is estimated that mining royalties impose a toll of 6 per cent., calculated on the price of coal at the pit's mouth, or considerably more than half the total diminished production which could result from this humane Act of labour legislation.

But we are asked: "Why stop here? Why don't your arguments apply elsewhere?" and we are told of people whose conditions of life are worse than some of those of coal-miners. Why stop here? Who ever said we would stop here? I welcome and support this measure, not only for its own sake, but much more because it is, I believe, simply the precursor of the general movement which is in progress all over the world, and in other industries besides this, towards reconciling the conditions of labour with the well-ascertained laws of science and health. If we are told that because we support this measure we shall be inflicting an injury or injustice on other classes of the population, I say there is a great solidarity among all classes of manual labourers. I believe that when they consider this matter they will see that all legitimate interests are in harmony, that no

---

[1]   Mr. Bonar Law.

one class can obtain permanent advantage by undue strain on another, and that in the end their turn will come for shorter hours, and will come the sooner because they have aided others to obtain that which they desire themselves.

When the House is asked to contemplate gloomy pictures of what will follow on this Bill, let them recur to the example of Parliaments gone by. When the Ten Hours Bill was introduced in 1847, a Bill which affected the hours of adult males inferentially, the same lugubrious prophecies were indulged in from both sides of the House. Distinguished economists came forward to prove that the whole profit of the textile industry was reaped after the eleventh hour. Famous statesmen on both sides spoke strongly against the measure. The Parliament, in 1847, was in the same sort of position as we are to-day in this respect, but how differently circumstanced in other respects. That Parliament did not enjoy the wide and accurate statistical information in every branch of labour which enables us to-day to move forward with discretion and prudence. They were not able to look to the general evidences of commercial security and expansion on which modern politicians can rely. They could not show, as we can show, overwhelming examples of owlish prophets dazzlingly disproved; they could not point, as we can point, to scores of cases where not only increased efficiency, but a positive increase in output has followed the reduction of the hours of labour. The principle was new, the future was vague. But the Parliament of those days did not quail. They trusted to broad, generous instincts of common sense; they drew a good, bold line; and we to-day enjoy in a more gentle, more humane, more skilful, more sober, and more civilised population the blessings which have followed their acts. Now it is our turn. Let us vote for the Second Reading of this Bill, and in so doing establish a claim upon the respect of Parliaments to come, such as we ourselves owe to Parliaments of the past.[1]

---

1   This concluded the debate, and the Second Reading was carried by 390 to 120.

UNEMPLOYMENT
KINNAIRD HALL, DUNDEE, *OCTOBER 10, 1908*

(Originally published in *The Times*)

$\mathcal{W}$hat is the political situation which unfolds itself to our reflections to-night? I present it to you without misgivings or reserve. For nearly three years a Liberal Administration, more democratic in its character, more widely selected in its *personnel*, more Radical in the general complexion of its policy, than any that has previously been known to British history, has occupied the place of power. During the whole of that period no single serious administrative mistake, either at home or abroad, has embarrassed or discredited the conduct of public affairs. Three Parliamentary Sessions, fruitful beyond precedent in important legislation, have been surmounted with dignity and dispatch. The authority and influence of Great Britain among foreign Powers have been prudently guarded, and are now appreciably augmented, and that authority and influence have been consistently employed, and will be in the future employed, in soothing international rivalries and suspicion, in asserting a proper respect for public law, in preserving a just and harmonious balance amongst great Powers, and in forwarding as opportunities have served, whether in the Near East or in the Congo, causes of a generous and disinterested humanitarianism.

The British Empire itself has enjoyed under Liberal rule a period of prosperous tranquillity, favourable both to development and consolidation; and it is no exaggeration to say that it was never more strong or more peacefully united than at the present moment. The confidence which the whole country, irrespective of party, feels in Sir Edward Grey in the present European crisis, is the measure of our success in foreign affairs. The gathering of the Convention of a United South Africa is in itself a vindication of colonial policy. Each year for which we have been responsible has been marked by some great and beneficent event which has commanded the acquiescence—or at least silenced the dissent—of many of our professed opponents. In 1906 the charter of trade unions; in 1907, the conciliation and settlement of South Africa; in 1908, the establishment of old-age pensions. These are large matters; they will take their place in the history book; and on them alone, if necessary, I would confidently base the claims of his Majesty's Government to respect, if not to renown, in future times.

But although we do not meet to-night in any atmosphere of crisis, nor in any expectation of a general election, nevertheless I feel, and I dare say you feel too, that we have reached a climacteric in the life of this Parliament. The next six months will probably determine the whole remaining fortunes of the Government, and decide whether a gradual but progressive decline will slowly carry the Administration in the natural course to the grave where so many others are peacefully slumbering, or whether, deriving fresh vigour from its exertions, it will march forward conquering and to conquer.

I said a few minutes ago that this session had been marked by a measure of great and cardinal importance. Surely no one will deny the magnitude and significance of the step which has been taken in the establishment of a system of old-age pensions. It marks the assertion in our social system of an entirely new principle in regard to poverty, and that principle, once asserted, cannot possibly be confined within its existing limits. Old-age pensions will carry us all a very long way. They have opened a door which will not soon or easily be closed. The members of both Houses of Parliament have been led to the verge of the cruel abyss of poverty, and have been in solemn session assembled to contemplate its depths and its gloom. All alike have come to gaze; none have remained unmoved. There are some distinguished and eminent men, men whose power and experience I cannot impugn, who have started back appalled by what they have seen, and whose only idea is to slam the door on the grim and painful prospect which has been revealed to their eyes.

But that is not the only spirit which has been awakened in our country; there are others, not less powerful, and a greater number, who will never allow that door to be closed; they have got their feet in it, they are resolved that it shall be kept open. Nay, more, they are prepared to descend into the abyss, and grapple with its evils—as sometimes you see after an explosion at a coal mine a rescue party advancing undaunted into the smoke and steam. Now there is the issue on which the future of this Parliament hangs—"Forward or back?" Voices sound loud and conflicting in our ears; the issue, the sharpest and simplest, the most tremendous that can be put to a generation of men—"Forward or backward?"—is the issue which confronts us at the present time, and on it the future of the Government is staked. There are faint-hearted friends behind; there are loud-voiced foes in front. The brewer's dray has been pulled across the road, and behind it are embattled a formidable confederation of vested interests. A mountainous obstacle of indifference and apathy bars our advance. What is your counsel? Forward or Back?

Let it be remembered that aged poverty is not the only evil with which, so far as our means allow, we have to grapple. What is the problem of the hour? It can be comprised in one word—Unemployment. After two years of unexampled trade expansion, we have entered upon a period of decline. We are not alone in this. A reaction from overtrading is general all over the world. Both Germany and the United States are suffering from a similar commercial contraction, and in both countries, in spite of their high and elaborate protective tariffs, a trade set-back has been accompanied by severe industrial dislocation and unemployment. In the United States of America, particularly, I am informed that unemployment has recently been more general than in this country. Indeed the financial collapse in the United States last autumn has been the most clearly marked of all the causes to which the present trade depression may be assigned.

It is not yet possible to say that the end of that period of depression is in sight; but there are some significant indications which I think justify the hope that it will be less severe and less prolonged than has been known in other trade cycles, or than some people were at first inclined to believe. But the problem of unemployment is not confined to periods of trade depression, and will not be solved by trade revival; and it is to that problem in its larger and more permanent aspects that I desire to draw your attention for a short time to-night.

There is no evidence that the population of Great Britain has increased beyond the means of subsistence. On the contrary, our wealth is increasing faster than our numbers. Production is active; industry grows, and grows with astonishing vigour and rapidity. Enterprise in this country requires no artificial stimulant; if it errs at all, it is from time to time upon the side of overtrading and overproduction. There is no ground for believing that this country is not capable of supporting an increasing population in a condition of expanding prosperity.

It must, however, be remembered that the British people are more than any other people in the world a manufacturing people. It is certain that our population could never have attained its present vast numbers, nor our country have achieved its position in the world, without an altogether unusual reliance upon manufacture as opposed to simple agriculture. The ordinary changes and transitions inseparable from the active life and growth of modern industry, therefore, operate here with greater relative intensity than in other countries. An industrial disturbance is more serious in Great Britain than in other countries, for it affects a far larger proportion of the people, and in their distresses the urban democracy are not sustained by the same solid backing of country-folk and peasant cultivators that we see in other lands. It has, therefore, become a paramount necessity for us to make scientific provision against the fluctuations and set-backs which are inevitable in world commerce and in national industry.

We have lately seen how the backwash of an American monetary disturbance or a crisis in the Near East or in the Far East, or some other cause influencing world trade, and as independent of our control as are the phases of the moon, may easily have the effect of letting loose upon thousands of humble families and households all the horrors of a state of siege or a warlike blockade. Then there are strikes and trade disputes of all kinds which affect vast numbers of people altogether unconcerned in the quarrel. Now, I am not going to-night to proclaim the principle of the "right to work." There is not much use in proclaiming a right apart from its enforcement; and when it is enforced there is no need to proclaim it. But what I am here to assert, and to assert most emphatically, is the responsibility of Government towards honest and law-abiding citizens; and I am surprised that that responsibility should ever be challenged or denied.

When there is a famine in India, when owing to some unusual course of nature the sky refuses its rains and the earth its fruits, relief works are provided in the provinces affected, trains of provisions are poured in from all parts of that great Empire, aid and assistance are given to the population involved, not merely to enable them to survive the period of famine, but to resume their occupations at its close. An industrial disturbance in the manufacturing districts and the great cities of this country presents itself to the ordinary artisan in exactly the same way as the failure of crops in a large province in India presents itself to the Hindu cultivator. The means by which he lives are suddenly removed, and ruin in a form more or less swift and terrible stares him instantly in the face. That is a contingency which seems to fall within the most primary and fundamental obligations of any organisation of Government. I do not know whether in all countries or in all ages that responsibility could be maintained, but I do say that here and now in this wealthy country and in this scientific age it does in my opinion exist, is not discharged, ought to be discharged, and will have to be discharged.

The social machinery at the basis of our industrial life is deficient, ill-organised, and incomplete. While large numbers of persons enjoy great wealth, while the mass of the artisan classes are abreast of and in advance of their fellows in other lands, there is a minority, considerable in numbers, whose condition is a disgrace to a scientific and professedly Christian

95

civilisation, and constitutes a grave and increasing peril to the State. Yes, in this famous land of ours, so often envied by foreigners, where the grace and ease of life have been carried to such perfection, where there is so little class hatred and jealousy, where there is such a wide store of political experience and knowledge, where there are such enormous moral forces available, so much wisdom, so much virtue, so much power, we have not yet succeeded in providing that necessary apparatus of insurance and security, without which our industrial system is not merely incomplete, but actually inhumane.

I said that disturbances of our industrial system are often started from outside this country by causes utterly beyond our control. When there is an epidemic of cholera, or typhoid, or diphtheria, a healthy person runs less risk than one whose constitution is prepared to receive the microbes of disease, and even if himself struck down, he stands a far greater chance of making a speedy recovery. The social and industrial conditions in Great Britain at this present time cannot be described as healthy. I discern in the present industrial system of our country three vicious conditions which make us peculiarly susceptible to any outside disturbance of international trade. First, the lack of any central organisation of industry, or any general and concerted control either of ordinary Government work, or of any extraordinary relief works. It would be possible for the Board of Trade to foretell with a certain amount of accuracy the degree of unemployment likely to be reached in any winter. It ought to be possible for some authority in some Government office—which I do not care—to view the whole situation in advance, and within certain limits to exert a powerful influence over the general distribution of Government contracts.

There is nothing economically unsound in increasing temporarily and artificially the demand for labour during a period of temporary and artificial contraction. There is a plain need of some averaging machinery to regulate and even-up the general course of the labour market, in the same way as the Bank of England, by its bank rate, regulates and corrects the flow of business enterprise. When the extent of the depression is foreseen, the extent of the relief should also be determined. There ought to be in permanent existence certain recognised industries of a useful, but uncompetitive character, like, we will say, afforestation, managed by public departments, and capable of being expanded or contracted according to the needs of the labour market, just as easily as you can pull out the stops or work the pedals of an organ. In this way, you would not eliminate unemployment, you certainly would not prevent the creation of unemployables; but you would considerably limit the scale of unemployment, you would reduce the oscillation of the industrial system, you would increase its stability, and by every step that you took in that direction you would free thousands of your fellow-countrymen from undeserved agony and ruin, and a far greater number from the haunting dread of ruin. That is the first point—a gap, a hiatus in our social organisation—to which I direct your attention to-night, and upon which the intelligence of this country ought to be concentrated.

The second vicious condition is positive and not negative. I mean the gross, and, I sometimes fear, increasing evil of casual labour. We talk a great deal about the unemployed, but the evil of the *under-employed* is the tap-root of unemployment. There is a tendency in many trades, almost in all trades, to have a fringe of casual labour on hand, available as a surplus whenever there is a boom, flung back into the pool whenever there is a slump. Employers and foremen in many trades are drawn consciously or unconsciously to distribute their work among a larger number of men than they regularly require, because this obviously increases their bargaining power with them, and supplies a convenient reserve for periods of brisk business activity.

And what I desire to impress upon you, and through you upon this country, is that the casual unskilled labourer who is habitually under-employed, who is lucky to get three, or at the outside four, days' work in the week, who may often be out of a job for three or four weeks at a time, who in bad times goes under altogether, and who in good times has no hope of security and no incentive to thrift, whose whole life and the lives of his wife and children are embarked in a sort of blind, desperate, fatalistic gamble with circumstances beyond his comprehension or control, that this poor man, this terrible and pathetic figure, is not as a class the result of accident or chance, is not casual because he wishes to be casual, is not casual as the consequence of some temporary disturbance soon put right. No; the casual labourer is here because he is wanted here. He is here in answer to a perfectly well-defined demand. He is here as the result of economic causes which have been too long unregulated. He is not the natural product, he is an article manufactured, called into being, to suit the requirements, in the Prime Minister's telling phrase, of all industries at particular times and of particular industries at all times.

I suppose no Department has more means of learning about these things than the Board of Trade, which is in friendly touch at every stage all over the country both with capital and labour. I publish that fact deliberately. I invite you to consider it, I want it to soak in. It appears to me that measures to check the growth and diminish the quantity of casual labour must be an essential part of any thorough or scientific attempt to deal with unemployment, and I would not proclaim this evil to you without having reason to believe that practicable means exist by which it can be greatly diminished.

If the first vicious condition which I have mentioned to you is lack of industrial organisation, if the second is the evil of casual labour, there is a third not less important. I mean the present conditions of boy labour. The whole underside of the labour market is deranged by the competition of boys or young persons who do men's work for boys' wages, and are turned off so soon as they demand men's wages for themselves. That is the evil so far as it affects the men; but how does it affect the boys, the youth of our country, the heirs of all our exertion, the inheritors of that long treasure of history and romance, of science and knowledge—aye, of national glory, for which so many valiant generations have fought and toiled—the youth of Britain, how are we treating them in the twentieth century of the Christian era? Are they not being exploited? Are they not being demoralised? Are they not being thrown away?

Whereas the youth of the wealthier class is all kept under strict discipline until eighteen or nineteen, the mass of the nation runs wild after fourteen years of age. No doubt at first employment is easy to obtain. There is a wide and varied field; there are a hundred odd jobs for a lad; but almost every form of employment now open to young persons affords them no opening, is of no use to them whatever when they are grown up, and in a great number of cases the life which they lead is demoralising and harmful. And what is the consequence? The consequence may be measured by this grim fact, that out of the unemployed applying for help under the Unemployed Workmen Act, no less than twenty-eight per cent. are between twenty and thirty years of age, that is to say, men in the first flush of their strength and manhood already hopelessly adrift on the dark and tumultuous ocean of life. Upon this subject, I say to you deliberately that no boy or girl ought to be treated merely as cheap labour, that up to eighteen years of age every boy and girl in this country should, as in the old days of apprenticeship, be learning a trade as well as earning a living.

All attempts to deal with these and similar evils involve the expenditure of money. It is no use abusing capitalists and rich people. They are neither worse nor better than any one else. They function quite naturally under the conditions in which they find themselves. When the conditions are vicious, the consequence will be evil; when the conditions are reformed, the evil will be abated. Nor do I think the wealthy people of Great Britain would be ungenerous or unwilling to respond to the plain need of this nation for a more complete or elaborate social organisation. They would have a natural objection to having public money wasted or spent on keeping in artificial ease an ever-growing class of wastrels and ne'er-do-weels. No doubt there would also be a selfish element who would sullenly resist anything which touched their pocket. But I believe that if large schemes, properly prepared and scientifically conceived for dealing with the evils I have mentioned were presented, and if it could be shown that our national life would be placed upon a far more stable and secure foundation, I believe that there would be thousands of rich people who would cheerfully make the necessary sacrifices. At any rate, we shall see.

The year that lies before us must be a year of important finance. No doubt that finance will be a subject of fierce and protracted discussion; but I shall certainly not exclude from my mind, in weighing the chances of social reform, that strong element of patriotism which is to be found among the more fortunate of our fellow-countrymen, and which has honourably distinguished them from the rich people of other countries I could name.

I have been dealing with three, and only three, of the evil causes which principally affect labour conditions in Great Britain at the present time. Do not forget, however, as the Prime Minister has reminded us, how intimate is the co-relation of all social reforms, how vital it is to national health and security that we should maintain an adequate and independent population upon the land, and how unsatisfactory, in Scotland, at any rate, are the present conditions for small holdings. Do not forget, either, how fatal to the social, moral, and political progress of British democracy is the curse of intemperance. There is not a man or woman who lifts a voice and exerts an influence in support either of land or of temperance reform, who will not be doing something not only to alleviate the sufferings of the poor, but to stimulate the healthy advance of British prosperity.

But see how vast is the range of this question of unemployment with which we are confronted. See now how intricate are its details and its perplexities; how foolish it would be to legislate in panic or haste; how vain it would be to trust to formulas and prejudices; how earnest must be the study; how patient and laborious the preparation; how scientific the spirit, how valiant the action, if that great and hideous evil of insecurity by which our industrial population are harassed is to be effectually diminished in our national life. See now, also, what sort of politicians those are, whichever extreme of politics they may belong to, who tell you that they have an easy, simple, and unfailing remedy for such an evil. What sort of unscrupulous and reckless adventurers they are who tell you that tariff reform, that a trumpery ten per cent. tariff on foreign manufactures, and a tax on wheat would enable them to provide "work for all." I was very glad to see that Mr. Balfour frankly and honestly dissociated himself, the other night at Dumfries, from the impudent political cheap-jacks who are touting the country on behalf of the Tory Party, by boldly declaring that tariff reform, or "fiscal reform," as he prefers to call it, would be no remedy for unemployment or trade oscillations.

Now that Mr. Balfour has made that admission, for which we thank him, and for which we respect him, I will make one in my turn. If tariff reform or protection, or fiscal reform, or whatever you choose to call it, is no remedy for unemployment—and it is pretty clear from the experience of other countries who have adopted it on a large scale that it is not—neither is free trade by itself a remedy for unemployment. The evil lies deeper, the causes are more complex than any within the reach of import duties or of no import duties, and its treatment requires special measures of a social, not less than of an economic character which are going to carry us into altogether new and untrodden fields in British politics.

I agree most whole-heartedly with those who say that in attempting to relieve distress or to regulate the general levels of employment, we must be most careful not to facilitate the very disorganisation of industry which causes distress. But I do not agree with those who say that every man must look after himself, and that the intervention by the State in such matters as I have referred to will be fatal to his self-reliance, his foresight, and his thrift. We are told that our non-contributory scheme of old-age pensions, for instance, will be fatal to thrift, and we are warned that the great mass of the working classes will be discouraged thereby from making any effective provision for their old age. But what effective provision have they made against old age in the past? If terror be an incentive to thrift, surely the penalties of the system which we have abandoned ought to have stimulated thrift as much as anything could have been stimulated in this world. The mass of the labouring poor have known that unless they made provision for their old age betimes they would perish miserably in the workhouse. Yet they have made no provision; and when I am told that the institution of old-age pensions will prevent the working classes from making provision for their old age, I say that cannot be, for they have never been able to make such provision. And I believe our scheme, so far from preventing thrift, will encourage it to an extent never before known.

It is a great mistake to suppose that thrift is caused only by fear; it springs from hope as well as from fear; where there is no hope, be sure there will be no thrift. No one supposes that five shillings a week is a satisfactory provision for old age. No one supposes that seventy is the earliest period in a man's life when his infirmities may overwhelm him. We have not pretended to carry the toiler on to dry land; it is beyond our power. What we have done is to strap a lifebelt around him, whose buoyancy, aiding his own strenuous exertions, ought to enable him to reach the shore.

And now I say to you Liberals of Scotland and Dundee two words—"Diligence and Daring." Let that be your motto for the year that is to come. "Few," it is written, "and evil are the days of man." Soon, very soon, our brief lives will be lived. Soon, very soon, we and our affairs will have passed away. Uncounted generations will trample heedlessly upon our tombs. What is the use of living, if it be not to strive for noble causes and to make this muddled world a better place for those who will live in it after we are gone? How else can we put ourselves in harmonious relation with the great verities and consolations of the infinite and the eternal? And I avow my faith that we are marching towards better days. Humanity will not be cast down. We are going on—swinging bravely forward along the grand high road—and already behind the distant mountains is the promise of the sun.

THE SOCIAL FIELD
BIRMINGHAM, *JANUARY 13, 1909*[1]

(Originally published in *The Times*)

I am very glad to come here to-night to wish good luck in the New Year to the Liberals of Birmingham. Good luck is founded on good pluck, and that is what I think you will not fail in. Birmingham Liberals have for twenty years been over-weighted by the influence of remarkable men and by the peculiar turn of events. This great city, which used to be the home of militant Radicalism, which in former days supplied with driving power the cause of natural representation against hereditary privilege, has been captured by the foe. The banner of the House of Lords has been flung out over the sons and grandsons of the men who shook all England in the struggle for the great Reform Bill; and while old injustice has but been replaced by new, while the miseries and the privations of the poor continue in your streets, while the differences between class and class have been even aggravated in the passage of years, Birmingham is held by the enemy and bound to retrogression in its crudest form.

But this is no time for despondency. The Liberal Party must not allow itself to be overawed by the hostile Press which is ranged against it. Boldly and earnestly occupied, the platform will always beat the Press. Still less should we allow ourselves to be perturbed by the fortuitous and sporadic results of by-electoral warfare. I suppose I have fought as many by-elections as most people, and I know that all the advantages lie with the attacking force. The contests are complicated by personal and local influences. The discussions turn upon the incidents of current legislation. There are always grievances to be urged against the Government of the

---

[1]   In the interval between this and the preceding speech the House of Lords had rejected the Licensing Bill.

day. After a great victory, all parties, and particularly the Liberals, are prone to a slackening of effort and organisation; after a great defeat all parties, and especially the Tories, are spurred to supreme exertions.

These factors are common to all by-elections, under all Governments; but never, I venture to say, has it been more important to an Opposition to gain by-electoral successes than during the present Parliament. It is their only possible line of activity. In the House of Commons they scarcely show their noses. In divisions they are absent; in debate—well, I do not think we need say much about that; and it is only by a combination of by-electoral incidents properly advertised by the Party Press on the one hand, and the House of Lords' manipulation upon the other, that the Conservative Party are able to keep their heads above water. And when I speak of the importance to the Opposition of by-elections, let me also remind you that never before have by-electoral victories been so important, not only to a great Party, but to a great trade.

Therefore, while I am far from saying that we should be content with recent manifestations of the opinion of the electorate, while I do not at all deny that they involve a sensible reaction of feeling of an unfavourable character, and while I urge the most strenuous exertions upon all concerned in party organisation, I assert that there is no reason, as the history of this country abundantly shows, why a general election, at a well-chosen moment, and upon some clear, broad, simple issue, should not retrieve and restore the whole situation.

There could be no question of a Government, hitherto undisturbed by internal disagreement and consistently supported in the House of Commons by a large, united, and intact majority, being deflected one hair's breadth from its course by the results of by-elections. We have our work to do, and while we have the power to carry it forward, we have no right, even if we had the inclination, to leave it uncompleted. Certainly we shall not be so foolish, or play so false to those who have supported us, as to fight on any ground but that of our own choosing, or at any time but that most advantageous to the general interest of the Progressive cause.

The circumstances of the period are peculiar. The powers of the House of Lords to impede, and by impeding to discredit, the House of Commons are strangely bestowed, strangely limited, and still more strangely exercised. There are little things which they can maul; there are big things they cannot touch; there are Bills which they pass, although they believe them to be wrong; there are Bills which they reject, although they know them to be right. The House of Lords can prevent the trams running over Westminster Bridge; but it cannot prevent a declaration of war. It can reject a Bill prohibiting foreign workmen being brought in to break a British strike; it cannot amend a Bill to give old-age pensions to 600,000 people. It can thwart a Government in the minute details of its legislation; it cannot touch the whole vast business of finance. It can prevent the abolition of the plural voter; but it could not prevent the abolition of the police. It can refuse a Constitution to Ireland, but not, luckily, to Africa.

Lord Lansdowne, in his leadership of the House of Lords during the present Parliament, has put forward claims on its behalf far more important and crude than ever were made by the late Lord Salisbury. No Tory leader in modern times has ever taken so high a view of its rights, and at the same time no one has shown a more modest conception of its duties. In destroying the Education Bill of 1906 the House of Lords asserted its right to resist the opinion of a majority of members of the House of Commons, fresh from election, upon a subject which had been one of the most prominent issues of the election. In rejecting the Licensing Bill of 1908 they have paraded their utter unconcern for the moral welfare of the mass of their fellow-countrymen.

There is one feature in the guidance of the House of Lords by Lord Lansdowne which should specially be noticed, and that is the air of solemn humbug with which this ex-Whig is always at pains to invest its proceedings. The Nonconformist child is forced into the Church school in single-school areas in the name of parents' rights and religious equality. The Licensing Bill is rejected in the highest interests of temperance. Professing to be a bulwark of the commercial classes against Radical and Socialistic legislation, the House of Lords passes an Old-Age Pensions Bill, which it asserts will be fatal alike to public finance and public thrift, a Mines Eight Hours Bill, which it is convinced will cripple British industry, and a Trades Disputes Bill, which it loudly declared tyrannous and immoral. Posing as a Chamber of review remote from popular passion, far from the swaying influences of the electorate, it nevertheless exhibits a taste for cheap electioneering, a subserviency to caucus direction, and a party spirit upon a level with many of the least reputable elective Chambers in the world; and beneath the imposing mask of an assembly of notables backed by the prescription and traditions of centuries we discern the leer of the artful dodger, who has got the straight tip from the party agent.

It is not possible for reasonable men to defend such a system or such an institution. Counter-checks upon a democratic Assembly there may be, perhaps there should be. But those counter-checks should be in the nature of delay, and not in the nature of arrest; they should operate evenly and equally against both political parties, and not against only one of them; and above all they should be counter-checks conceived and employed in the national interest and not in a partisan interest. These abuses and absurdities have now reached a point when it is certain that reform, effective and far-reaching, must be the necessary issue at a general election; and, whatever may be the result of that election, be sure of this, that no Liberal Government will at any future time assume office without securing guarantees that that reform shall be carried out.

There is, however, one reason which would justify a Government, circumstanced and supported as we are, in abandoning prematurely the trust confided to us by the country. When a Government is impotent, when it is destitute of ideas and devoid of the power to give effect to them, when it is brought to a complete arrest upon the vital and essential lines of its policy, then I entirely agree that the sooner it divests itself of responsibilities which it cannot discharge, the better for the country it governs and the Party it represents. No one who looks back over the three busy years of legislation which have just been completed can find any grounds for such a view of our position; and although we have sustained checks and vexations from circumstances beyond our control which have prevented us settling, as we otherwise would have done, the problems of licensing and of education, no lover of progress who compares the Statute-book as it stands to-day with its state in 1905, need feel that he has laboured in vain.

No one can say that we have been powerless in the past. The trade unionist as he surveys the progress of his organisation, the miner as the cage brings him to the surface of the ground, the aged pensioner when he visits the post office with his cheque-book, the Irish Catholic whose son sees the ranges of a University career thrown open, the child who is protected in his home and in the street, the peasant who desires to acquire a share of the soil he tills, the youthful offender in the prison, the citizen as he takes his seat on the county bench, the servant who is injured in domestic service, all give the lie to that—all can bear witness to the workings of a tireless social and humanitarian activity, which, directed by knowledge and backed by power, tends steadily to make our country a better place for the many, without at the same time making it a bad place for the few.

But, if we have been powerful in the past, shall we then be powerless in the future? Let the year that has now opened make its answer to that. We shall see before many months are passed whether his Majesty's Government, and the House of Commons, by which it is supported, do not still possess effective means to carry out their policy, not only upon those important political issues in which we have been for the time being thwarted, but also in that still wider and, in my opinion, more important field of social organisation into which, under the leadership of the Prime Minister, we shall now proceed to advance.

I do not, of course, ignore the fact that the House of Lords has the power, though not the constitutional right, to bring the government of the country to a standstill by rejecting the provision which the Commons make for the financial service of the year. That is a matter which does not rest with us, it rests with them. If they want a speedy dissolution, they know where to find one. If they really believe, as they so loudly proclaim, that the country will hail them as its saviours, they can put it to the proof. If they are ambitious to play for stakes as high as any Second Chamber has ever risked, we shall not be wanting. And, for my part, I should be quite content to see the battle joined as speedily as possible upon the plain, simple issue of aristocratic rule against representative government, between the reversion to protection and the maintenance of free trade, between a tax on bread and a tax on—well, never mind. And if they do not choose, or do not dare to use the powers they most injuriously possess, if fear, I say, or tactics, or prudence, or some lingering sense of constitutional decency, restrains them, then for Heaven's sake let us hear no more of these taunts, that we, the Liberal Party, are afraid to go to the country, that we do not possess its confidence, and that we are impotent to give effect to the essential purposes of our policy.

Subject to such a constitutional outrage as I have indicated, his Majesty's Government will claim their right and use their power to present the Liberal case as a whole to the judgment of the whole body of electors. That case is already largely developed. How utterly have all those predictions been falsified that a Liberal Government would be incapable of the successful conduct of Imperial affairs! Whether you look at our position in Europe, or at the difficult conduct of Indian administration, or the relations which have been preserved, and in some cases restored, with our self-governing Colonies, the policy of the Government has been attended with so much success that it has not only commanded the approval of impartial persons, but has silenced political criticism itself.

It was in South Africa that we were most of all opposed and most of all distrusted, and by a singular inversion it is in South Africa that the most brilliant and memorable results have been achieved. Indeed, I think that the gift of the Transvaal and Orange River Constitutions and the great settlement resulting therefrom will be by itself as a single event sufficient to vindicate in the eyes of future generations the administration of Sir Henry Campbell-Bannerman, and to dignify his memory in Parliaments and periods which we shall not see. But our work abroad is not yet completed, has not yet come to its full fruition. If we should continue, as I expect we shall, to direct public affairs for the full five years which are the normal and the healthy period of British Administrations, we may look for a further advance and improvement in all the great external spheres of Imperial policy. We may look in India for a greater sense of confidence and solidarity between the people and the Government. We shall salute the sunrise of South Africa united under the British Crown.

And in Europe I trust that Sir Edward Grey will have crowned his work at the Foreign Office by establishing a better and kindlier feeling between the British and the German peoples. That will be the record of policy beyond the seas on which we shall appeal for judgment and for justice.

If it be said that, contrary to general expectation, our policy has prospered better abroad than at home, you have not far to look for the reason. Abroad we have enjoyed full responsibility, a free hand, and fair-play; at home we have had a divided authority, a fettered hand, and the reverse of fair-play. We have been hampered and we have been harassed. We have done much; we could have done much more.

Our policy at home is less complete and less matured than it is abroad. But it so happens that many of the most important steps which we should now take, are of such a character that the House of Lords will either not be able or will not be anxious to obstruct them, and could not do so except by courting altogether novel dangers. The social field lies open. There is no great country where the organisation of industrial conditions more urgently demands attention. Wherever the reformer casts his eyes he is confronted with a mass of largely preventable and even curable suffering. The fortunate people in Britain are more happy than any other equally numerous class have been in the whole history of the world. I believe the left-out millions are more miserable. Our vanguard enjoys all the delights of all the ages. Our rearguard straggles out into conditions which are crueller than barbarism. The unemployed artisan, the casual labourer, and the casual labourer's wife and children, the sweated worker, the infirm worker, the worker's widow, the under-fed child, the untrained, undisciplined, and exploited boy labourer—it is upon these subjects that our minds should dwell in the early days of 1909.

The Liberal Party has always known the joy which comes from serving great causes. It must also cherish the joy which comes from making good arrangements. We shall be all the stronger in the day of battle if we can show that we have neglected no practicable measure by which these evils can be diminished, and can prove by fact and not by words that, while we strive for civil and religious equality, we also labour to build up—so far as social machinery can avail—tolerable basic conditions for our fellow-countrymen. There lies the march, and those who valiantly pursue it need never fear to lose their hold upon the heart of Britain.

THE APPROACHING CONFLICT

NOTTINGHAM, *JANUARY 30, 1909*

(Originally published in *The Manchester Guardian*)

*W*e are met together at a time when great exertions and a high constancy are required from all who cherish and sustain the Liberal cause. Difficulties surround us and dangers threaten from this side and from that. You know the position which has been created by the action of the House of Lords. Two great political Parties divide all England between them in their conflicts. Now it is discovered that one of these Parties possesses an unfair weapon—that one of these Parties, after it is beaten at an election, after it is deprived of the support and confidence of the country, after it is destitute of a majority in the representative Assembly, when it sits in the shades of Opposition without responsibility, or representative authority, under the frown, so to speak, of the Constitution, nevertheless possesses a weapon, an instrument, a tool, a utensil—call it what you will—with which it can harass, vex, impede, affront, humiliate, and finally destroy the most serious labours of the other. When it is realised that the Party which possesses this prodigious and unfair advantage is in the main the Party of the rich against the poor, of the classes and their dependants against the masses, of the lucky, the wealthy, the happy, and the strong against the left-out and the shut-out millions of the weak and poor, you will see how serious the constitutional situation has become.

A period of supreme effort lies before you. The election with which this Parliament will close, and towards which we are moving, is one which is different in notable features from any other which we have known. Looking back over the politics of the last thirty years, we hardly ever see a Conservative Opposition approaching an election without a programme, on paper at any rate, of social and democratic reform. There was Lord Beaconsfield with his policy of "health and the laws of health." There was the Tory democracy of Lord Randolph Churchill in 1885 and 1886, with large, far-reaching plans of Liberal and democratic reform, of a generous policy to Ireland, of retrenchment and reduction of expenditure upon naval and military armaments—all promises to the people, and for the sake of which he resigned rather than play them false. Then you have the elections of 1892 and 1895. In each the Conservative Party, whether in office or opposition, was, under the powerful influence of Mr. Chamberlain, committed to most extensive social programmes, of what we should call Liberal and Radical reforms, like the Workmen's Compensation Act and Old-Age Pensions, part of which were carried out by them and part by others.

But what social legislation, what plans of reform do the Conservative Party offer now to the working people of England if they will return them to power? I have studied very carefully the speeches of their leaders—if you can call them leaders—and I have failed to discover a single plan of social reform or reconstruction. Upon the grim and sombre problems of the Poor Law they have no policy whatever. Upon unemployment no policy whatever; for the evils of intemperance no policy whatever, except to make sure of the public-house vote; upon the question of the land, monopolised as it is in the hands of so few, denied to so many, no policy whatever; for the distresses of Ireland, for the relations between the Irish and British peoples, no policy whatever unless it be coercion. In other directions where they have a policy, it is worse than no policy. For Scotland the Lords' veto, for Wales a Church repugnant to the conscience of the overwhelming majority of the Welsh people, crammed down their throats at their own expense.

Yet we are told they are confident of victory, they are persuaded that the country has already forgotten the follies and even the crimes of the late Administration, and that the general contempt and disgust in which they were dismissed from power has already passed away. They are already busy making their Cabinet, who is to be put in and, what is not less important, who is to be put out. Lists of selection and lists of proscription are being framed. The two factions into which they are divided, the Balfourites and the tariff reformers, are each acutely conscious of one another's infirmities, and, through their respective organs, they have succeeded in proving to their apparent satisfaction what most of us have known, and some of us have said for a long time past, that they are an uncommonly poor lot all round.

It would be bad enough if a Party so destitute, according to its own statement, of political merit were to return with the intention of doing nothing but repeating and renewing our experiences under Mr. Balfour's late Administration, of dragging through empty sessions, of sneering at every philanthropic enthusiasm, of flinging a sop from time to time to the brewers or the parsons or the landed classes. But those would not be the consequences which would follow from the Tory triumph. Consequences far more grave, immeasurably more disastrous, would follow. We are not offered an alternative policy of progress, we are not confronted even with a policy of standstill, we are confronted with an organised policy of constructive reaction. We are to march back into those shades from which we had hoped British civilisation and British science had finally emerged.

If the Conservative Party win the election they have made it perfectly clear that it is their intention to impose a complete protective tariff, and to raise the money for ambitious armaments and colonial projects by taxing the poor. They have declared, with a frankness which is, at any rate, remarkable, that they will immediately proceed to put a tax on bread, a tax on meat, a tax on timber, and an innumerable schedule of taxes on all manufactured articles imported into the United Kingdom; that is to say, that they will take by all these taxes a large sum of money from the pockets of the wage-earners, by making them pay more for the food they eat, the houses they live in, and the comforts and conveniences which they require in their homes, and that a great part of this large sum of money will be divided between the landlords and the manufacturers in the shape of increased profits; and even that part of it which does reach the Exchequer is to be given back to these same classes in the shape of reductions in income-tax and in direct taxation. If you face the policy with which we are now threatened by the Conservative Party fairly and searchingly, you will see that it is nothing less than a deliberate attempt on the part of important sections of the propertied classes to transfer their existing burdens to the shoulders of the masses of the people, and to gain greater profits for the investment of their capital by charging higher prices.

It is very natural that a Party nourishing such designs should be apprehensive of criticism and of opposition; but I must say I have never heard of a Party which was in such a jumpy, nervous state as our opponents are at this present time. If one is led in the course of a speech, as I sometimes am, to speak a little firmly and bluntly about the Conservative tariff reformers, they become almost speechless with indignation. They are always in a state of incipient political apoplexy, while as for the so-called Liberal Unionists, whenever they are criticised, they never leave off whining and say that it is unchivalrous to attack them while Mr. Chamberlain is disabled. Sorry I am that he is out of the battle, not only on personal, but on public grounds. His fiercest opponents would welcome his re-entry into the political arena, if only for the fact that we should then have a man to deal with, and some one whose statement of the case for his side would be clear and bold, whose speeches would be worth reading and worth answering, instead of the melancholy marionettes whom the wire-pullers of the Tariff Reform League are accustomed to exhibit on provincial platforms. But I hope you will not let these pretexts or complaints move you or prevent you from calling a spade a spade, a tax a tax, a protective tariff a gigantic dodge to cheat the poor, or the Liberal Unionist party the most illiberal thing on record.

But if the tariff reformers are so touchy and intolerant that they resent the slightest attack or criticism from their opponents as if it were sacrilege, that is nothing to the fury which they exhibit when any of their friends on the Conservative side begin to ask a few questions. One would have thought at least that matters of such gravity and such novelty should be considered fairly on their merits. But what does Mr. Austen Chamberlain say? He tells us that no hesitation will be tolerated from Unionist Members of Parliament in regard to any tariff reform proposals which may in a future Parliament be submitted—by whoever may be the Chancellor of the Exchequer. No hesitation will be tolerated. Not opposition, not criticism, not dissent, but no hesitation will be tolerated. The members of the Unionist Party are to go to the next Parliament, not as honest gentlemen, free to use their minds and intelligences. They are to go as the pledged, tied-up delegates of a caucus, forced to swallow without hesitation details of a tariff which they have not even seen; denied the right which every self-respecting man should claim, to give their vote on grand and cardinal issues according to their faith and their conscience. And in order that those who would refuse to be bound by these dishonouring conditions may be smelt out and excluded from the House of Commons, a secret society of nameless but probably interested busybodies is hard at work in all the dirtiest sewers of political intrigue.

But, after all, these methods are an inseparable part of the process of carrying a protectionist tariff. The whole question resolves itself into a matter of "business is business," and the predatory interests which have banded themselves together to finance and organise the tariff campaign cannot be expected to put up with the conscientious scruples and reasonable hesitations of Members of Parliament. It will be a cash transaction throughout, with large profits and quick delivery. Every little would-be monopolist in the country is going to have his own association to run his own particular trade. Every constituency will be forced to join in the scramble, and to secure special favours at the expense of the commonwealth for its special branches of industry. All the elections of the future will turn on tariffs. Why, you can see the thing beginning already. That egregious Tariff Commission have been dividing all the loot among themselves before the battle has been won—dividing the lion's skin while the beast lives—and I was reading only the other day that the Conservatives of Norwood have decided that they could not support their Member any longer, because, forsooth, he would not pledge himself to vote for a special tax on foreign imported chairs and window panes. It is the same in every country.

Such is the great conspiracy with which the British democracy is now confronted—an attempt to place the main burden of taxation upon the shoulders of wage-earners and not on income-drawers, a disastrous blow at the prosperity, the freedom, the flexibility, and the expansive power of British industry, and a deadly injury to the purity of English public life. The Conservative Party tell us that if they win the victory they will screw a protective tariff on our necks. What do we say? What of the House of Lords? We say that if we win, we will smash to pieces the veto of the House of Lords. If we should obtain a majority at the next election—and I have good hopes that if we act with wisdom and with union, and, above all, with courage, we shall undoubtedly obtain an effective majority—the prize we shall claim will be a final change in the relations of the two Houses of Parliament, of such a character as to enable the House of Commons to make its will supreme within the lifetime of a single Parliament; and except upon that basis, or for the express purpose of effecting that change, we will not accept any responsibility for the conduct of affairs.

But there is another issue which must not be overlooked. I mean the social issue. We have taken a great step already. I must say that he is rather a sour kind of man who can find nothing to notice in the Old-Age Pensions Act except its little flaws and petty defects. I think you will feel, on the contrary, that the establishment of the pensions system is a marvellous and impressive example of the power which British Governments possess. Without a hitch, perfectly smoothly, punctual to the minute, regular as clockwork, nearly 600,000 aged persons are being paid their pensions every week. That is a wonderful and beneficent achievement, a good job well worth some risk and sweat to finish. Nearly eight millions of money are being sent circulating through unusual channels, long frozen by poverty, circulating in the homes of the poor, flowing through the little shops which cater to their needs, cementing again family unions which harsh fate was tearing asunder, uniting the wife to the husband, and the parent to the children. No; in spite of Socialistic sneer and Tory jeer and glorious beer, and all the rest of it, I say it is a noble and inspiring event, for which this Parliament will be justly honoured by generations unborn. I said just now that a Tory tariff victory meant marching backwards, but there are some things they cannot undo. We may be driven from power. We may desire to be released from responsibility. Much of our work may be cut short, much may be overturned. But there are some things which Tory reaction will not dare to touch, and, like the settlement and reconciliation of South Africa, so the Old-Age Pensions Act will live and grow and ripen as the years roll by, far beyond the reach of Party warfare and far above the changing moods of faction.

There are many political injustices in this country and many absurd, oppressive, or obsolete practices. But the main aspirations of the British people are at this present time social rather than political. They see around them on every side, and almost every day, spectacles of confusion and misery which they cannot reconcile with any conception of humanity or justice. They see that there are in the modern state a score of misfortunes that can happen to a man without his being in fault in any way, and without his being able to guard against them in any way. They see, on the other hand, the mighty power of science, backed by wealth and power, to introduce order, to provide safeguards, to prevent accidents, or at least to mitigate their consequences. They know that this country is the richest in the world; and in my sincere judgment the British democracy will not give their hearts to any Party that is not able and willing to set up that larger, fuller, more elaborate, more thorough social organisation, without which our country and its people will inevitably sink through sorrow to disaster and our name and fame fade upon the pages of history.

We have done some of that work, and we are going to do more. In moving forward to this great struggle which is approaching, we are going to carry our social policy along with us. We are not going to fight alone upon the political and constitutional issue, nor alone upon the defence of free trade. We are going, fearless of the consequences, confident of our faith, to place before the nation a wide, comprehensive, interdependent scheme of social organisation—to place it before the people not merely in the speeches or placards of a Party programme, but by a massive series of legislative proposals and administrative acts. If we are interrupted or impeded in our march, the nation will know how to deal with those who stand in the path of vital and necessary reforms. And I am confident that in the day of battle the victory will be to the earnest and to the persevering; and then again will be heard the doleful wail of Tory rout and ruin, and the loud and resounding acclamations with which the triumphant armies of democracy will march once again into the central place of power.

THE SECOND READING OF THE
ANTI-SWEATING BILL[1]

HOUSE OF COMMONS, *APRIL 28, 1909*

*J*t is a serious national evil that any class of his Majesty's subjects should receive in return for their utmost exertions less than a living wage.

It was formerly supposed that the workings of the laws of supply and demand would in the regular and natural course of events, and by a steady progression, eliminate that evil, and achieve adequate minimum standards. Modern opinion has found it necessary greatly to refine upon these broad generalisations of the truth, and the first clear division that we make to-day in questions of wages, is that between a healthy and unhealthy condition of bargaining.

Where, as in the great staple trades of this country, you have powerful organisations on both sides, with responsible leaders able to bind their constituents to their decisions, conjoined with automatic scales, or arbitration or conciliation in case of a deadlock, there you have a healthy condition of bargaining, which increases the competitive power of the industry, which continually weaves more closely together the fortunes of Capital and Labour, and which enforces a constant progression in the standards of living and of productive power. But where, as in what we call "Sweated trades," you have no organisation at all on either side, no parity of bargaining between employers and employed, where the good employer is continually undercut by the bad, and the bad again by the worse; where the worker whose whole livelihood depends on the trade is undercut by the worker to whom it is only a second string; where the feebleness and ignorance of the workers and their isolation from each other render them an easy prey to the tyranny of bad masters, and middlemen one step above them upon the lowest rungs of the ladder, and themselves held in the grip

---

1   Otherwise called "The Trade Boards Bill."

of the same relentless forces—there you have a condition not of progress but of progressive degeneration. And just as in the former case the upward tendency will be constant if it is not interrupted by external power, so in the latter case the demoralisation will continue in a squalid welter for periods which are quite indefinite so far as our brief lives are concerned.

We have seen from the investigations of the last twenty years, when the phenomena of sweating have been under close and scientific review, that there is no power of self-cure within the area of the evil. We have seen that while the general advance in the standards of work and wages has on the whole been constant, these morbid and diseased patches, which we call the Sweated Trades, have not shared in that improvement, but have remained in a state of chronic depression and degeneration. The same shocking facts, in some cases the same pitiful witnesses, were brought before the Select Committee last year as before Lord Dunraven's Committee in 1888. Indeed I am advised that in some respects wages and conditions are worse than they were twenty years ago. Nor are these melancholy facts confined to any one country. Sweating is not a peculiarity of Great Britain. Practically the same trades experience the same evils in all other industrial countries. France, Germany, Austria, and America reproduce with great exactness under similar economic conditions the same social evils, and in those countries, as in ours, Sweated Industries—by which I mean trades where there is no organisation, where wages are exceptionally low, and conditions subversive of physical health and moral welfare—cast dark shadows in what is, upon the whole, the growing and broadening light of civilisation.

There is a clear reason for this, which is in itself at once a justification for the special treatment which we propose for these trades, and a means of marking them off more or less definitely from the ordinary trades. In the case of any great staple trade in this country, if the rate of wages became unnaturally low compared to other industries, and the workers could not raise it by any pressure on their part, the new generation at any rate would exercise a preference for better pay and more attractive forms of industry. The gradual correction of depressed conditions over large periods of time is thus possible. But in these sweated industries there is no new generation to come to the rescue. They are recruited from a class rather than from a section of the community. The widow, the women folk of the poorest type of labourer, the broken, the weak, the struggling, the diseased—those are the people who largely depend upon these trades, and they have not the same mobility of choice, exerted, tardily though it be, by a new generation, but which is undoubtedly operative upon the great staple trades of the country. That is an explanation which accounts for the same evils being reproduced under similar conditions in different countries, separated widely from one another and marked by great differences of general conditions.

I ask the House to regard these industries as sick and diseased industries. I ask Parliament to deal with them exactly in the same mood and temper as we should deal with sick people. It would be cruel to prescribe the same law for the sick as for the sound. It would be absurd to apply to the healthy the restrictions required for the sick. Further, these sweated trades are not inanimate abstractions. They are living, almost sentient, things. Let the House think of these sweated trades as patients in a hospital ward. Each case must be studied and treated entirely by itself. No general rule can be applied. There is no regulation dose which will cure them all. You cannot effect quicker cures by giving larger doses. Different medicines, different diets, different operations are required for each; and consideration, encouragement, nursing, personal effort are necessary for all. Great flexibility and variety of procedure, and a wide discretionary power, entrusted to earnest and competent people, must characterise any attempt to legislate on this subject.

The central principle of this Bill is the establishment of Trade Boards, which will be charged with the duty of fixing a minimum wage. I am very anxious to give these Trade Boards the utmost possible substance and recognition. They will be formed on the principle of equality of representation for employers and employed, with a skilled official chairman or nucleus. That is the principle I have adopted in the new Arbitration Court recently established. That is the principle which will govern the system of Labour Exchanges, shortly to be introduced, and other measures which may come to be associated with Labour Exchanges, and I think it is an excellent principle.

At the same time, do not let us suppose that these Trade Boards will, in the first instance, be very strong or representative bodies. They are to be formed in trades mainly worked by women, where no organisation has ever yet taken root, where there are as yet no means of finding and focusing an effective trade opinion. Where possible, they will be partly elective; in many cases they will, I expect, have to begin by being almost entirely nominated. In some cases it will be upon the official members alone that the main burden will fall. I could not ask the House to confer upon bodies of this nebulous character, not representative, not elective in any democratic sense, responsible not to constituents, nor to a public department, nor to Parliament itself in any way, the absolute and final power of enforcing by the whole apparatus of the law any decision, whether wise or foolish, upon wage questions to which they may come by the narrowest majority. The work which we entrust to them wholly and finally is sufficiently difficult and important. We direct them by this Bill to prescribe minimum rates of wages. They are to find the minimum rate.

For that purpose they are as well qualified as any body that we could devise. In this sphere their jurisdiction will be complete. The Board of Trade will not retry the question of what is the right minimum rate. Another and quite different question will be decided by the Board of Trade. They will decide whether the minimum rate which has been prescribed by the Trade Board commands sufficient support in the trade to make its enforcement by inspection and prosecution likely to be effective.

That is the division between the responsibility which the Trade Boards will have and the responsibility which we shall reserve to ourselves. I shall be quite ready in Committee to express that intention, which is in the Bill, in a simpler and stronger manner, and to make the function of the Board of Trade a positive and not a negative one, so that when the Trade Board has fixed the minimum rate of wages it shall, after an interval of six months, acquire the force of law, and shall be enforced by compulsory powers, unless in the meanwhile the Board of Trade decides or rules otherwise. For my part, I gladly give an assurance that it is our intention to put the compulsory provisions of this Bill into full effect upon at least one of the trades in the schedule, at as early a date as possible, in order to bring about the fulfilment of a much-needed and long-overdue experiment.

Now I come to the probationary period, and I know that there are a great many who have stated that it is mere waste of time. I, on the contrary, have been led to the opinion that it is vital to any practical or effective policy against sweating. It is no use to attempt, in trades as complex and obscure as these with which we are dealing, to substitute outside authority for trade opinion. The only hope lies in the judicious combination of the two, each acting and reacting upon the other. A mere increase of the penal provisions and inspection would be a poor compensation for the active support of a powerful section within the trade itself. It is upon the probationary period that we rely to enable us to rally to the Trade Board and to its minimum wage the best employers in the trade. In most instances the best employers in the trade are already paying wages equal or superior to the probable minimum which the Trade Board will establish. The inquiries which I have set on foot in the various trades scheduled have brought to me most satisfactory assurances from nearly all the employers to whom my investigators have addressed themselves.

For the enforcement of this Act, and for the prevention of evasion and collusion, I rely upon the factory inspectors, who will report anything that has come to their notice on their rounds and who will make themselves a channel for complaints. I rely still more upon the special peripatetic inspectors and investigators who will be appointed under the Act by the Board of Trade, who will have to conduct prosecutions under the Act, and who will devote all their time to the purposes of the Act. These officers will incidentally clothe the Trade Boards with real authority, once the rate has been enforced, in that they will be responsible to the Trade Board, and not to some powerful Department of Government external to the Trade Board itself. I rely further upon the support of the members of the Trade Boards themselves, who will act as watch-dogs and propagandists. I rely upon the driving power of publicity and of public opinion. But most of all I put my faith in the practical effect of a powerful band of employers, perhaps a majority, who, whether from high motives or self-interest, or from a combination of the two—they are not necessarily incompatible ideas—will form a vigilant and instructed police, knowing every turn and twist of the trade, and who will labour constantly to protect themselves from being undercut by the illegal competition of unscrupulous rivals.

An investigator in the East End of London writes:

"The people who can check evasion are the large firms. Their travellers form a magnificent body of inspectors, who ought to see that the Act is enforced. The checking of evasion will have to be carried out, not so much by visiting workshops and home-workers as by hearing where cheap, low-class goods are coming into the market, and tracing the goods back to the contractors who made them."

There are solid reasons on which we on this side of the House who are Free Traders rely with confidence, when we associate ourselves with this class of legislation. First of all, we must not imagine that this is the only European country which has taken steps to deal with sweating. The first exhibition of sweated products was held in Berlin, and it was from that exhibition that the idea was obtained of holding that most valuable series of exhibitions throughout this country which created the driving power which renders this Bill possible. I am advised that German legislation on some of these questions has even anticipated us. In other countries legislation is pending on principles not dissimilar from those which we advocate. In Bavaria and Baden the latest reports are to the effect that the official Government Reports of Inquiries recommend almost the same and in some cases stronger provisions than those to which we now ask the assent of the House of Commons. This may be said in a different form of Austria. All this movement which is going on throughout Europe, and which is so pregnant with good, will be powerfully stimulated by our action in this country, and that stimulus will not only facilitate our work by removing the argument which causes hon. gentlemen opposite anxiety, but it will also, I think, redound to the credit of this country that it took a leading and prominent position in what is a noble and benignant work.

I was delighted to hear the Leader of the Opposition say, in a concise and cogent sentence, that he could easily conceive many sweated trades in which the wages of the workers could be substantially raised without any other change except a diminution of price. Sir, the wages of a sweated worker bear no accurate relation to the ultimate price. Sometimes they vary in the same places for the same work done at the same time. And sometimes the worst sweating forms a part of the production of articles of luxury sold at the very highest price. We believe further, however, that decent conditions make for industrial efficiency and increase rather than diminish competitive power. "General low wages," said Mill, "never caused any country to undersell its rivals; nor did general high wages ever hinder it." The employers who now pay the best wages in these sweated trades maintain themselves not only against the comparatively small element of foreign competition in these trades, but against what is a far more formidable competition for this purpose—the competition of those employers who habitually undercut them by the worst processes of sweating. I cannot believe that the process of raising the degenerate and parasitical portion of these trades up to the level of the most efficient branches of the trade, if it is conducted by those conversant with the conditions of the trade and interested in it, will necessarily result in an increase of the price of the ultimate product. It may, even as the right hon. gentleman has said, sensibly diminish it through better methods.

Sir, it is on these grounds, and within these limits, that I ask for a Second Reading for this Bill.

The principles and objects are scarcely disputed here. Let us go into Committee and set to work upon the details, actuated by a single-minded desire to produce a practical result. It is by the evidences of successful experiment that, more than any other way, we shall forward and extend the area of our operations; and in passing this Bill the House will not only deal manfully with a grave and piteous social evil, but it will also take another step along that path of social organisation into which we have boldly entered, and upon which the Parliaments of this generation, whatever their complexion, will have to march.

LABOUR EXCHANGES AND
UNEMPLOYMENT INSURANCE

HOUSE OF COMMONS, *MAY 19, 1909*

*T*he functions of Government in relation to industrial life may be divided into three categories—discipline, organisation, and relief. The control and regulation of industrial conditions by penal and disciplinary powers belong to the Home Office, the relieving and curative processes are entrusted to the Local Government Board, and the organisation of industry falls to the province of the Board of Trade. The proposals which I now submit to the House are concerned only with organisation; they can be judged only in relation to that section of the subject; they do not pretend to stretch beyond it, or to include other not less important aspects; and I ask that they shall not be impugned, because, in dealing with the evils which properly fall within that sphere, they do not extend to other evils that lie without it.

I ask permission to introduce a Bill for the establishment of a national system of Labour Exchanges. There is high authority for this proposal. The Majority and Minority representatives of the Poor Law Commission, differing in so much else, are agreed unanimously in its support. "In the forefront of our proposals," says the Majority Report, "we place Labour Exchanges." "This National Labour Exchange," says the Minority Report, "though in itself no adequate remedy, is the foundation of all our proposals. It is, in our view, an indispensable condition of any real reform." The National Conference of Trade Union Delegates, convened by the Parliamentary Committee of the Trade Union Congress, of March 19, 1909, resolved unanimously: "That this Conference of Trade Union delegates, representing 1,400,000 members, approves of the establishment of Labour Exchanges on a national basis, under the control of the Board of Trade, provided that the managing board contains at least an equal proportion of employers and representatives of Trade Unions." The Central Unemployed Body for London, by a Resolution in June 1908, declared in favour of a national system of Labour Exchanges. Economists as divergent in opinion as Professor Ashley, of Birmingham, and Professor Chapman, of Manchester, have all approved and urged the project publicly in the strongest terms. Several of the principal members of the late Government have, either in evidence before the Poor Law Commission or in public speeches, expressed themselves in favour of Labour Exchanges, and the Report of the delegates of the Labour Party to Germany strongly approves of the system which they found there, namely: "the co-ordination and systematic management of Public Labour Exchanges."

The British authorities which I have mentioned are reinforced by the example of many foreign countries; and as early as 1904 the Board of Trade, in its reports on agencies and methods of dealing with unemployed in foreign countries, drew attention to the very considerable extension of Labour Exchanges in the last three years in Germany, Austria, Switzerland, France, and Belgium. Since then Norway has been added to the list. Mr. W. Bliss, in the Bulletin of the *Washington Bureau of Labour* for May, 1908, in the course of a survey of the whole field of unemployment and of possible remedies, says, "The most important agencies for providing work for the unemployed who are employable, but have no prospect of returning to their former positions, are the public employment bureaux. These are largely developed in a number of European countries, and especially in Germany, where they have grown rapidly in the last twenty years, both in numbers and in efficiency." So that the House will see that we have behind us this afternoon not only a practical consensus of opinion among authorities at home in favour of the policy, but the spectacle of its successful practice on an extensive scale, and over a period of years, in the greatest industrial community of the Continent, and its extension in various degrees to many other countries.

I do not, therefore, propose to occupy the time of the House with any elaborate justification of the merits of the Bill. Those we may discuss at our leisure later. I confine myself only to a few general observations. Two main defects in modern industrial conditions which were emphasised by the Royal Commission were the lack of mobility of labour and lack of information. With both of these defects the National System of Labour Exchanges is calculated to deal. Modern industry has become national. Fresh means of transport knit the country into one, as it was never knit before. Labour alone in its search for markets has not profited; the antiquated, wasteful, and demoralising method of personal application— that is to say, the hawking of labour—persists. Labour Exchanges will give labour for the first time a modernised market. Labour Exchanges, in the second place, will increase and will organise the mobility of labour. But let me point out that to increase the *mobility* of labour is not necessarily to increase the *movement* of labour. Labour Exchanges will not increase the movement of labour; they will only render that movement, when it has become necessary, more easy, more smooth, more painless, and less wasteful.

Labour Exchanges do not pretend to any large extent to create new employment. Their main function will be to organise the existing employment, and by organising the existing employment to reduce the friction and wastage, resulting from changes in employment and the movement of workers, to a minimum. By so doing they will necessarily raise the general economic standard of our industrial life.

So far as the second defect, "lack of information," is concerned, a system of Labour Exchanges promises to be of the highest value. In proportion as they are used, they will give absolutely contemporary information upon the tendencies of the demand for labour, both in quality and in quantity, as between one trade and another, as between one season and another, as between one cycle and another, and as between one part of the country and another. They will tell the worker where to go for employment. They will tell him, what is scarcely less important, where it is useless to go in search of employment. Properly co-ordinated and connected with the employment bureaux of the various education authorities, which are now coming into existence in Scotland and in England, they will afford an increasing means of guiding the new generation into suitable, promising, and permanent employment, and will divert them from overstocked or declining industries. They will put an end to that portion of unemployment that is merely local or accidental in character. They are the only means of grappling with the evils of casual employment, with all its demoralising consequences. They are capable of aiding the process of dovetailing one seasonal trade into another. A system of Labour Exchanges, dispensing with the need for wandering in search of work, will make it possible, for the first time, to deal stringently with vagrancy. And, lastly, Labour Exchanges are indispensable to any system of Unemployment Insurance, as indeed to any other type of honourable assistance to the unemployed, since they alone can provide an adequate test of the desire for work and of the reality of unemployment. The authority of both Reports of the Poor Law Commission may be cited upon these points; and I shall present this Bill to the House as an important piece of social and industrial machinery, the need for which has long been apparent, and the want of which has been widely and painfully felt.

I said that in the creation of such a system we may profit by the example of Germany; we may do more, we may improve upon the example of Germany. The German Exchanges, though co-ordinated and encouraged to some extent by State and Imperial Governments, are mainly municipal in their scope. Starting here with practically a clear field and with the advantage of the experiment and the experience of other lands to guide us, we may begin upon a higher level and upon a larger scale. There is reason to believe that the utility of a system like Labour Exchanges, like utility of any other market, increases in proportion to its range and scope. We therefore propose, as a first principle, that our system shall be uniform and national in its character; and here, again, we are supported both by the Minority and by the Majority Reports of the Royal Commission.

A Departmental Committee at the Board of Trade has, during the last six months, been working out the scheme in close detail. The whole country will be divided into ten or twelve principal divisions, each with a Divisional Clearing House, and each under a Divisional Chief, all co-ordinated with the National Clearing House in London. Distributed among these 10 Divisions in towns of, let us say, 100,000 or upwards will be between 30 and 40 First-class Labour Exchanges; in towns of 50,000 to 100,000 between 40 and 50 Second-class Exchanges; and about 150 minor offices, consisting of Third-class Exchanges, Sub-Offices, and Waiting-rooms, which last will be specially used in connection with Dock decasualisation.

The control and direction of the whole system will be under the Board of Trade. But in order to secure absolute impartiality as between the interests of capital and labour, Joint Advisory Committees, to contain in equal numbers representatives of employers and work-people, will be established in the principal centres. Thus we shall apply to the local management of Labour Exchanges the same principle of parity of representation between workmen and employers under impartial guidance and chairmanship, that we have adopted in the administration of the Trade Boards Bill, and that, *mutatis mutandis*, is the governing feature of the Courts of Arbitration which have recently been set up. If this Bill should obtain the assent of Parliament without undue delay, I should hope to bring the system into simultaneous operation over the whole country, so far as practicable, in the early months of next year. Temporary premises will be procured in all cases in the first instance; but a programme of building has been prepared, which in ten years will by a gradual process enable in all the principal centres these temporary premises to be replaced by permanent buildings.

The expense of this system will no doubt be considerable. Its ordinary working will not need a sum less than about £170,000 per year, and during the period when the building is going on the expenditure will rise to about £200,000 per year.

We hope that the Labour Exchanges will become industrial centres in each town. We hope they will become the labour market. They may, where necessary, provide an office where the Trade Board, if there is one, will hold its meetings. We desire to co-operate with trade unions on cordial terms, while preserving strict impartiality between capital and labour in disputed matters. It may, for instance, be possible for trade unions to keep their vacant-book in some cases at the exchanges. The structure of those Exchanges may in some cases be such as to enable us to have rooms which can be let to trade unions at a rent, for benefit and other meetings, so as to avoid the necessity under which all but the strongest unions lie at the present time of conducting their meetings in licensed premises. The Exchanges may, as they develop, afford facilities for washing, clothes-mending, and for non-alcoholic refreshments to persons who are attending them. Separate provision will be made for men and for women, and for skilled and for unskilled labour. Boy labour will be dealt with in conjunction with the local Education Authorities; and travelling expenses may be advanced on loan, if the management of the Exchange think fit, to persons for whom situations have been found.

So much for the policy of Labour Exchanges. That is a policy complete in itself. It would be considerable if it stood alone; but it does not stand alone. As my right hon. friend the Chancellor of the Exchequer has announced in his Budget speech, the Government propose to associate with the policy of Labour Exchanges a system of Unemployment Insurance.

The House knows that the Minority Report advocates a system of compulsory labour exchanges, that no person shall engage any man for less than a month except through a Labour Exchange. That is not the proposal we are making. We are making a proposal of voluntary Labour Exchanges. I am quite ready to admit that no system of voluntary Labour Exchanges can deal adequately with the evils and difficulties of casual labour; but there is one conclusive reason against compulsory Labour Exchanges at the present time. To establish a system of compulsory Labour Exchanges in order to eliminate casual labour, and so to divide among a certain proportion of workers all available employment, would be absolutely and totally to cast out at the other end a surplus of unemployed: and to do this before preparations have been made for dealing with that surplus, would be to court an administrative breakdown which could not fail to be attended with the gravest possible disaster. Until poor law reform has made further progress, to establish a compulsory system of Labour Exchanges would only increase and not diminish the miseries with which we are seeking to cope.

We have, therefore, decided that our system of labour exchanges shall be voluntary in its character. For that very reason there is a great danger, to which I have never shut my eyes, that the highest ranks of labour, skilled workers, members of strong trade unions, would not think it necessary to use the Exchanges, but would use the very excellent apparatus which they have established themselves; that therefore this expensive system of

Exchanges which we are calling into being would come to be used only by the poorest of the workers in the labour market, and, consequently, would gradually relapse and fall back into the purely distress machinery and non-economic machinery from which we are labouring to extricate and separate it. It is for that reason, quite apart from the merits of the scheme of unemployment insurance, that the Government are very anxious to associate with their system of Labour Exchanges a system of unemployed insurance. If Labour Exchanges depend for their effective initiation and establishment upon unemployment insurance being associated with them, it is equally true to say that no scheme of unemployment insurance can be worked except in conjunction with some apparatus for finding work and testing willingness to work, like Labour Exchanges. The two systems are complementary; they are man and wife; they mutually support and sustain each other.

So I come to Unemployment Insurance. It is not practicable at the present time to establish a universal system of unemployment insurance. We, therefore, have to choose at the very outset of this subject between insuring some workmen in all trades or all workmen in some. In the first case we should have a voluntary, and in the second a compulsory system. The risk of unemployment varies so much between one man and another owing to relative skill, character, demeanour, and other qualities, that any system of State-aided voluntary insurance is utilised mainly by those most liable to be unemployed, and, consequently, a preponderance of bad risks is established against the Insurance Office fatal to its financial stability. On the other hand, a compulsory system of insurance, which did not add to the contribution of the worker a substantial contribution from outside, would almost certainly break down, because of the refusal of the higher class of worker to assume, unsupported, a share of the burden of the weaker members of the community.

We have decided to adopt the second alternative, and our insurance system will, in consequence, be based upon four main principles. It will involve contributions from workmen and employers; it will receive a substantial subvention from the State; it will be organised by trades; it will be compulsory upon all—employers and employed, skilled and unskilled, unionists and non-unionists alike—within those trades. The hon. Member for Leicester[1] with great force showed that to confine a scheme of unemployment insurance merely to trade unionists would be trifling with the subject. It would only be aiding those who have, thank God, been most able to aid themselves, without at the same time assisting

---

[1]   Mr. Ramsay MacDonald.

those who hitherto, under existing conditions, have not been able to make any effective provision.

To what trades ought we, as a beginning, to apply this system of compulsory contributory unemployment insurance? There is a group of trades specially marked out for the operation of such a policy. They are trades in which unemployment is not only high, but chronic, for even in the best of times it persists; in which it is not only high and chronic, but marked by seasonal and cyclical fluctuations, and in which, wherever and howsoever it occurs, it takes the form not of short time or of any of those devices for spreading wages and equalising or averaging risks, but of a total, absolute, periodical discharge of a certain proportion of the workers. The group of trades which we contemplate to be the subject of our scheme are these: house-building, and works of construction, engineering, machine- and tool-making, ship-building and boat-building, making of vehicles, and mill-sawing.

That is a very considerable group of industries. They comprise, probably at the present time, 2¼ millions of adult males. Two and a quarter millions of adult males are, roughly speaking, one-third of the population of these three kingdoms engaged in purely industrial work; that is to say, excluding commercial, professional, agricultural, and domestic occupations. Of the remaining two-thirds of the industrial population, nearly one-half are employed in the textile trades, in mining, on the railways, in the merchant marine, and in other trades, which either do not present the same features of unemployment which we see in these precarious trades, or which, by the adoption of short time or other arrangements, avoid the total discharge of a proportion of workmen from time to time. So that this group of trades to which we propose to apply the system of unemployment insurance, roughly speaking, covers very nearly half of the whole field of unemployment; and that half is, on the whole, perhaps the worse half.

The financial and actuarial basis of the scheme has been very carefully studied by the light of all available information. The report of the actuarial authorities whom I have consulted leaves me in no doubt that, even after all allowance has been made for the fact that unemployment may be more rife in the less organised and less highly skilled trades than in the trade unions who pay unemployment benefits—which is by no means certain—there is no doubt whatever that a financially sound scheme can be evolved which, in return for moderate contributions, will yield adequate benefits. I do not at this stage propose to offer any figures of contributions or benefits to the House. I confine myself to stating that we propose to aim at a scale of benefits which would be somewhat lower both in amount and in duration of payments, than that which the best-organised trade unions provide for their own members, but which, at the same time, should afford a substantial weekly payment extending over by far the greater part of the average period of unemployment of all unemployed persons in these trades.

In order to enable such a scale of benefits to be paid, we should have to raise a total sum of something between 5d. and 6d. per week per head, and this sum will be met by contributions, not necessarily equal, from the State, the workman, and the employer. For such sacrifices, which are certainly not extortionate, and which, fairly adjusted, will not hamper industry nor burden labour, nor cause an undue strain on public finance, we believe it possible to relieve a vast portion of our industrial population from a haunting and constant peril which gnaws the very heart of their prosperity and contentment.

The House will see the connection of this to the Labour Exchanges. The machinery of the insurance scheme has been closely studied, and, as at present advised, we should propose to follow the example of Germany in respect of Insurance Cards or Books, to which stamps will be affixed week by week. When a worker in an insured trade loses his employment, all he will have to do is to take his card to the Labour Exchange, which, working in conjunction with the Insurance Office, will find him a job or pay him his benefit.

The relation of the whole scheme of insurance to the present voluntary efforts of trade unions requires, and will receive, the most anxious consideration, and I am in hopes that we shall be able to make proposals which would absolutely safeguard trade unions from the unfair competition of a national insurance fund, and will indeed act as a powerful encouragement to voluntary organisations which are providing unemployed benefit.

I have thought it right to submit these not inconsiderable proposals in general outline to the House of Commons at this early stage, in order that the proposals for Labour Exchanges which we are now putting forward may be properly understood, and may not be underrated or misjudged. We cannot bring the system of unemployment insurance before Parliament in a legislative form this year for five reasons: We have not now got the time; we have not yet got the money; the finance of such a system has to be adjusted and co-ordinated with the finance of the other insurance schemes upon which the Chancellor of the Exchequer is engaged; the establishment of a system of Labour Exchanges is the necessary forerunner and foundation of a system of insurance; and, lastly, no such novel departure as unemployment insurance could possibly be taken without much further consultation and negotiation with the trade unions and employers specially concerned than the conditions of secrecy under which we have been working have yet allowed. This business of conference and consultation of the fullest character will occupy the winter, when the Board of Trade will confer with all parties affected, so that the greatest measure of agreement may be secured for our proposals when they are next year presented in their final form.

It is only necessary for me to add that the pressure and prospect of these heavy duties have required me to make a re-arrangement of the Labour Department of the Board of Trade. I propose to divide it into three sections. The first will be concerned with Wages questions and Trade disputes, with Arbitration, Conciliation, and with the working of the Trade Boards Bill, should it become law; the second, with Statistics, the Census of Production, Special Inquiries, and *The Labour Gazette*; and the third, with Labour Exchanges and Unemployment Insurance.

One of the functions of the last section will be to act as a kind of intelligence bureau, watching the continual changes of the labour market here and abroad, and suggesting any measure which may be practicable, such as co-ordination and distribution of Government contracts and municipal work, so as to act as a counterpoise to the movement of the ordinary labour market, and it will also, we trust, be able to conduct examinations of schemes of public utility, so that such schemes can, if decided upon by the Government and the Treasury, be set on foot at any time with knowledge and forethought, instead of the haphazard, hand-to-mouth manner with which we try to deal with these emergencies at the present time.

Such are the proposals which we submit in regard to the organisation section of this problem. I have carefully confined myself to that section. I have not trespassed at all upon the other no less important or scarcely less important branches, and I am quite certain this Parliament will gladly devote whatever strength it possesses to attempting to grapple with these hideous problems of social chaos, which are marring the contentment and honour of our country, and which, neglected, may fatally affect its life and its strength.

III - THE BUDGET

THE BUDGET RESOLUTIONS

HOUSE OF COMMONS, *MAY 4, 1903*

*T*he Leader of the Opposition this afternoon told us that we were at the beginning of what would be a very complex and a very protracted discussion. If that discussion continues as it has begun, the Government will have no reason to complain of it. We have made extensive and even daring proposals. Those proposals have been accepted and, on the whole, even acclaimed by the public at large, and they have not been substantially challenged in this House. The Leader of the Opposition, it is true, devoted his reasoned and temperate speech to making a careful inquiry into the foundations and the character of certain of the taxes by which my right hon. friend proposes to raise the revenue for the year; and I gathered he accepted, with such reservations as are proper to all engaged in a large discussion, and as are particularly appropriate to a Party leader, the general principle of differentiation of taxation in regard to the amount of property, but that he demurred to and condemned differentiation in regard to the character of property. The right hon. gentleman singled out for special censure and animadversion the two sets of taxes in relation to land and to the licensed trade. He used an expression about some of the forms of taxation proposed by the Chancellor of the Exchequer which was a striking one. He said that they diverged from the principles which have hitherto dominated civilised society.

Even at the risk of that accusation we on this side of the House have always taken and will always assert an entirely different position in regard to the taxation of land and of liquor licences from that of the taxation of other classes of property. The immemorial custom of nearly every modern State, the mature conclusions of many of the greatest thinkers, have placed the tenure, transfer, and obligations of land in a wholly different category from other classes of property. The mere obvious physical distinction between land, which is a vital necessity of every human being and which at the same time is strictly limited in extent, and other property is in itself sufficient to justify a clear differentiation in its treatment, and in the view taken by the State of the conditions which should govern the tenure of land from that which should regulate traffic in other forms of property. When the right hon. gentleman seeks by comparisons to show that the same reasoning which has been applied to land ought also in logic and by every argument of symmetry to be applied to the unearned increment derived from other processes which are at work in our modern civilisation, he only shows by each example he takes how different are the conditions which attach to the possession of land and speculation in the value of land from those which attach to other forms of business speculation.

"If," he inquires, "you tax the unearned increment on land, why don't you tax the unearned increment from a large block of stocks? I buy a piece of land; the value rises; I buy stocks; their value rises." But the operations are entirely dissimilar. In the first speculation the unearned increment derived from land arises from a wholly sterile process, from the mere withholding of a commodity which is needed by the community. In the second case, the investor in a block of shares does not withhold from the community what the community needs. The one operation is in restraint of trade and in conflict with the general interest, and the other is part of a natural and healthy process, by which the economic plant of the world is nourished and from year to year successfully and notably increased.

Then the right hon. gentleman instanced the case of a new railway and a country district enriched by that railway. The railway, he explained, is built to open up a new district; and the farmers and landowners in that district are endowed with unearned increment in consequence of the building of the railway. But if after a while their business aptitude and industry creates a large carrying trade, then the railway, he contends, gets its unearned increment in its turn. But the right hon. gentleman cannot call the increment unearned which the railway acquires through the regular service of carrying goods, rendering a service on each occasion in proportion to the tonnage of goods it carries, making a profit by an active extension of the scale of its useful business—he cannot surely compare that process with the process of getting rich merely by sitting still. It is clear that the analogy is not true.

We are further told that the Budget proposals proceed on the assumption that there is a corner in land, and that communities are denied the opportunity of getting the land required, whereas, it is asserted, there is in fact nothing approaching a corner in land. I do not think the Leader of the Opposition could have chosen a more unfortunate example than Glasgow. He said that the demand of that great community for land was for not more than forty acres a year. Is that the only demand of the people of Glasgow for land? Does that really represent the complete economic and natural demand for the amount of land a population of that size requires to live on? I will admit that at present prices it may be all that they can afford to purchase in the course of a year. But there are one hundred and twenty thousand persons in Glasgow who are living in one-room tenements; and we are told that the utmost land those people can absorb economically and naturally is forty acres a year. What is the explanation? Because the population is congested in the city the price of land is high upon the suburbs, and because the price of land is high upon the suburbs the population must remain congested within the city. That is the position which we are complacently assured is in accordance with the principles which have hitherto dominated civilised society.

But when we seek to rectify this system, to break down this unnatural and vicious circle, to interrupt this sequence of unsatisfactory reactions, what happens? We are not confronted with any great argument on behalf of the owner. Something else is put forward, and it is always put forward in these cases to shield the actual landowner or the actual capitalist from the logic of the argument or from the force of a Parliamentary movement. Sometimes it is the widow. But that personality has been used to exhaustion. It would be sweating in the cruellest sense of the word, overtime of the grossest description, to bring the widow out again so soon. She must have a rest for a bit; so instead of the widow we have the market-gardener—the market-gardener liable to be disturbed on the outskirts of great cities, if the population of those cities expands, if the area which they require for their health and daily life should become larger than it is at present.

I should like to point out to the Committee that the right hon. gentleman, in using this argument about the market-gardener, recognises very clearly—and I think beyond the possibility of a withdrawal—the possibility of these cities expanding and taking up a larger area of ground in consequence of the kind of taxation which my right hon. friend in his land taxes seeks to impose. But let that pass. What is the position disclosed by the argument? On the one hand we have one hundred and twenty thousand persons in Glasgow occupying one-room tenements; on the other, the land of Scotland. Between the two stands the market-gardener, and we are solemnly invited, for the sake of the market-gardener, to keep that great population congested within limits that are unnatural and restricted to an annual supply of land which can bear no relation whatever to their physical, social, and economic needs—and all for the sake of the market-gardener, who can perfectly well move farther out as the city spreads, and who would not really be in the least injured.

We take the view that land cannot be regarded as an ordinary commodity, nor are we prepared to place publicans' licences in the same position as ordinary property. A licence is a gift from the State, and the licensed trade is subject to special restrictions and special taxation; this has been recognised by all parties and by all Governments. The position in regard to licences, as we know perfectly well, has been sensibly and, indeed, entirely altered in the course of the last few years. We have seen the assertion on the part of the licensed trade of their right to convert their annual tenancy of a licence from what it has been understood to be, to a freehold, and in that position they must face the logical consequences of the arguments they have used and of their action. If there are any hardships to them in the taxation proposed, let the hardships be exposed to Parliament and they will be considered in no spirit of prejudice or malice. Do not, however, let us have attempts to represent that the tax which involves an increase in the cost of production extinguishes the profits of the industry. It does not necessarily affect the profits of the industry; it is not a deduction from resultant profits; it is an incident in the turnover. If there are hard cases and special instances, we are prepared to meet them with the closest attention and with a desire to avoid severity or anything like the appearance of harsh treatment of individuals. But we decline to regard licences or land on the same footing as ordinary property. Licences are not to be regarded as ordinary private property, but as public property which ought never to have been alienated from the State.

No one will deny that we are making very considerable proposals to Parliament for the finance of the year; but the Conservative Party have gravely compromised their power of resistance. Those who desire to see armaments restricted to the minimum consistent with national security, those who labour to combat the scares of war, and to show how many alarms have no foundation,—those are not ill-situated, if they choose to make criticisms on the scale and scope of the finance required for the year's expenditure. But an Opposition that day after day exposes the First Lord of the Admiralty and the Prime Minister to a rain of questions and cross-questions, the only object of which, or an important object of which, is to promote a feeling of insecurity, involving demands for new expenditure of an almost indefinite character, those who, like the right hon. Member for Dover,[1] hurry to and fro in the land saying—or was it singing?—"We want eight, and we won't wait"—they, at least, are not in the best position to tell the taxpayer to call on some one else. Surely a reputation for patriotism would be cheaply gained by clamouring for ships that are not needed, to be paid for with money that is to come from other people.

There is another set of arguments to which I should like to refer. We have been long told that this Budget would reveal the bankruptcy of free-trade finance, and the Leader of the Opposition, seeking from time to time for

---

[1]   Mr. Wyndham.

a sound economic foothold in the fiscal quicksands in which he is being engulfed, has endeavoured to rest the sole of his foot on tariff for revenue. The adoption of a policy of tariff reform, we have been told, had become absolutely necessary if the revenue of the country was to be obtained and if a natural expansion were to be imparted to it. But now, if we may judge from the newspapers, one of the complaints made against the free-trade system and the free-trade Budget of my right hon. friend is not that the revenue will expand too little, but that there is the possibility that it will expand too much. It is not that we have reached the limits of practicable free-trade taxation, but that the taxation we now ask Parliament to assent to, will yield in the second year a much more abundant return than in the first year, and that in subsequent years the yield will increase still further. In the words of *The Times* newspaper: "The Chancellor of the Exchequer has laid broad and deep the basis of further revenue for future years."

Those who lately taunted us with being arrested by a dead wall of Cobdenite principles are now bewailing that we have opened up broad avenues of financial advance. They came to bewail the deficit of this year: they remained to censure the surplus of next. We may, no doubt, in the future hear arguments of how protection will revive industry and increase employment, as we have heard them in the past; but there is one argument which I should think it unlikely would be effectively used against us in the future, and that is that a free-trade system cannot produce revenue, because one of the criticisms which is emphatically directed against this Budget is on account of that very expansiveness of revenue which it was lately declared a free-trade system never could produce.

But that is not the only vindication of free-trade finance which is at hand. How have foreign countries stood the late depression in trade? The shortfall of the revenue from the estimates in this country was last year less than two millions, in Germany it was eight millions, and in the United States over nineteen millions. Let the House see what fair-weather friends these protectionist duties are. In times of depression they shrink. In times of war they may fail utterly. When they are wanted, they dwindle, when they are wanted most urgently, they fade and die away altogether.

And what is true of the taxation of manufactured articles as a foundation for any fiscal policy is true still more of the taxation of food, and of no country is it so true as of this island. For if you were ever engaged in a war which rendered the highways of the ocean insecure the rise in prices would be such that all food taxes would have to be swept away at once by any Government which desired to use the whole vigour of its people in prosecuting the war. This year, with its trade depression and its excellent maintenance of the revenue, has seen the vindication of free trade as a revenue-producing instrument; next year will see its triumph.

I have no apprehensions about the Budget which is now before the Committee. As Mr. Gladstone said, in introducing the Reform Bill of 1884, what is wanted to carry this measure is concentration and concentration only, and what will lose this measure is division and division only. And I venture to think that it will not only be a demonstration of the soundness of the economic fiscal policy we have long followed, but it will also be a demonstration of the fiscal and financial strength of Great Britain which will not be without its use and value upon the diplomatic and perhaps even upon the naval situation in Europe.

The right honourable Member for East Worcestershire[1] said this Budget was the work of several sessions, if not indeed of several Parliaments. The statement is exaggerated. The proposals outlined do not in any degree transcend the limits of the practical. A social policy may be very large, but at the same time it may be very simple. All these projects of economic development, of labour exchanges, of insurance for invalidity, and unemployment, which depend on money grants, may require very careful and elaborate administrative adjustment; but so far as Parliament is concerned they do not impose difficulties or make demands upon the time of the House in any way comparable to those which are excited by the passage of an Education or a Licensing Bill, and I see no reason whatever why we should not anticipate that in the course of this session and next session we should be able to establish a wide and general system of national insurance, which, more than any other device within the reach of this generation of the workers of our country, will help to hold off from them some of the most fatal and most cruel perils which smash their households and ruin the lives of families and of workmen.

On many grounds we may commend this Budget to the House. It makes provision for the present. It makes greater provision for the future. Indirect taxation reaches the minimum. Food taxation reaches the minimum since the South African war. Certainly the working classes have no reason to complain. Nothing in the Budget touches the physical efficiency and energy of labour. Nothing in it touches the economy of the cottage home. Middle-class people with between £300 and £2,000 a year are not affected in any considerable degree, except by the estate duties, and in that not to a large extent, while in some cases they are distinctly benefited in the general way of taxation. The very rich are not singled out for peculiar, special, or invidious forms of imposition.

The chief burden of the increase of taxation is placed upon the main body of the wealthy classes in this country, a class which in number and in wealth is much greater than in any other equal community, if not, indeed,

1   Mr. Austen Chamberlain.

in any other modern State in the whole world; and that is a class which, in opportunities of pleasure, in all the amenities of life, and in freedom from penalties, obligations, and dangers, is more fortunate than any other equally numerous class of citizens in any age or in any country. That class has more to gain than any other class of his Majesty's subjects from dwelling amid a healthy and contented people, and in a safely guarded land.

I do not agree with the Leader of the Opposition, that they will meet the charges which are placed upon them for the needs of this year by evasion and fraud, and by cutting down the charities which their good feelings have prompted them to dispense. The man who proposes to meet taxation by cutting down his charities, is not the sort of man who is likely to find any very extensive source of economy in the charities which he has hitherto given. As for evasion, I hope the right hon. gentleman and his supporters underrate the public spirit which animates a proportion at any rate of the class which would be most notably affected by the present taxation. And there is for their consolation one great assurance which is worth much more to them than a few millions, more or less, of taxation. It is this—that we are this year taking all that we are likely to need for the policy which is now placed before the country, and which will absorb the energies of this Parliament. And, so far as this Parliament is concerned, it is extremely unlikely, in the absence of a national calamity, that any further demand will be made upon them, or that the shifting and vague shadows of another impending Budget will darken the prospects of improving trade.

When all that may be said on these grounds has been said, we do not attempt to deny that the Budget raises some of the fundamental issues which divide the historic Parties in British politics. We do not want to embitter those issues, but neither do we wish to conceal them. We know that hon. gentlemen opposite believe that the revenue of the country could be better raised by a protective tariff. We are confident that a free-trade system alone would stand the strain of modern needs and yield the expansive power which is necessary at the present time in the revenue. And our proof shall be the swift accomplishment of the fact. The right hon. gentleman opposite and his friends seek to arrest the tendency to decrease the proportion of indirect to direct taxation which has marked, in unbroken continuity, the course of the last sixty years. We, on the other hand, regard that tendency as of deep-seated social significance, and we are resolved that it shall not be arrested. So far as we are concerned, we are resolved that it shall continue until in the end the entire charge shall be defrayed from the profits of accumulated wealth and by the taxation of those popular indulgences which cannot be said in any way to affect the physical efficiency of labour. The policy of the Conservative Party is to multiply and extend the volume and variety of taxes upon food and necessaries. They will repose themselves, not only, as we are still forced to do, on tea and sugar, but upon bread and meat—not merely upon luxuries and comforts, but also on articles of prime necessity. Our policy is not to increase, but whenever possible to decrease, and ultimately to abolish altogether, taxes on articles of food and the necessaries of life.

If there is divergence between us in regard to the methods by which we are to raise our revenue, there is also divergence in regard to the objects on which we are to spend them. We are, on both sides, inclined to agree that we are approaching, if we have not actually entered on, one of the climacterics of our national life. We see new forces at work in the world, and they are not all friendly forces. We see new conditions abroad and around us, and they are not all favourable conditions; and I think there is a great deal to be said for those who on both sides of politics are urging that we should strive for a more earnest, more strenuous, more consciously national life. But there we part, because the Conservative Party are inclined too much to repose their faith for the future security and pre-eminence of this country upon naval and military preparations, and would sometimes have us believe that you can make this country secure and respected by the mere multiplication of ironclad ships. We shall not exclude that provision, and now indeed ask the Committee to enable us to take the steps to secure us that expansion of revenue which will place our financial resources beyond the capacity of any Power that we need to take into consideration. But we take a broader view. We are not going to measure the strength of great countries only by their material resources. We think that the supremacy and predominance of our country depend upon the maintenance of the vigour and health of its population, just as its true glory must always be found in the happiness of its cottage homes. We believe that if Great Britain is to remain great and famous in the world, we cannot allow the present social and industrial disorders, with their profound physical and moral reactions, to continue unchecked. We propose to you a financial scheme, but we also advance a policy of social organisation. It will demand sacrifices from all classes; it will give security to all classes. By its means we shall be able definitely to control some of the most wasteful processes in our social life, and without it our country will remain exposed to vital dangers, against which fleets and armies are of no avail.

THE BUDGET AND NATIONAL INSURANCE

THE FREE TRADE HALL, MANCHESTER, *MAY 23, 1909*

(Originally published in *The Manchester Guardian*)

Considering that you have all been ruined by the Budget, I think it very kind of you to receive me so well. When I remember all the injuries you have suffered—how South Africa has been lost; how the gold mines have been thrown away; how all the splendid army which Mr. Brodrick got together has been reduced to a sham; and how, of course, we have got no navy of any kind whatever, not even a fishing smack, for the thirty-five millions a year we give the Admiralty; and when I remember that in spite of all these evils the taxes are so oppressive and so cruel that any self-respecting Conservative will tell you he cannot afford either to live or die, I think it remarkable that you should be willing to give me such a hearty welcome back to Manchester. Yes, sir, when I think of the colonies we have lost, of the Empire we have alienated, of the food we have left untaxed, and the foreigners we have left unmolested, and the ladies we have left outside, I confess I am astonished to find you so glad to see me here again.

It is commonly said that our people are becoming hysterical, and that Britain is losing her old deep-seated sagacity for judging men and events. That is not my view. I have been taught that the dock always grows near the nettle. I am inclined to think that in a free community every evil carries with it its own corrective, and so I believe that sensationalism of all kinds is playing itself out, and, overdoing, is itself undone. And the more our scaremongers cry havoc, and panic, and airships, and sea-serpents, and all the other things they see floating around, the greater is the composure and the greater is the contempt with which the mass of the nation receives these revelations, and the more ready they are to devote their mind to the large and serious problems of national and social organisation which press for solution and for action at the present time, and upon which his Majesty's Government have notable proposals to make.

I come to you this afternoon to speak about the political situation and the Budget, or rather I come to speak to you about the Budget, because the Budget is the political situation; and I ask you, as if it were at an election, whether you will support the policy of the Budget or not. Let us look into it.

What is the position in which we find ourselves? After reducing the taxes on coal, on tea, on sugar, and on the smaller class of incomes by nearly £7,000,000 a year, and after paying back £40,000,000 of debt in three years, we find that new circumstances and new needs make it necessary that we should obtain fresh revenue for the service of the State.

What are the reasons for this demand? There are three reasons—and only three. Old-age pensions, the navy, and the decrease in the revenue derived from alcoholic liquor. From those three causes we require sixteen millions more money this year than we did last year. Now who has a right—this is my first question—to reproach us for that? Certainly the Conservative Party have no right.

Take first the case of old-age pensions. I do not think their record is a very good one on that. They promised old-age pensions to win the general election of 1895. They were in power for ten years and they made no effort to redeem their pledge. Again, Mr. Chamberlain, in 1903, promised old-age pensions as a part of his Tariff Reform proposal, but the Conservative Party refused to agree to the inclusion of old-age pensions in that programme and forced that great man in the height of his power and his career to throw out old-age pensions from the Tariff Reform programme and to write a letter to the newspapers to say that he had done so.

We, the Liberal Party, did not promise old-age pensions at the election of 1906. The subject was scarcely mentioned by any of the candidates who are now your Members. Certainly it did not occupy at all a prominent position. We did not promise old-age pensions; we gave old-age pensions. When the Old-Age Pensions Bill was before the House of Commons, what was the attitude of the Conservative Party? Did they do anything to try to reduce or control the expenditure of that great departure? On the contrary. As my right honourable friend the Chancellor of the Exchequer has told the House of Commons, amendments to the Old-Age Pensions Bill were moved or received the official support of the Whips of the Conservative Party which would have raised the cost of that scheme to fourteen millions a year. And the Liberal Government, which was making this great effort, which was doing the work, which was keeping the Tory promise, was reproached and was derided for not accepting the proposals which these irresponsible philanthropists, these social reformers on the cheap, these limited-liability politicians, were so ready to move. And Lord Halsbury, the late Lord Chancellor, one of the leaders of the Conservative Party, a man with a powerful influence in their councils, said in a public speech that the old-age pensions as proposed by the Government were so paltry as to be almost a mockery.

I do not think any fair-minded or impartial man, or any average British jury, surveying the record of the Conservative Party upon old-age pensions, could come to any other conclusion than that they had used this question for popularity alone; that they never meant to give old-age pensions; that they only meant to get votes by promising to give them; that they would have stopped them being given if they could; that while the Bill was on its way they tried to embarrass the Government, and to push things to unpractical extremes; and now, even when the pensions have been given, they would not pay for them if they could help it. Let me say that I think the conclusion, which I believe any jury would come to, would perhaps be rather harsh upon the Conservative Party. I believe they meant better than their record; I am willing to admit that. But their record is before us, and it is a bad one, and upon the facts I have no hesitation in saying that it is not open to them to protest—they have not even an inch of foothold to protest—against any expenditure which we may now have to incur in order to defray the consequences of the policy of old-age pensions. So much for the first cause of the increased expenditure.

I pass to the navy. The Naval Estimates have risen by three millions this year. I regret it; but I am prepared to justify it. There will be a further increase next year. I regret it; but within proper limits necessary to secure national safety I shall be prepared to justify it; but I hope you will not expect me to advocate a braggart and sensational policy of expenditure upon armaments. I have always been against that, as my father was before me.

In my judgment, a Liberal is a man who ought to stand as a restraining force against an extravagant policy. He is a man who ought to keep cool in the presence of Jingo clamour. He is a man who believes that confidence between nations begets confidence, and that the spirit of peace and goodwill makes the safety it seeks. And, above all, I think a Liberal is a man who should keep a sour look for scaremongers of every kind and of every size, however distinguished, however ridiculous—and sometimes the most distinguished are the most ridiculous—a cold, chilling, sour look for all of them, whether their panic comes from the sea or from the air or from the earth or from the waters under the earth.

His Majesty's Government are resolved that the defensive measures of this country shall be prescribed by the policy of Ministers responsible to

Parliament, and by the calculations, subject to that policy, of the experts on whom those Ministers rely, and not by the folly and the clamour of Party politicians or sensational journalists. In that determination we as a Government are united, and we shall remain united. Yet it is clear that the increase in the Naval Estimates of this year must be followed by another increase in those of next year. That is deplorable. It will impose upon our finances a strain which some other nations would not find it very easy to bear, but which, if the necessity be proved, this country will not be unwilling, and will certainly not be unable to support.

Well, but what have the Conservative Party got to say about it? Have they any right to complain of the taxes which are necessary for the maintenance of our naval power? Do we not see that they are ever exerting themselves to urge still greater expenditure upon the nation? He is a poor sort of fellow, a penny-plain-twopence-coloured kind of patriot who goes about shouting for ships, and then grudges the money necessary to build them. And when Mr. Balfour tells us that "gigantic sacrifices" are required, and that those gigantic sacrifices "must begin now," and then at the same time objects to the taxes by which the Government proposes to raise the money, he puts himself in a very queer position.

I have dealt with two of the causes which have led to our demand for further revenue—old-age pensions and the navy. Upon neither of them have the Conservative Party any ground for attacking us. What is the third? Ah, gentlemen, I agree that there is one cause of the prospective deficit for which we are budgeting for which the Conservative Party is in no way responsible. I mean the decline in the consumption of alcoholic liquors. Nothing that they have said and nothing that they have done has, in intention or in fact, contributed to the drying up of that source of revenue. On the contrary, by their legislation, by the views they have taken of the rights of the licensed trade, by their resistance to every measure of temperance reform, by their refusal even to discuss in the House of Lords the great Licensing Bill of last year, by their association with the brewers and with the liquor traffic generally, they have done all they could—I do them the justice to admit it—to maintain the Customs and Excise from alcoholic liquors at the highest level. If the habits of the people, under the influences of a wider culture, of variety, of comfort, of brighter lives, and of new conceptions, have steadily undergone a beneficent elevation and amelioration, it has been in spite of every obstacle that wealth and rank and vested interest could interpose.

The money has to be found. There is no Party in the State who can censure us because of that. Our proposals for enlarging the public revenue are just and fair to all classes. They will not, in spite of all these outcries you hear nowadays, sensibly alter the comfort or status, or even the elegance of any class in our great and varied community. No man, rich or poor, will eat a worse dinner for our taxes.

Of course, from a narrow, electioneering point of view, there are a great many people—I believe they are wrong—who think we should have done much better if we had put another penny on the income tax instead of increasing the tax upon tobacco. Well, I have come here this afternoon to tell you that we think it right that the working classes should be asked to pay a share towards the conduct of a democratic State. And we think that taxes on luxuries, however widely consumed, are a proper channel for such payment to be made. We believe that the working classes are able to pay by that channel, and we believe, further, that they are ready to pay. We do not think that in this old, wise country they would have respected any Government which at a time like this had feared to go to them for their share.

I have a good confidence that this Budget is going to go through. If there are hardships and anomalies in particular cases or particular quarters, we are ready to consider them. They will emerge in the discussions of the House of Commons, and we have every desire to consider them and to mitigate them. But we believe in the situation in which we find ourselves in this country, and in the general situation of the world at the present time—that the taxes on incomes over £3,000 a year, upon estates at death, on motor-cars before they cause death, upon tobacco, upon spirits, upon liquor licences, which really belong to the State, and ought never to have been filched away; and, above all, taxes upon the unearned increment in land are necessary, legitimate, and fair; and that without any evil consequences to the refinement or the richness of our national life, still less any injury to the sources of its economic productivity, they will yield revenue sufficient in this year and in the years to come to meet the growing needs of Imperial defence and of social reform.

This Budget will go through. It will vindicate the power of the House of Commons. It will show, what some people were inclined to forget, that in our Constitution a Government, supported by a House of Commons and the elected representatives of the people, has in fact a full control of national affairs, and has the means of giving effect to its intentions, to its policy, and to its pledges in every sphere of public affairs.

That is one thing which the passage of this Budget will show. Let not that be overlooked. But that is not the only thing; the Budget will do more than that. It will reveal the financial strength of Britain. At a time when every European country is borrowing merely for the needs of ordinary annual expenditure, when all these disturbing naval programmes, which are injuring the peace of the world and the security and progress of civilisation, are being supported by borrowed money; and when the credit of Germany has fallen below that of Italy, this country, which has necessarily to make the biggest expenditure for naval defence of any country, will be found, under a Free Trade system and by our proposals, able not only to pay its way, but to pay off the debts of the past—to pay off the debts of our predecessors—even in the worst of times at the rate of something like £7,000,000 a year.

I have spoken to you of the causes which in the past have led up to this Budget. I have spoken to you of its present justification. What of the future? If I had to sum up the immediate future of democratic politics in a single word I should say "Insurance." That is the future—Insurance against dangers from abroad. Insurance against dangers scarcely less grave and much more near and constant which threaten us here at home in our own island. I had the honour and opportunity a few days ago of explaining to the House of Commons our proposals for unemployment insurance. That is a considerable matter. It stands by itself. It is a much simpler question than invalidity insurance; but it is a great matter by itself. Indeed, I thought while I was explaining it to the House of Commons that I had not made such an important speech since I had the honour of explaining the details of the Transvaal Constitution.

Well, what is the proposal? The proposal is that you should make a beginning. We have stood still too long. We should begin forthwith, taking some of the greatest trades of the country in which unemployment is most serious, in which fluctuations are most severe, in which there are no short-time arrangements to mitigate the severity to the individual; and that a system of compulsory contributory insurance, with a large subvention from the State, should be introduced into those great industries.

But our proposals go farther than that. The State assistance to unemployment insurance will not be limited to those trades in which it is compulsory. Side by side with the compulsory system we shall offer facilities to voluntary insurance schemes in other trades, managed by trade unions or by societies or groups of workmen. Moreover, we contemplate that the State insurance office should undertake, if desired, the insurance against unemployment of any individual workman in any trade outside of those for which compulsory powers are required, and should afford to these individuals an equivalent support to that which is given in the trades which are subject to the compulsory system.

Of course you will understand that the terms, that can be offered under a voluntary or partial system, are not so good as those which can be obtained in the compulsory system of a great trade. Where all stand together, it is much better for each. But still it is certain that individuals who take advantage of the insurance policy which will be introduced, and I trust carried through Parliament next year, will be able to secure terms which will be much more favourable than any which are open to them by their unaided contributions at the present time, because their contributions will be reinforced by the contributions of the State. Further, if our beginning proves a success the attempt and the system will not stop there. It will be extended, and in proportion as experience and experiment justify its extension, in proportion as the people of this country desire its extension, it must eventually cover, in course of years, the whole of our great industrial community.

Well now, it is said that in adopting the policy of contributory insurance the Government have admitted that they were wrong in establishing old-age pensions upon the non-contributory basis. Now I do not think that is true. There is no inconsistency or contradiction between a non-contributory system of old-age pensions and a contributory system of insurance against unemployment, sickness, invalidity, and widowhood. The circumstances and conditions are entirely different. The prospect of attaining extreme old age, of living beyond threescore years and ten, which is the allotted span of human life, seems so doubtful and remote to the ordinary man, when in the full strength of manhood, that it has been found in practice almost impossible to secure from any very great number of people the regular sacrifices which are necessary to guard against old age.

But unemployment, accident, sickness, and the death of the bread-winner are catastrophes which may reach any household at any moment. Those vultures are always hovering around us, and I do not believe there is any sensible, honest man who would not wish to guard himself against them, if it were in his power to make the necessary contribution, and if he were sure—this is a very important point—that he would not by any accident or fraud or muddle be done out of the security he had paid for. And if we choose to adopt one system of State-aid for dealing with one class of need, and quite a different system for dealing with quite a different class of need, it does not lie with any one, least of all does it lie with those who have impartially neglected every problem and every solution, to reproach us with inconsistency.

But I go farther. The Old-Age Pensions Act, so far from being in conflict with a scheme of contributory insurance, is really its most helpful and potent ally. The fact that at seventy the State pension is assured to all those who need it, makes a tremendous difference to every form of insurance confined to the years before seventy, whether for old age or for invalidity. I asked an eminent actuary the other day to make me some calculations. They are rough, general calculations, and no doubt they might be more exact. But roughly, I believe it to be no exaggeration to say that the rates to cover a man till seventy are in many cases scarcely half what they would be, if they had to cover him till death. Do you see what that means? It is a prodigious fact. It is the sort of fact by the discovery of which people make gigantic fortunes; and I suggest to you that we should make this gigantic fortune for John Bull. It means that the whole field of insurance has become much more fruitful than it ever was before, that there is a new class of insurance business possible which never was possible before. It means that the whole field of insurance is far more open to the poorest class of people than it was before, and that with a proper system the benefits of the Old-Age Pensions Act would not be confined to the actual pensioners who are drawing their money, but would extend forwards in anticipation to all other classes and to all other people, and that so far as five shillings a week is concerned—that is not much unless you have not got it—the actuarial position of every man and woman in this country has been enormously improved by the Old-Age Pensions Act.

It is of that improvement that we mean to take advantage next year. Next year, when Free Trade will have yielded the necessary funds to the revenue, we mean to move forward into this great new field. But let me say one thing which is of the utmost importance. We must remember that the field of insurance is already largely covered by a great mass of benevolent and friendly societies, just as the field of unemployment insurance is already occupied to some extent by trade unions, and the Government would not approve of any development or extension of the policy of insurance which did not do full justice to existing institutions, or which did not safeguard those institutions, to whom we owe so inestimable and incommensurable a debt, or caused any sudden disturbance or any curtailment of their general methods of business. On the contrary, we believe that when our proposals are put in their full detail before the country, they will be found to benefit and encourage and not to injure those agencies which have so long been voluntarily and prosperously at work.

The decisive question is this—will the British working classes embrace the opportunities which will shortly be offered to them? They are a new departure; they involve an element of compulsion and of regulation which is unusual in our happy-go-lucky English life. The opportunity may never return. For my own part, I confess to you, my friends in Manchester, that I would work for such a policy and would try to carry it through even if it were a little unpopular at first, and would be willing to pay the forfeit of a period of exclusion from power, in order to have carried such a policy through; because I know that there is no other way within the reach of this generation of men and women by which the stream of preventable misery can be cut off.

If I had my way I would write the word "Insure" over the door of every cottage, and upon the blotting-book of every public man, because I am convinced that by sacrifices which are inconceivably small, which are all within the power of the very poorest man in regular work, families can be secured against catastrophes which otherwise would smash them up for ever. I think it is our duty to use the strength and the resources of the State to arrest the ghastly waste not merely of human happiness but of national health and strength which follows when a working man's home which has taken him years to get together is broken up and scattered through a long spell of unemployment, or when, through the death, the sickness, or the invalidity of the bread-winner, the frail boat in which the fortunes of the family are embarked founders, and the women and children are left to struggle helplessly on the dark waters of a friendless world. I believe it is well within our power now, before this Parliament is over, to establish vast and broad throughout the land a mighty system of national insurance which will nourish in its bosom all worthy existing agencies and will embrace in its scope all sorts and conditions of men.

I think it is not untrue to say that in these years we are passing through a decisive period in the history of our country. The wonderful century which followed the Battle of Waterloo and the downfall of the Napoleonic domination, which secured to this small island so long and so resplendent a reign, has come to an end. We have arrived at a new time. Let us realise it. And with that new time strange methods, huge forces, larger combinations—a Titanic world—have sprung up around us. The foundations of our power are changing. To stand still would be to fall; to fall would be to perish. We must go forward. We will go forward. We will go forward into a way of life more earnestly viewed, more scientifically organised, more consciously national than any we have known. Thus alone shall we be able to sustain and to renew through the generations which are to come, the fame and the power of the British race.

LAND AND INCOME TAXES IN THE BUDGET

EDINBURGH, *JULY 17, 1909*

(Originally published in *The Times*)

*W*e are often assured by sagacious persons that the civilisation of modern States is largely based upon respect for the rights of private property. If that be true, it is also true that such respect cannot be secured, and ought not, indeed, to be expected, unless property is associated in the minds of the great mass of the people with ideas of justice and of reason.

It is, therefore, of the first importance to the country—to any country—that there should be vigilant and persistent efforts to prevent abuses, to distribute the public burdens fairly among all classes, and to establish good laws governing the methods by which wealth may be acquired. The best way to make private property secure and respected is to bring the processes by which it is gained into harmony with the general interests of the public. When and where property is associated with the idea of reward for services rendered, with the idea of recompense for high gifts and special aptitudes displayed or for faithful labour done, then property will be honoured. When it is associated with processes which are beneficial, or which at the worst are not actually injurious to the commonwealth, then property will be unmolested; but when it is associated with ideas of wrong and of unfairness, with processes of restriction and monopoly, and other forms of injury to the community, then I think that you will find that property will be assailed and will be endangered.

A year ago I was fighting an election in Dundee. In the course of that election I attempted to draw a fundamental distinction between the principles of Liberalism and of Socialism, and I said "Socialism attacks capital; Liberalism attacks monopoly." And it is from that fundamental distinction that I come directly to the land proposals of the present Budget.

It is quite true that the land monopoly is not the only monopoly which exists, but it is by far the greatest of monopolies; it is a perpetual monopoly, and it is the mother of all other forms of monopoly. It is quite true that unearned increments in land are not the only form of unearned or undeserved profit which individuals are able to secure; but it is the principal form of unearned increment, derived from processes, which are not merely not beneficial, but which are positively detrimental to the general public. Land, which is a necessity of human existence, which is the original source of all wealth, which is strictly limited in extent, which is fixed in geographical position—land, I say, differs from all other forms of property in these primary and fundamental conditions.

Nothing is more amusing than to watch the efforts of our monopolist opponents to prove that other forms of property and increment are exactly the same and are similar in all respects to the unearned increment in land. They talk to us of the increased profits of a doctor or a lawyer from the growth of population in the towns in which they live. They talk to us of the profits of a railway through a greater degree of wealth and activity in the districts through which it runs. They tell us of the profits which are derived from a rise in stocks and shares, and even of those which are sometimes derived from the sale of pictures and works of art, and they ask us—as if it were their only complaint—"Ought not all these other forms to be taxed too?"

But see how misleading and false all these analogies are. The windfalls which people with artistic gifts are able from time to time to derive from the sale of a picture—from a Vandyke or a Holbein—may here and there be very considerable. But pictures do not get in anybody's way. They do not lay a toll on anybody's labour; they do not touch enterprise and production at any point; they do not affect any of those creative processes upon which the material well-being of millions depends. And if a rise in stocks and shares confers profits on the fortunate holders far beyond what they expected, or, indeed, deserved, nevertheless, that profit has not been reaped by withholding from the community the land which it needs, but, on the contrary, apart from mere gambling, it has been reaped by supplying industry with the capital without which it could not be carried on.

If the railway makes greater profits, it is usually because it carries more goods and more passengers. If a doctor or a lawyer enjoys a better practice, it is because the doctor attends more patients and more exacting patients, and because the lawyer pleads more suits in the courts and more important suits. At every stage the doctor or the lawyer is giving service in return for his fees; and if the service is too poor or the fees are too high, other doctors and other lawyers can come freely into competition. There is constant service, there is constant competition; there is no monopoly, there is no injury to the public interest, there is no impediment to the general progress.

Fancy comparing these healthy processes with the enrichment which comes to the landlord who happens to own a plot of land on the outskirts or at the centre of one of our great cities, who watches the busy population around him making the city larger, richer, more convenient, more famous every day, and all the while sits still and does nothing! Roads are made, streets are made, railway services are improved, electric light turns night into day, electric trams glide swiftly to and fro, water is brought from reservoirs a hundred miles off in the mountains—and all the while the landlord sits still. Every one of those improvements is effected by the labour and at the cost of other people. Many of the most important are effected at the cost of the municipality and of the ratepayers. To not one of those improvements does the land monopolist, as a land monopolist, contribute, and yet by every one of them the value of his land is sensibly enhanced.

He renders no service to the community, he contributes nothing to the general welfare, he contributes nothing even to the process from which his own enrichment is derived. If the land were occupied by shops or by dwellings, the municipality at least would secure the rates upon them in aid of the general fund; but the land may be unoccupied, undeveloped, it may be what is called "ripening"—ripening at the expense of the whole city, of the whole country—for the unearned increment of its owner. Roads perhaps have to be diverted to avoid this forbidden area. The merchant going to his office, the artisan going to his work, have to make a detour or pay a tram fare to avoid it. The citizens are losing their chance of developing the land, the city is losing its rates, the State is losing its taxes which would have accrued, if the natural development had taken place—and that share has to be replaced at the expense of the other ratepayers and taxpayers; and the nation as a whole is losing in the competition of the world—the hard and growing competition in the world—both in time and money. And all the while the land monopolist has only to sit still and watch complacently his property multiplying in value, sometimes manifold, without either effort or contribution on his part. And that is justice!

But let us follow the process a little farther. The population of the city grows and grows still larger year by year, the congestion in the poorer quarters becomes acute, rents and rates rise hand in hand, and thousands of families are crowded into one-roomed tenements. There are 120,000 persons living in one-roomed tenements in Glasgow alone at the present time. At last the land becomes ripe for sale—that means that the price is too tempting to be resisted any longer—and then, and not till then, it is sold by the yard or by the inch at ten times, or twenty times, or even fifty times, its agricultural value, on which alone hitherto it has been rated for the public service.

The greater the population around the land, the greater the injury which they have sustained by its protracted denial, the more inconvenience which has been caused to everybody, the more serious the loss in economic strength and activity, the larger will be the profit of the landlord when the sale is finally accomplished. In fact you may say that the unearned increment on the land is on all-fours with the profit gathered by one of those American speculators who engineer a corner in corn, or meat, or cotton, or some other vital commodity, and that the unearned increment in land is reaped by the land monopolist in exact proportion, not to the service, but to the disservice done.

It is monopoly which is the keynote; and where monopoly prevails, the greater the injury to society, the greater the reward of the monopolist will be. See how this evil process strikes at every form of industrial activity. The municipality, wishing for broader streets, better houses, more healthy, decent, scientifically planned towns, is made to pay, and is made to pay in exact proportion, or to a very great extent in proportion, as it has exerted itself in the past to make improvements. The more it has improved the town, the more it has increased the land value, and the more it will have to pay for any land it may wish to acquire. The manufacturer purposing to start a new industry, proposing to erect a great factory offering employment to thousands of hands, is made to pay such a price for his land that the purchase-price hangs round the neck of his whole business, hampering his competitive power in every market, clogging him far more than any foreign tariff in his export competition; and the land values strike down through the profits of the manufacturer on to the wages of the workman. The railway company wishing to build a new line finds that the price of land which yesterday was only rated at its agricultural value has risen to a prohibitive figure the moment it was known that the new line was projected; and either the railway is not built, or, if it is, is built, only on terms which largely transfer to the landowner the profits which are due to the shareholders and the advantages which should have accrued to the travelling public.

It does not matter where you look or what examples you select, you will see that every form of enterprise, every step in material progress, is only undertaken after the land monopolist has skimmed the cream off for himself, and everywhere to-day the man, or the public body, who wishes to put land to its highest use is forced to pay a preliminary fine in land values to the man who is putting it to an inferior use, and in some cases to no use at all. All comes back to the land value, and its owner for the time being is able to levy his toll upon all other forms of wealth and upon every form of industry. A portion, in some cases the whole, of every benefit which is laboriously acquired by the community is represented in the land value, and finds its way automatically into the landlord's pocket. If there is a rise in wages, rents are able to move forward, because the workers can afford to pay a little more. If the opening of a new railway or a new tramway, or the institution of an improved service of workmen's trains, or a lowering of fares, or a new invention, or any other public convenience affords a benefit to the workers in any particular district, it becomes easier for them to live, and therefore the landlord and the ground landlord, one on top of the other, are able to charge them more for the privilege of living there.

Some years ago in London there was a toll-bar on a bridge across the Thames, and all the working people who lived on the south side of the river, had to pay a daily toll of one penny for going and returning from their work. The spectacle of these poor people thus mulcted of so large a proportion of their earnings appealed to the public conscience: an agitation was set on foot, municipal authorities were roused, and at the cost of the ratepayers the bridge was freed and the toll removed. All those people who used the bridge were saved 6d. a week. Within a very short period from that time the rents on the south side of the river were found to have advanced by about 6d. a week, or the amount of the toll which had been remitted. And a friend of mine was telling me the other day that in the parish of Southwark about £350 a year, roughly speaking, was given away in doles of bread by charitable people in connection with one of the churches, and as a consequence of this the competition for small houses, but more particularly for single-roomed tenements is, we are told, so great that rents are considerably higher than in the neighbouring district.

All goes back to the land, and the landowner, who in many cases, in most cases, is a worthy person utterly unconscious of the character of the methods by which he is enriched, is enabled with resistless strength to absorb to himself a share of almost every public and every private benefit, however important or however pitiful those benefits may be.

I hope you will understand that when I speak of the land monopolist, I am dealing more with the process than with the individual landowner. I have no wish to hold any class up to public disapprobation. I do not think that the man who makes money by unearned increment in land, is morally a worse man than any one else, who gathers his profit where he finds it, in this hard world under the law and according to common usage. It is not the individual I attack; it is the system. It is not the man who is bad; it is the law which is bad. It is not the man who is blameworthy for doing what the law allows and what other men do; it is the State which would be blameworthy, were it not to endeavour to reform the law and correct the practice. We do not want to punish the landlord. We want to alter the law. Look at our actual proposal.

We do not go back on the past. We accept as our basis the value as it stands to-day. The tax on the increment of land begins by recognising and franking all past increment. We look only to the future; and for the future we say only this: that the community shall be the partner in any further increment above the present value after all the owner's improvements have been deducted. We say that the State and the municipality should jointly levy a toll upon the future unearned increment of the land. A toll of what? Of the whole? No. Of a half? No. Of a quarter? No. Of a fifth—that is the proposal of the Budget. And that is robbery, that is plunder, that is communism and spoliation, that is the social revolution at last, that is the overturn of civilised society, that is the end of the world foretold in the Apocalypse! Such is the increment tax about which so much chatter and outcry are raised at the present time, and upon which I will say that no more fair, considerate, or salutary proposal for taxation has ever been made in the House of Commons.

But there is another proposal concerning land values which is not less important. I mean the tax on the capital value of undeveloped urban or suburban land. The income derived from land and its rateable value under the present law depend upon the use to which the land is put. In consequence, income and rateable value are not always true or complete measures of the value of the land. Take the case to which I have already referred, of the man who keeps a large plot in or near a growing town idle for years, while it is "ripening"—that is to say, while it is rising in price through the exertions of the surrounding community and the need of that community for more room to live. Take that case. I daresay you have formed your own opinion upon it. Mr. Balfour, Lord Lansdowne, and the Conservative Party generally, think that that is an admirable arrangement. They speak of the profits of the land monopolist, as if they were the fruits of thrift and industry and a pleasing example for the poorer classes to imitate. We do not take that view of the process. We think it is a dog-in-the-manger game. We see the evil, we see the imposture upon the public, and we see the consequences in crowded slums, in hampered commerce, in distorted or restricted development, and in congested centres of population, and we say here and now to the land monopolist who is holding up his land—and the pity is, it was not said before—you shall judge for yourselves whether it is a fair offer or not—we say to the land monopolist: "This property of yours might be put to immediate use with general advantage. It is at this minute saleable in the market at ten times the value at which it is rated. If you choose to keep it idle in the expectation of still further unearned increment, then at least you shall be taxed at the true selling value in the meanwhile." And the Budget proposes a tax of a halfpenny in the pound on the capital value of all such land; that is to say, a tax which is a little less in equivalent, than the income-tax would be upon the property, if the property were fully developed.

That is the second main proposal of the Budget with regard to the land; and its effects will be, first, to raise an expanding revenue for the needs of the State; secondly that, half the proceeds of this tax, as well as of the other land taxes, will go to the municipalities and local authorities generally to relieve rates; thirdly, the effect will be, as we believe, to bring land into the market, and thus somewhat cheapen the price at which land is obtainable for every object, public and private. By so doing we shall liberate new springs of enterprise and industry, we shall stimulate building, relieve overcrowding, and promote employment.

These two taxes, both in themselves financially, economically, and socially sound, carry with them a further notable advantage. We shall obtain a complete valuation of the whole of the land in the United Kingdom. We shall procure an up-to-date Doomsday-book showing the capital value, apart from buildings and improvements, of every piece of land. Now, there is nothing new in the principle of valuation for taxation purposes. It was established fifteen years ago in Lord Rosebery's Government by the Finance Act of 1894, and it has been applied ever since without friction or inconvenience by Conservative administrations.

And if there is nothing new in the principle of valuation, still less is there anything new or unexpected in the general principles underlying the land proposals of the Budget. Why, Lord Rosebery declared himself in favour of taxation of land values fifteen years ago. Lord Balfour has said a great many shrewd and sensible things on this subject which he is, no doubt, very anxious to have overlooked at the present time. The House of Commons has repeatedly affirmed the principle, not only under Liberal Governments, but—which is much more remarkable—under a Conservative Government. Four times during the last Parliament Mr. Trevelyan's Bill for the taxation of land values was brought before the House of Commons and fully discussed, and twice it was read a second time during the last Parliament, with its great Conservative majority, the second time by a majority of no less than ninety votes. The House of Lords, in adopting Lord Camperdown's amendment to the Scottish Valuation Bill, has absolutely conceded the principle of rating undeveloped land upon its selling value, although it took very good care not to apply the principle; and all the greatest municipal corporations in England and Scotland—many of them overwhelmingly Conservative in complexion—have declared themselves in favour of the taxation of land values; and now, after at least a generation of study, examination, and debate, the time has come when we should take the first step to put these principles into practical effect. You have heard the saying "The hour and the man." The hour has come, and with it the Chancellor of the Exchequer.

I have come to Scotland to exhort you to engage in this battle and devote your whole energy and influence to securing a memorable victory. Every nation in the world has its own way of doing things, its own successes and its own failures. All over Europe we see systems of land tenure which economically, socially, and politically are far superior to ours; but the benefits that those countries derive from their improved land systems are largely swept away, or at any rate neutralised, by grinding tariffs on the necessaries of life and the materials of manufacture. In this country we have long enjoyed the blessings of Free Trade and of untaxed bread and meat, but against these inestimable benefits we have the evils of an unreformed and vicious land system. In no great country in the new world or the old have the working people yet secured the double advantage of free trade and free land together, by which I mean a commercial system and a land system from which, so far as possible, all forms of monopoly have been rigorously excluded. Sixty years ago our system of national taxation was effectively reformed, and immense and undisputed advantages accrued therefrom to all classes, the richest as well as the poorest. The system of local taxation to-day is just as vicious and wasteful, just as great an impediment to enterprise and progress, just as harsh a burden upon the poor, as the thousand taxes and Corn Law sliding scales of the "hungry 'forties." We are met in an hour of tremendous opportunity. "You who shall liberate the land," said Mr. Cobden, "will do more for your country than we have done in the liberation of its commerce."

You can follow the same general principle of distinguishing between earned and unearned increment through the Government's treatment of the income-tax. There is all the difference in the world between the income which a man makes from month to month or from year to year by his continued exertion, which may stop at any moment, and will certainly stop, if he is incapacitated, and the income which is derived from the profits of accumulated capital, which is a continuing income irrespective of the exertion of its owner. Nobody wants to penalise or to stigmatise income derived from dividends, rent, or interest; for accumulated capital, apart from monopoly, represents the exercise of thrift and prudence, qualities which are only less valuable to the community than actual service and labour. But the great difference between the two classes of income remains. We are all sensible of it, and we think that that great difference should be recognised when the necessary burdens of the State have to be divided and shared between all classes.

The application of this principle of differentiation of income-tax has enabled the present Government sensibly to lighten the burden of the great majority of income-tax payers. Under the late Conservative

Government about 1,100,000 income-tax payers paid income-tax at the statutory rate of a shilling in the pound. Mr. Asquith, the Prime Minister, when Chancellor of the Exchequer, reduced the income-tax in respect of earned incomes under £2,000 a year from a shilling to ninepence, and it is calculated that 750,000 income-tax payers—that is to say, nearly three-quarters of the whole number of income-tax payers—who formerly paid at the shilling rate have obtained an actual relief from taxation to the extent of nearly £1,200,000 a year in the aggregate. The present Chancellor of the Exchequer in the present Budget has added to this abatement a further relief—a very sensible relief, I venture to think you will consider it—on account of each child of parents who possess under £500 a year, and that concession involved a further abatement and relief equal to £600,000 a year. That statement is founded on high authority, for it figured in one of the Budget proposals of Mr. Pitt, and it is to-day recognised by the law of Prussia.

Taking together the income-tax reforms of Mr. Asquith and Mr. Lloyd-George, taking the two together—because they are all part of the same policy, and they are all part of our treatment as a Government of this great subject—it is true to say that very nearly three out of every four persons who pay income-tax will be taxed after this Budget, this penal Budget, this wicked, monstrous, despoliatory Budget—three out of every four persons will be taxed for income-tax at a lower rate than they were by the late Conservative Government.

You will perhaps say to me that may be all very well, but are you sure that the rich and the very rich are not being burdened too heavily? Are you sure that you are not laying on the backs of people who are struggling to support existence with incomes of upwards of £3,000 a year, burdens which are too heavy to be borne? Will they not sink, crushed by the load of material cares, into early graves, followed there even by the unrelenting hand of the death duties collector? Will they not take refuge in wholesale fraud and evasion, as some of their leaders ingenuously suggest, or will there be a general flight of all rich people from their native shores to the protection of the hospitable foreigner? Let me reassure you on these points.

The taxes which we now seek to impose to meet the need of the State will not appreciably affect, have not appreciably affected, the comfort, the status, or even the style of living of any class in the United Kingdom. There has been no invidious singling out of a few rich men for special taxation. The increased burden which is placed upon wealth is evenly and broadly distributed over the whole of that wealthy class who are more numerous in Great Britain than in any other country in the world, and who, when this Budget is passed, will still find Great Britain the best country to live in. When I reflect upon the power and influence that class possesses, upon the general goodwill with which they are still regarded by their poorer neighbours, upon the infinite opportunities for pleasure and for culture which are open to them in this free, prosperous, and orderly commonwealth, I cannot doubt that they ought to contribute, and I believe that great numbers of them are willing to contribute, in a greater degree than heretofore, towards the needs of the navy, for which they are always clamouring, and for those social reforms upon which the health and contentment of the whole population depend.

And after all, gentlemen, when we are upon the sorrows of the rich and the heavy blows that have been struck by this wicked Budget, let us not forget that this Budget, which is denounced by all the vested interests in the country and in all the abodes of wealth and power, after all, draws nearly as much from the taxation of tobacco and spirits, which are the luxuries of the working classes, who pay their share with silence and dignity, as it does from those wealthy classes upon whose behalf such heartrending outcry is made.

I do not think the issue before the country was ever more simple than it is now. The money must be found; there is no dispute about that. Both parties are responsible for the expenditure and the obligations which render new revenue necessary; and, as we know, we have difficulty in resisting demands which are made upon us by the Conservative Party for expenditure upon armaments far beyond the limits which are necessary to maintain adequately the defences of the country, and which would only be the accompaniment of a sensational and aggressive policy in foreign and in Colonial affairs. We declare that the proposals we have put forward are conceived with a desire to be fair to all and harsh to none. We assert they are conceived with a desire to secure good laws regulating the conditions by which wealth may be obtained and a just distribution of the burdens of the State. We know that the proposals which we have made will yield all the money that we need for national defence, and that they will yield an expanding revenue in future years for those great schemes of social organisation, of national insurance, of agricultural development, and of the treatment of the problems of poverty and unemployment, which are absolutely necessary if Great Britain is to hold her own in the front rank of the nations. The issue which you have to decide is whether these funds shall be raised by the taxation of a protective tariff upon articles of common use and upon the necessaries of life, including bread and meat, or whether it shall be raised, as we propose, by the taxation of luxuries, of superfluities, and monopolies.

I have only one word more to say, and it is rendered necessary by the observations which fell from Lord Lansdowne last night, when, according to the Scottish papers, he informed a gathering at which he was the principal speaker that the House of Lords was not obliged to swallow the Budget whole or without mincing.[1] I ask you to mark that word. It is a characteristic expression. The House of Lords means to assert its right to mince. Now let us for our part be quite frank and plain. We want this Budget Bill to be fairly and fully discussed; we do not grudge the weeks that have been spent already; we are prepared to make every sacrifice—I speak for my honourable friends who are sitting on this platform—of personal convenience in order to secure a thorough, patient, searching examination of proposals the importance of which we do not seek to conceal. The Government has shown itself ready and willing to meet reasonable argument, not merely by reasonable answer, but when a case is shown, by concessions, and generally in a spirit of goodwill. We have dealt with this subject throughout with a desire to mitigate hardships in special cases, and to gain as large a measure of agreement as possible for the proposals we are placing before the country. We want the Budget not merely to be the work of the Cabinet and of the Chancellor of the Exchequer; we want it to be the shaped and moulded plan deliberately considered by the House of Commons. That will be a long and painful process to those who are forced from day to day to take part in it. We shall not shrink from it. But when that process is over, when the Finance Bill leaves the House of Commons, I think you will agree with me that it ought to leave the House of Commons in its final form. No amendments, no excision, no modifying or mutilating will be agreed to by us. We will stand no mincing, and unless Lord Lansdowne and his landlordly friends choose to eat their own mince, Parliament will be dissolved, and we shall come to you in a moment of high consequence for every cause for which Liberalism has ever fought. See that you do not fail us in that hour.

---

[1]   Lord Lansdowne has since been at pains to explain that he did not use the word "mincing." That word ought to have been "wincing" or "hesitation"—it is not clear which.

THE BUDGET AND THE LORDS

NORWICH, *JULY 26, 1909*

(Originally published in *The Manchester Guardian*)

The Budget is the great political issue of the day. It involves all other questions; it has brought all other issues to a decisive test. *The Daily Mail* has stated that the Budget is hung up. So it is. It is hung up in triumph over the High Peak; it is hung up as a banner of victory over Dumfries, over Cleveland, and over Mid-Derby. The miniature general election just concluded has shown that the policy embodied in the Budget, and which inspires the Budget, has vivified and invigorated the Liberal Party, has brought union where there was falling away, has revived enthusiasm where apathy was creeping in.

You cannot but have been impressed with the increasing sense of reality which political affairs have acquired during the last few months. What is it they are doing at Westminster? Across and beyond the complicated details of finance, the thousand amendments and more which cover the order paper, the absurd obstruction, the dry discussions in Committee, the interminable repetition of divisions, the angry scenes which flash up from time to time, the white-faced members sitting the whole night through and walking home worn out in the full light of morning—across and beyond all this, can you not discern a people's cause in conflict? Can you not see a great effort to make a big step forward towards that brighter and more equal world for which, be sure, those who come after us will hold our names in honour? That is the issue which is being decided from week to week in Westminster now, and it is in support of that cause that we are asking from you earnest and unswerving allegiance.

I do not think that there is any great country in the world where there are so many strong forces of virtue and vitality as there are in our own country. But there is scarcely any country in the world where there is so little organisation. Look at our neighbour and friendly rival Germany. I see that great State organised for peace and organised for war to a degree to which we cannot pretend. We are not organised as a nation, so far as I can see, for anything except party politics, and even for purposes of party politics we are not organised so well as they are in the United States. A more scientific, a more elaborate, a more comprehensive social organisation is indispensable to our country if we are to surmount the trials and stresses which the future years will bring. It is this organisation that the policy of the Budget will create. It is this organisation that the loss of the Budget will destroy.

But, we are told, "it presses too heavily upon the land-owning classes." I have heard it said that in the French Revolution, if the French nobility, instead of going to the scaffold with such dignity and fortitude, had struggled and cried and begged for mercy, even the hard hearts of the Paris crowd would have been melted, and the Reign of Terror would have come to an end. There is happily no chance of our aristocracy having to meet such a fate in this loyal-hearted, law-abiding, sober-minded country. They are, however, asked to discharge a certain obligation. They are asked to contribute their share to the expenses of the State. That is all they are asked to do. Yet what an outcry, what tribulation, what tears, what wrath, what weeping and wailing and gnashing of teeth, and all because they are asked to pay their share.

One would suppose, to listen to them, that the whole of the taxation was being raised from, or was about to be raised from the owners of agricultural estates. What are the facts? Nearly half the taxation of the present Budget is raised by the taxation of the luxuries of the working classes. Are they indignant? Are they crying out? Not in the least. They are perfectly ready to pay their share, and to pay it in a manly way, and two hundred thousand of them took the trouble to go to Hyde Park the other day in order to say so.

What are the facts about agricultural land? It is absolutely exempt from the operations of the new land taxation so long as agricultural land is worth no more for other purposes than it is for agricultural purposes: that is to say, so long as agricultural land is agricultural land and not urban or suburban land, it pays none of the new land taxation. It is only when its value for building purposes makes its continued agricultural use wasteful and uneconomic, it is only when it becomes building land and not agricultural land, and when because of that change it rises enormously in price and value—it is only then that it contributes under the new land taxation its share to the public of the increment value which the public has given to it.

Then take the death duties. One would suppose from what one hears in London and from the outcry that is raised, that the whole of the death duties were collected from the peers and from the county families. Again I say, look at the facts. The Inland Revenue report for last year shows that £313,000,000 of property passing on death became subject to death duties, and of that sum £228,000,000 was personalty and not real estate, leaving only £85,000,000 real estate, and of that £85,000,000 only £22,000,000 was agricultural land. These death duties are represented as being levied entirely upon a small class of landed gentry and nobility, but, as a matter of fact, there is collected from that class in respect of agricultural land only seven per cent. of the whole amount of money which the Exchequer derives from death duties.[1]

I decline, however, to judge the question of the House of Lords simply and solely by any action they may resolve to take upon the Budget. We must look back upon the past. We remember the ill-usage and the humiliation which the great majority that was returned by the nation to support Sir Henry Campbell-Bannerman in 1906 has sustained in the last three years at the hands of the House of Lords. That Assembly must be judged by their conduct as a whole. Lord Lansdowne has explained, to the amusement of the nation, that he claimed no right on behalf of the House of Lords to "mince" the Budget. All, he tells us, he has asked for, so far as he is concerned, is the right to "wince" when swallowing it. Well, that is a much more modest claim. It is for the Conservative Party to judge whether it is a very heroic claim for one of their leaders to make. If they are satisfied with the wincing Marquis, we have no reason to protest. We should greatly regret to cause Lord Lansdowne and his friends any pain. We have no wish whatever to grudge them any relief which they may obtain by wincing or even by squirming. We accord them the fullest liberty in that respect.

After all, the House of Lords has made others wince in its time. Even in the present Parliament they have performed some notable exploits. When the House of Lords rejected the Bill to prevent one man casting his vote two or three times over in the same election, every one in this country who desired to see a full and true representation of the people in Parliament might well have winced. When the House of Lords rejected or mutilated beyond repair the Land Valuation Bills for England and for Scotland, every land reformer in the country might have winced. When

---

[1]   Since the date of this speech the new concessions, doubling the allowance exempted from income tax for the expenses of agricultural estates, have been made public.

the House of Lords destroyed Mr. Birrell's Education Bill of 1906, every man who cared for religious equality and educational peace might have winced. When they contemptuously flung out, without even discussing it or examining it, the Licensing Bill, upon which so many hopes were centred and upon which so many months of labour had been spent, they sent a message of despair to every temperance reformer, to every social and philanthropic worker, to every church, to every chapel, to every little Sunday school throughout the land. If it should now prove to be their turn, if the measure they have meted out to others should be meted out to them again, however much we might regret their sorrows, we could not but observe the workings of poetic justice.

But I hope the House of Lords and those who back them will not be under any illusions about the Budget and the position of the Government. The Government is in earnest about the Budget. The Budget carries with it their fortunes and the fortunes of the Liberal Party. Careful argument, reasonable amendment, amicable concession, not affecting the principles at stake—all these we offer while the Bill is in the House of Commons. But when all that is said and done, as the Bill leaves the House of Commons so it must stand. It would be a great pity if Lord Curzon, the Indian pro-Consul, or the London *Spectator*—it would be a great pity if those potentates were to make the great mistake of supposing that the Government would acquiesce in the excision of the land clauses of the Budget by the House of Lords. Such a course is unthinkable. Any Liberal Government which adopted it would be swiftly ruined. The land proposals of the Government have not been made without long deliberation and full responsibility. We shall not fail to carry them effectively through the House of Commons; still less shall we accept any amendment at the hands of the House of Lords.

Is it not an extraordinary thing that upon the Budget we should even be discussing at all the action of the House of Lords? The House of Lords is an institution absolutely foreign to the spirit of the age and to the whole movement of society. It is not perhaps surprising in a country so fond of tradition, so proud of continuity, as ourselves that a feudal assembly of titled persons, with so long a history and so many famous names, should have survived to exert an influence upon public affairs at the present time. We see how often in England the old forms are reverently preserved after the forces by which they are sustained and the uses to which they were put and the dangers against which they were designed have passed away. A state of gradual decline was what the average Englishman had come to associate with the House of Lords. Little by little, we might have expected, it would have ceased to take a controversial part in practical politics. Year by year it would have faded more completely into the past to which it belongs until, like Jack-in-the-Green or Punch-and-Judy, only a picturesque and fitfully lingering memory would have remained.

And during the last ten years of Conservative government this was actually the case. But now we see the House of Lords flushed with the wealth of the modern age, armed with a party caucus, fortified, revived, resuscitated, asserting its claims in the harshest and in the crudest manner, claiming to veto or destroy even without discussion any legislation, however important, sent to them by any majority, however large, from any House of Commons, however newly elected. We see these unconscionable claims exercised with a frank and undisguised regard to party interest, to class interest, and to personal interest. We see the House of Lords using the power which they should not hold at all, which if they hold at all, they should hold in trust for all, to play a shrewd, fierce, aggressive party game of electioneering and casting their votes according to the interest of the particular political party to which, body and soul, they belong.

It is now suggested—publicly in some quarters, privately in many quarters—that the House of Lords will not only use without scruple their veto in legislation but they propose to extend their prerogatives; they are going to lay their hands upon finance, and if they choose they will reject or amend the Budget. I have always thought it a great pity that Mr. Gladstone made a compromise with the House of Lords over the Franchise Bill of 1884. I regret, and I think many of my hon. friends in the House of Commons will regret, looking back upon the past, that the present Government did not advise a dissolution of Parliament upon the rejection of the Education Bill in 1906. A dissolution in those circumstances would not merely have involved the measure under discussion, but if the Government of that day had received the support of the electors at the poll their victory must have carried with it that settlement and reform of the relations between the two Houses of Parliament which is necessary to secure the effective authority of the House of Commons. That is the question which, behind and beyond all others, even the Budget, even Free Trade, even the land—that is the question which, as the Prime Minister has said, is the dominant issue of our time.

Opportunity is fickle, opportunity seldom returns; but I think you will agree with me that if the House of Lords, not content with its recent exploits with the legislative veto, were to seize on the new power which its backers claim for it over finance—if, not content with the extreme assertions of its own privileges, it were to invade the most ancient privileges of the House of Commons—if, as an act of class warfare, for it would be nothing less, the House of Lords were to destroy the Budget, and thus not only create a Constitutional deadlock of novel and unmeasured gravity, but also plunge the whole finance of the country into unparalleled confusion, then, in my judgment, opportunity, clear, brilliant, and decisive, would return, and we should have the best chance we have ever had of dealing with them once for all.

These circumstances may never occur. I don't believe they will occur. If we only all stand firm together I believe the Budget will be carried. I believe the Budget will vindicate the strength of the Government supported by the House of Commons. I believe it will vindicate the financial strength of this great country. I don't believe, if we pursue our course without wavering or weakening, there is any force in this country which can stand against us. The Conservative Whip in the House of Lords, a friend of mine, Lord Churchill, said the other day that the House of Lords when they received the Budget would do their duty. I hope they will. But in any case be sure of this—that the Government and the House of Commons will do their duty. Then if there is anything more to be done, see that you are ready to do your duty too.

THE SPIRIT OF THE BUDGET

LEICESTER, *SEPTEMBER 5, 1909*

(Originally published in *The Times*)

I have done my best to study the political history of the last forty or fifty years, and I cannot find any Government which, at the end of its fourth year, enjoyed the same measure of support, prestige, and good fortune that we do. The only Administration which could compare in the importance and the volume of its legislation with the present Government is Mr. Gladstone's great Government of 1868. That was a Government of measures and of men; but no measure of that Government could equal in importance the Old-Age Pensions Act which we have placed on the Statute-book. The settlement of the Irish Church question by Disestablishment was not a more baffling and intricate business, than the settlement of the Irish University question which Mr. Birrell has achieved. The labour legislation of the Government of 1868, although very important, shows nothing which equals in importance the Trades Disputes Act, which we have carried through, and Mr. Cardwell's reforms in army organisation were not more successful, and were certainly much less generally accepted, than those which have been effected by Mr. Haldane. In the fourth year of its administration the Government of 1868 was genuinely unpopular. It had quarrelled with the Nonconformists without gaining the support of the Church; it had offended the liquor interest without satisfying the Temperance forces in the country; it had disturbed and offended many vested interests without arousing popular enthusiasm.

Indeed, if you look back, you will find that the fourth year in the history of a Government is always a very critical and has often been a very unfortunate year. It is quite true that Mr. Disraeli's Government, which assumed office in 1874, did enjoy in its fourth year a fleeting flush of success, which, however, proved illusory. With that single exception, every other modern Government that has lasted so long, has occupied an unsatisfactory position in its fourth year. The Government of 1880 in the year 1884 was brought very low, and was deeply involved in disastrous enterprises beyond the sea which ultimately resulted in sorrow and misfortune. The Conservative Government which took office in 1886 was by the year 1890, owing to its strange proceedings against Mr. Parnell, brought to the depths of humiliation. The Government of 1895 was in the year 1899 thoroughly unpopular, and if they had not plunged into the tumult of war in South Africa, they would very shortly have been dismissed from power. As for the Government of 1900, in the fourth year of Mr. Balfour's late Administration, I am sure I could not easily do justice to the melancholy position which they occupied.

Where do we stand to-day at the end of our fourth year of office? I put it plainly to you to consider, whether one is not justified in saying that we occupy a position of unexampled strength at the present time. The Government is strong in its administrative record, which reveals no single serious or striking mistake in all the complicated conduct of affairs. There have been no regrettable incidents by land or sea and none of those personal conflicts between the high officials that used to occur so frequently under a late dispensation. We have had no waste of public treasure and no bloodshed. We are strong in the consciousness of a persistent effort to sweep away anomalies and inequalities, to redress injustice, to open more widely to the masses of the people the good chances in life, and to safeguard them against its evil chances. We also claim that we are strong in the support and enthusiasm of a majority of our fellow-countrymen. We are strong in the triumph of our policy in South Africa; most of all we are strong in the hopes and plans which we have formed for the future.

It is about this future that I will speak to you this afternoon. And let me tell you that when I think about it, I do not feel at all inclined to plead exhaustion in consequence of the exertions we have made, or to dwell upon the successes which we have had in the past, or to survey with complacency the record of the Government or to ask you to praise us for the work which we have done. No; when I think of the work which lies before us, upon which we have already entered, of the long avenues of social reconstruction and reorganisation which open out in so many directions and ever more broadly before us, of the hideous squalor and misery which darken and poison the life of Britain, of the need of earnest action, of the prospects of effective and immediate action—when I dwell upon this, it is not of feelings of lassitude or exhaustion that I am conscious, but only of a vehement impulse to press onwards.

The social conditions of the British people in the early years of the twentieth century cannot be contemplated without deep anxiety. The anxiety is keen because it arises out of uncertainty. It is the gnawing anxiety of suspense. What is the destiny of our country to be? Nothing is settled either for or against us. We have no reason to despair; still less have we any reason to be self-satisfied. All is still in our hands for good or for ill. We have the power to-day to choose our fortune, and I believe there is no nation in the world, perhaps there never has been in history, any nation which at one and the same moment was confronted with such opposite possibilities, was threatened on the one hand by more melancholy disaster, and cheered on the other by more bright, yet not unreasonable hopes. The two roads are open. We are at the cross-ways. If we stand on in the old happy-go-lucky way, the richer classes ever growing in wealth and in number, and ever declining in responsibility, the very poor remaining plunged or plunging even deeper into helpless, hopeless misery, then I think there is nothing before us but savage strife between class and class, with an increasing disorganisation, with an increasing destruction of human strength and human virtue—nothing, in fact, but that dual degeneration which comes from the simultaneous waste of extreme wealth and of extreme want.

Now we have had over here lately colonial editors from all the Colonies of the British Empire, and what is the opinion which they expressed as to the worst thing they saw in the old country? The representatives of every Colony have expressed the opinion that the worst they saw here, was the extreme of poverty side by side with the extreme of luxury. Do not you think it is very impressive to find an opinion like that, expressed in all friendship and sincerity, by men of our own race who have come from lands which are so widely scattered over the surface of the earth, and are the product of such varied conditions? Is it not impressive to find that they are all agreed, coming as they do from Australia, or Canada, or South Africa, or New Zealand, that the greatest danger to the British Empire and to the British people is not to be found among the enormous fleets and armies of the European Continent, nor in the solemn problems of Hindustan; it is not the Yellow peril nor the Black peril nor any danger in the wide circuit of colonial and foreign affairs. No, it is here in our midst, close at home, close at hand in the vast growing cities of England and Scotland, and in the dwindling and cramped villages of our denuded countryside. It is there you will find the seeds of Imperial ruin and national decay—the unnatural gap between rich and poor, the divorce of the people from the land, the want of proper discipline and training in our youth, the exploitation of boy labour, the physical degeneration which seems to follow so swiftly on civilised poverty, the awful jumbles of an obsolete Poor Law, the horrid havoc of the liquor traffic, the constant insecurity in the means of subsistence and employment which breaks the heart of many a sober, hard-working man, the absence of any established minimum standard of life and comfort among the workers, and, at the other end, the swift increase of vulgar, joyless luxury—here are the enemies of Britain. Beware lest they shatter the foundations of her power.

Then look at the other side, look at the forces for good, the moral forces, the spiritual forces, the civic, the scientific, the patriotic forces which make for order and harmony and health and life. Are they not tremendous too? Do we not see them everywhere, in every town, in every class, in every creed, strong forces worthy of Old England, coming to her rescue, fighting for her soul? That is the situation in our country as I see it this afternoon—two great armies evenly matched, locked in fierce conflict with each other all along the line, swaying backwards and forwards in strife—and for my part I am confident that the right will win, that the generous influences will triumph over the selfish influences, that the organising forces will devour the forces of degeneration, and that the British people will emerge triumphant from their struggles to clear the road and lead the march amongst the foremost nations of the world.

Well, now, I want to ask you a question. I daresay there are some of you who do not like this or that particular point in the Budget, who do not like some particular argument or phrase which some of us may have used in advocating or defending it. But it is not of these details that I speak; the question I want each of you to ask himself is this: On which side of this great battle which I have described to you, does the Budget count? Can any of you, looking at it broadly and as a whole, looking on the policy which surrounds it, and which depends upon it, looking at the arguments by which it is defended, as well as the arguments by which it is opposed—can any one doubt that the Budget in its essential character and meaning, in its spirit and in its practical effect, would be a tremendous reinforcement, almost like a new army coming up at the end of the day, upon the side of all those forces and influences which are fighting for the life and health and progress of our race?

In the speeches which I have made about the country since the Budget was introduced I have explained and defended in detail the special financial proposals upon which we rely to provide the revenue for the year. You are, no doubt, generally acquainted with them. There is the increase in the income-tax of twopence, the further discrimination between earned and unearned income, and the super-tax of sixpence on incomes of over £5,000 a year. There are the increases in estate duties and in the legacy duties, and there are the new duties on stamps; there is the tax on motor-cars and petrol, the proceeds of which are to go to the improvement of the roads and the abatement of the dust nuisance; there are the taxes on working class indulgences—namely, the increase in the tax on tobacco and on whisky, which enable the working man to pay his share, as indeed he has shown himself very ready to do; there are the taxes on liquor licences, which are designed to secure for the State a certain special proportion of the monopoly value created wholly by the State and with which it should never have parted; and, lastly, there are the three taxes upon the unearned increment in land, upon undeveloped land, upon the unearned increment in the reversion of leases, and then there is the tax upon mining royalties.

Now these are the actual proposals of the Budget, and I do not think that, if I had the time, I should find any great difficulty in showing you that there are many good arguments, a great volume of sound reason, which can be adduced in support of every one of these proposals. Certainly there is no difficulty in showing that since the Budget has been introduced there has been no shock to credit, there has been no dislocation of business, there has been no setback in the beginning of that trade revival about the approach of which I spoke to you, when I was in Leicester at the beginning of the year and which there are now good reasons for believing is actually in progress. The taxes which have been proposed have not laid any burden upon the necessaries of life like bread or meat, nor have they laid any increased burden upon comforts like tea and sugar. There is nothing in these taxes which makes it harder for a labouring man to keep up his strength or for the small man of the middle class to maintain his style of living. There is nothing in these taxes which makes it more difficult for any hard-working person, whether he works with his hands or his head, to keep a home together in decent comfort. No impediment has been placed by these taxes upon enterprise; no hampering restrictions interrupt the flow of commerce. On the contrary, if the tax upon spirits should result in a diminution in the consumption of strong drink, depend upon it, the State will gain, and all classes will gain. The health of millions of people, the happiness of hundreds of thousands of homes, will be sensibly improved, and money that would have been spent upon whisky will flow into other channels, much less likely to produce evil and much more likely to produce employment. And if the tax on undeveloped land, on land, that is to say, which is kept out of the market, which is held up idly in order that its owner may reap unearned profit by the exertions and through the needs of the surrounding community, if that tax should have the effect of breaking this monopoly and of making land cheaper, a tremendous check on every form of productive activity will have been removed. All sorts of enterprises will become economically possible which are now impossible owing to the artificially high price of land, and new forces will be liberated to stimulate the wealth of the nation.

But it is not on these points that I wish to dwell this afternoon. I want to tell you about the meaning and the spirit of the Budget. Upon the Budget and upon the policy of the Budget depends a far-reaching plan of social organisation designed to give a greater measure of security to all classes, but particularly to the labouring classes. In the centre of that plan stands the policy of national insurance. The Chancellor of the Exchequer has been for more than a year at work upon this scheme, and it is proposed—I hope next year, if there is a next year—it is proposed, working through the great friendly societies, which have done so much invaluable work on these lines, to make sure that, by the aid of a substantial subvention from the State, even the poorest steady worker or the poorest family shall be enabled to make provision against sickness, against invalidity, and for the widows and orphans who may be left behind.

Side by side with this is the scheme of insurance against unemployment which I hope to have the honour of passing through Parliament next year. The details of that scheme are practically complete, and it will enable upwards of two and a quarter millions of workers in the most uncertain trades of this country—trades like ship-building, engineering, and building—to secure unemployment benefits, which in a great majority of cases will be sufficient to tide them over the season of unemployment. This scheme in its compulsory form is limited to certain great trades like those I have specified, but it will be open to other trades, to trade unions, to workers' associations of various kinds, or even to individuals to insure with the State Unemployment Insurance Office against unemployment on a voluntary basis, and to secure, through the State subvention, much better terms than it would be possible for them to obtain at the present time.

It would be impossible to work a scheme of unemployment insurance except in conjunction with some effective method of finding work and of testing willingness to work, and that can only be afforded by a national system of labour exchanges. That Bill has already passed through Parliament, and in the early months of next year we shall hope to bring it into operation by opening, all over the country, a network of labour exchanges connected with each other and with the centre by telephone. We believe this organisation may secure for labour—and, after all, labour is the only thing the great majority of people have to sell—it will secure for labour, for the first time, that free and fair market which almost all other commodities of infinitely less consequence already enjoy, and will replace the present wasteful, heartbreaking wanderings aimlessly to and fro in search of work by a scientific system; and we believe that the influence of this system in the end must tend to standardising the conditions of wages and employment throughout the country.

Lastly, in connection with unemployment I must direct your attention to the Development Bill, which is now before Parliament, the object of which is to provide a fund for the economic development of our country, for the encouragement of agriculture, for afforestation, for the colonisation of England, and for the making of roads, harbours, and other public works. And I should like to draw your attention to a very important clause in that Bill, which says that the prosecution of these works shall be regulated, as far as possible, by the conditions of the labour market, so that in a very bad year of unemployment they can be expanded, so as to increase the demand for labour at times of exceptional slackness, and thus correct and counterbalance the cruel fluctuations of the labour market. The large sums of money which will be needed for these purposes are being provided by the Budget of Mr. Lloyd-George, and will be provided in an expanding volume in the years to come through the natural growth of the taxes we are imposing.

I have hitherto been speaking of the industrial organisation of insurance schemes, labour exchanges, and economic development. Now I come to that great group of questions which are concerned with the prevention and relief of distress. We have before us the reports of the majority and minority of the Royal Commission on the Poor Law, and we see there a great and urgent body of reforms which require the attention of Parliament. The first and most costly step in the relief of distress has already been taken by the Old-Age Pensions Act, supplemented, as it will be if the Budget passes, by the removal of the pauper disqualification. By that Act we have rescued the aged from the Poor Law. We have yet to rescue the children; we have yet to distinguish effectively between the *bonâ fide* unemployed workman and the mere loafer and vagrant; we have yet to transfer the sick, the inebriate, the feeble-minded and the totally demoralised to authorities specially concerned in their management and care.

But what I want to show you, if I have made my argument clear, is that all these schemes—which I can do little more than mention this afternoon, each one of which is important—are connected one with the other, fit into one another at many points, that they are part of a concerted and interdependent system for giving a better, fairer social organisation to the masses of our fellow-countrymen. Unemployment insurance, which will help to tide a workman over a bad period, is intimately and necessarily associated with the labour exchanges which will help to find him work and which will test his willingness to work. This, again, will be affected by the workings of the Development Bill, which, as I told you, we trust may act as a counterpoise to the rocking of the industrial boat and give a greater measure of stability to the labour market.

The fact that everybody in the country, man and woman alike, will be entitled, with scarcely any exception, to an old-age pension from the State at the age of seventy—that fact makes it ever so much cheaper to insure against invalidity or infirmity up to the age of seventy. And, with the various insurance schemes which are in preparation, we ought to be able to set up a complete ladder, an unbroken bridge or causeway, as it were, along which the whole body of the people may move with a certain assured measure of security and safety against hazards and misfortunes. Then, if provision can be arranged for widows and orphans who are left behind, that will be a powerful remedy against the sweating evil; for, as you know, these helpless people, who in every country find employment in particular trades, are unable to make any fair bargain for themselves, and their labour, and this consequently leads to the great evils which have very often been brought to the notice of Parliament. That, again, will fit in with the Anti-Sweating Bill we are passing through Parliament this year.

Now, I want you to see what a large, coherent plan we are trying to work out, and I want you to believe that the object of the plan and the results of it will be to make us a stronger as well as a happier nation. I was reading the other day some of the speeches made by Bismarck—a man who, perhaps more than any other, built up in his own lifetime the strength of a great nation—speeches which he made during the time when he was introducing into Germany those vast insurance schemes, now deemed by all classes and parties in Germany to be of the utmost consequence and value. "I should like to see the State" (said Prince Bismarck in 1881), "which for the most part consists of Christians, penetrated to some extent by the principles of the religion which it professes, especially as concerns the help one gives to his neighbour, and sympathy with the lot of old and suffering people." Then, again, in the year 1884 he said: "The whole matter centres in the question, 'Is it the duty of the State or is it not to provide for its helpless citizens?' I maintain that it is its duty, that it is the duty, not only of the 'Christian' State, as I ventured once to call it when speaking of 'Practical Christianity,' but of every State."

There are a great many people who will tell you that such a policy, as I have been endeavouring to outline to you this afternoon, will not make our country stronger, because it will sap the self-reliance of the working classes. It is very easy for rich people to preach the virtues of self-reliance to the poor. It is also very foolish, because, as a matter of fact, the wealthy, so far from being self-reliant, are dependent on the constant attention of scores, and sometimes even hundreds, of persons who are employed in waiting upon them and ministering to their wants. I think you will agree with me, on the other hand—knowing what you do of the life of this city and of the working classes generally—that there are often trials and misfortunes which come upon working-class families quite beyond any provision which their utmost unaided industry and courage could secure for them. Left to themselves, left absolutely to themselves, they must be smashed to pieces, if any exceptional disaster or accident, like recurring sickness, like the death or incapacity of the breadwinner, or prolonged or protracted unemployment, fall upon them.

There is no chance of making people self-reliant by confronting them with problems and with trials beyond their capacity to surmount. You do not make a man self-reliant by crushing him under a steam roller. Nothing in our plans will relieve people from the need of making every exertion to help themselves, but, on the contrary, we consider that we shall greatly stimulate their efforts by giving them for the first time a practical assurance that those efforts will be crowned with success.

I have now tried to show you that the Budget, and the policy of the Budget, is the first conscious attempt on the part of the State to build up a better and a more scientific organisation of society for the workers of this country, and it will be for you to say—at no very distant date—whether all this effort for a coherent scheme of social reconstruction is to be swept away into the region of lost endeavour.

That is the main aspect of the Budget to which I wish to draw your attention. But there is another significance of the highest importance which attaches to the Budget. I mean the new attitude of the State towards wealth. Formerly the only question of the tax-gatherer was, "How much have you got?" We ask that question still, and there is a general feeling, recognised as just by all parties, that the rate of taxation should be greater for large incomes than for small. As to how much greater, parties are no doubt in dispute. But now a new question has arisen. We do not only ask to-day, "How much have you got?" we also ask, "How did you get it? Did you earn it by yourself, or has it just been left you by others? Was it gained by processes which are in themselves beneficial to the community in general, or was it gained by processes which have done no good to any one, but only harm? Was it gained by the enterprise and capacity necessary to found a business, or merely by squeezing and bleeding the owner and founder of the business? Was it gained by supplying the capital which industry needs, or by denying, except at an extortionate price, the land which industry requires? Was it derived from active reproductive processes, or merely by squatting on some piece of necessary land till enterprise and labour, and national interests and municipal interests, had to buy you out at fifty times the agricultural value? Was it gained from opening new minerals to the service of man, or by drawing a mining royalty from the toil and adventure of others? Was it gained by the curious process of using political influence to convert an annual licence into a practical freehold and thereby pocketing a monopoly value which properly belongs to the State—how did you get it?" That is the new question which has been postulated and which is vibrating in penetrating repetition through the land.[1]

It is a tremendous question, never previously in this country asked so plainly, a new idea, pregnant, formidable, full of life, that taxation should not only have regard to the volume of wealth, but, so far as possible, to the character of the processes of its origin. I do not wonder it has raised a great stir. I do not wonder that there are heart-searchings and angry words because that simple question, that modest proposal, which we see embodied in the new income-tax provisions, in the land taxes, in the licence duties, and in the tax on mining royalties—that modest proposal means, and can only mean, the refusal of the modern State to bow down unquestioningly before the authority of wealth. This refusal to treat all forms of wealth with equal deference, no matter what may have been the process by which it was acquired, is a strenuous assertion in a practical form, that there ought to be a constant relation between acquired wealth and useful service previously rendered, and that where no service, but rather disservice, is proved, then, whenever possible, the State should make a sensible difference in the taxes it is bound to impose.

It is well that you should keep these issues clearly before you during the weeks in which we seem to be marching towards a grave constitutional crisis. But I should like to tell you that a general election, consequent upon the rejection of the Budget by the Lords, would not, ought not to be, and could not be fought upon the Budget alone. "Budgets come," as the late Lord Salisbury said in 1894—"Budgets come and Budgets go." Every Government frames its own expenditure for each year; every Government has to make its own provision to meet that expenditure. There is a Budget every year, and memorable as the Budget of my right hon. friend may be, far-reaching as is the policy depending upon it, the Finance Bill, after all, is in its character only an annual affair. But the rejection of the Budget by the House of Lords would not be an annual affair. It would be a violent rupture of constitutional custom and usage extending over three hundred years and recognised during all that time by the leaders of every Party in the State. It would involve a sharp and sensible breach with the traditions of the past; and what does the House of Lords depend upon if not upon the traditions of the past? It would amount to an attempt at revolution not by the poor, but by the rich; not by the masses, but by the privileged few; not in the name of progress, but in that of reaction; not for the purpose of broadening the framework of the State, but of greatly narrowing it. Such an attempt, whatever you may think of it, would be historic in its

---

[1] We do not, of course, ask it of the individual taxpayer. That would be an impossible inquisition. But the House of Commons asks itself when it has to choose between taxes on various forms of wealth, "By what process was it got?"

character, and the result of the battle fought upon it, whoever wins, must inevitably be not of an annual, but of a permanent and final character. The result of such an election must mean an alteration of the veto of the House of Lords; if they win they will have asserted their right, not merely to reject legislation of the House of Commons, but to control the finances of the country, and if they lose, we will deal with their veto once and for all.

We do not seek the struggle, we have our work to do; but if it is to come, it could never come better than now. Never again perhaps, certainly not for many years, will such an opportunity be presented to the British democracy. Never will the ground be more favourable; never will the issues be more clearly or more vividly defined. Those issues will be whether the new taxation, which is admitted on all sides to be necessary, shall be imposed upon luxuries, superfluities, and monopolies, or upon the prime necessaries of life; whether you shall put your tax upon the unearned increment on land or upon the daily bread of labour; whether the policy of constructive social reform on which we are embarked, and which expands and deepens as we advance, shall be carried through and given a fair chance, or whether it shall be brought to a dead stop and all the energies and attention of the State devoted to Jingo armaments and senseless foreign adventure. And, lastly, the issue will be whether the British people in the year of grace 1909 are going to be ruled through a representative Assembly, elected by six or seven millions of voters, about which almost every one in the country, man or woman, has a chance of being consulted, or whether they are going to allow themselves to be dictated to and domineered over by a minute minority of titled persons, who represent nobody, who are answerable to nobody, and who only scurry up to London to vote in their party interests, in their class interests, and in their own interests.

These will be the issues, and I am content that the responsibility for such a struggle, if it should come, should rest with the House of Lords themselves. But if it is to come, we shall not complain, we shall not draw back from it. We will engage in it with all our hearts and with all our might, it being always clearly understood that the fight will be a fight to the finish, and that the fullest forfeits, which are in accordance with the national welfare, shall be exacted from the defeated foe.

THE BUDGET AND PROPERTY

ABERNETHY, *OCTOBER 7, 1909*

(Originally published in *The Daily Telegraph*)

*T*his is a very fine gathering for a lonely glen, and it augurs well for the spirit of Liberalism. Much will be expected of Scotland in the near future. She will be invited to pronounce upon some of the largest and most complicated questions of politics and finance that can possibly engage the attention of thoughtful citizens, and her decision will perhaps govern events.

There is one contrast between Parties which springs to the eye at once. One Party has a policy, detailed, definite, declared, actually in being. The other Party has no policy. The Conservative Party has no policy which it can put before the country at the present time on any of the great controverted questions of the day. On most of the previous occasions when we have approached a great trial of strength, the Conservative Party have had a policy of their own which they could state in clear terms. You would naturally expect some reticence or reserve from the head of a Government responsible for the day-to-day administration of affairs. But what do you see at the present time? Mr. Asquith speaks out boldly and plainly on all the great questions which are being debated, and it is the Leader of the Opposition who has to take refuge in a tactical and evasive attitude. Why, Mr. Balfour is unable to answer the simplest questions. At Birmingham, the Prime Minister asked him in so many words: What alternative did he propose to the Budget? What did he mean by Tariff Reform? and what was his counsel to the House of Lords?

It would not be difficult to frame an answer to all these questions. Mr. Chamberlain, for instance, was quite ready with his answers to all of them.

At Glasgow in 1903 he stated what his Budget would have been, and he explained precisely what he meant by Tariff Reform. At Birmingham last month he was equally clear in urging the Lords to reject the Budget. There is no doubt whatever where Mr. Chamberlain and those who agree with him stand to-day. They would raise the extra taxation which is required, by protective import duties on bread, on meat, on butter, cheese, and eggs, and upon foreign imported manufactured articles; and in order to substitute their plan for ours they are prepared to urge the House of Lords to smash up the Budget and to smash up as much of the British Constitution and the British financial system as may be necessary for the purpose.

That is their policy; but, after all, it is Mr. Balfour who is the leader of the Conservative Party. He is the statesman who would have to form and carry on any administration which might be formed from that Party, and he will not state his policy upon any of the dominant questions of the day. Why will he not answer these simple questions? He is the leader, and it is because he wishes to remain the leader that he observes this discreet silence. He tells us he is in favour of Tariff Reform, he loves Tariff Reform, he worships Tariff Reform. He feels that it is by Tariff Reform alone that the civilisation of Great Britain can be secured, and the unity of the Empire achieved; but nothing will induce him to say what he means by Tariff Reform. That is a secret which remains locked in his own breast. He condemns our Budget, he clamours for greater expenditure, and yet he puts forward no alternative proposals by which the void in the public finances may be made good. And as for his opinion about the House of Lords, he dare not state his true opinion to-day upon that subject. I do not say that there are not good reasons for Mr. Balfour's caution. It sometimes happens that the politics of a Party become involved in such a queer and awkward tangle that only a choice of evils is at the disposal of its leader; and when the leader has to choose between sliding into a bog on the one hand and jumping over a precipice on the other, some measure of indulgence may be extended to him if he prefers to go on marking time, and indicating the direction in which his followers are to advance by a vague general gesture towards the distant horizon.

Whatever you may think about politics, you must at least, in justice to his Majesty's Government, recognise that their position is perfectly plain and clear. Some of you may say to me, "Your course, your policy may be clear enough, but you are burdening wealth too heavily by your taxes and by your speeches." Those shocking speeches! "You are driving capital out of the country." Let us look at these points one at a time. The capital wealth of Britain is increasing rapidly. Sir Robert Giffen estimated some years ago that the addition to the capital wealth of the nation was at least between two hundred and three hundred millions a year. I notice that the paid-up capital of registered companies alone, which was 1,013 millions sterling in 1893, has grown naturally and healthily to 2,123 millions sterling in 1908. And, most remarkable of all, the figures I shall submit to you, the gross amount of income which comes under the view of the Treasury Commissioners who are charged with the collection of income-tax, was in the year 1898-9 762 millions, and it had risen from that figure to 980 millions sterling in the year 1908-9: that is to say, that it had risen by 218 millions in the course of ten years.

From this, of course, a deduction has to be made for more efficient methods of collection. This cannot be estimated exactly; but it certainly accounts for much less than half the increase. Let us assume that it is a half. The increase is therefore 109 millions. I only wish that wages had increased in the same proportion. When I was studying those figures I have mentioned to you I looked at the Board of Trade returns of wages. Those returns deal with the affairs of upwards of ten millions of persons, and in the last ten years the increase in the annual wages of that great body of persons has only been about ten million pounds: that is to say, that the increase of income assessable to income-tax is at the very least more than ten times greater than the increase which has taken place in the same period in the wages of those trades which come within the Board of Trade returns.

When we come to the question of how burdens are to be distributed, you must bear these facts and figures in mind, because the choice is severely limited. You can tax wealth or you can tax wages—that is the whole choice which is at the disposal of the Chancellor of the Exchequer. Of course I know there are some people who say you can tax the foreigner—but I am quite sure that you will not expect me to waste your time in dealing with that gospel of quacks and creed of gulls. The choice is between wealth and wages, and we think that, in view of that great increase in accumulated wealth which has marked the last ten years, and is the feature of our modern life, it is not excessive or unreasonable at the present stage in our national finances to ask for a further contribution from the direct taxpayers of something under eight millions a year. That is the total of all the new taxes on wealth which our Budget imposes, and it is about equal to the cost of four of those *Dreadnoughts* for which these same classes were clamouring a few months ago. And it is less than one-thirteenth of the increased income assessable to income-tax in the last ten years.

It is because we have done this that we are the object of all this abuse and indignation which is so loudly expressed in certain quarters throughout the country at the present time. While the working-classes have borne the extra taxation upon their tobacco and whisky in silence, all this rage and fury is outpoured upon the Government by the owners of this ever-increasing fund of wealth, and we are denounced as Socialists, as Jacobins, as Anarchists, as Communists, and all the rest of the half-understood vocabulary of irritated ignorance, for having dared to go to the wealthy classes for a fair share of the necessary burdens of the country. How easy it would be for us to escape from all this abuse if we were to put the extra taxation entirely upon the wages of the working classes by means of taxes on bread and on meat. In a moment the scene would change, and we should be hailed as patriotic, far-sighted Empire-builders, loyal and noble-hearted citizens worthy of the Motherland, and sagacious statesmen versed in the science of government. See, now, upon what insecure and doubtful foundations human praise and human censure stand.

Well, then, it is said your taxes fall too heavily upon the agricultural landowner and the country gentleman. Now, there is no grosser misrepresentation of the Budget than that it hits the agricultural landowner, and I think few greater disservices can be done to the agricultural landowner, whose property has in the last thirty years in many cases declined in value, than to confuse him with the ground landlord in a great city, who has netted enormous sums through the growth and the needs of the population of the city. None of the new land taxes touch agricultural land, while it remains agricultural land. No cost of the system of valuation which we are going to carry into effect will fall at all upon the individual owner of landed property. He will not be burdened in any way by these proposals. On the contrary, now that an amendment has been accepted permitting death duties to be paid in land in certain circumstances, the owner of a landed estate, instead of encumbering his estate by raising the money to pay off the death duties, can cut a portion from his estate; and this in many cases will be a sensible relief. Secondly, we have given to agricultural landowners a substantial concession in regard to the deductions which they are permitted to make from income-tax assessment on account of the money which they spend as good landlords upon the upkeep of their properties, and we have raised the limit of deduction from 12 1/2 per cent. to 25 per cent. Thirdly, there is the Development Bill—that flagrant Socialistic measure which passed a second reading in the House of Lords unanimously—which will help all the countryside and all classes of agriculturists, and which will help the landlord in the country among the rest. So much for that charge.

Then it is said, "At any rate you cannot deny that the Budget is driving capital out of the country." I should like to point out to you that before the Budget was introduced, we were told that it was Free Trade that was driving capital out of the country. Let that pass. It is said we cannot deny that the Budget is driving capital out of the country. I deny it absolutely. To begin with, it is impossible to drive the greater part of our capital out of this country, for what is the capital of the country? The greatest part of that capital is the land, the state of cultivation which exists, the roads, the railways, the mines, the mills—this is the greatest part of the capital. The owners of that capital might conceivably, if they thought fit, depart from the country, but their possessions would remain behind.

I shall be asked, What about all this foreign investment that is going on? Is not British credit now being diverted abroad to foreign countries, to the detriment of our own country? Is not British capital fleeing from The Socialistic speeches of the Chancellor of the Exchequer, and the President of the Board of Trade, and taking refuge in Germany, where of course there are no Socialists, or in other countries, where there is never any disturbance, like France, or Spain, or Russia, or Turkey? Now let us look into that. There are only two ways in which capital can leave this country for foreign investments. It is no good sending bits of paper to the foreigner and expecting him to pay a dividend in return. There are only two ways—one is by exports made by British labour, and the other by bullion. Now, if the exports were to increase, surely that should be a cause of rejoicing, especially to our Tariff Reformers, who regard the increase in exports as the index of national prosperity. As for the second— the export of bullion—would you believe it, it is only a coincidence, but it is an amusing coincidence, there are actually six million pounds' worth more gold in the country now, than there were at the beginning of the year before the Budget was introduced. The active and profitable investment abroad which has marked the last two or three years, which is bound to swell the exports of the next few years, has not been attended by any starvation of home industry. On the contrary, the amount of money forthcoming for the development of new industries and now enterprises in this country during the last two or three years has compared very favourably with the years which immediately preceded them, when the Conservative Government was in power.

Property in Great Britain is secure. It would be a great mistake to suppose that that security depends upon the House of Lords. If the security of property in a powerful nation like our own were dependent upon the action or inaction of 500 or 600 persons, that security would long ago have been swept away. The security of property depends upon its wide diffusion among great numbers and all classes of the population, and it becomes more secure year by year because it is gradually being more widely distributed. The vital processes of civilisation require, and the combined interests of millions guarantee, the security of property. A society in which property was insecure would speedily degenerate into barbarism; a society in which property was absolutely secure, irrespective of all conceptions of justice in regard to the manner of its acquisition, would degenerate, not to barbarism, but death. No one claims that a Government should from time to time, according to its conceptions of justice, attempt fundamentally to recast the bases on which property is erected. The process must be a gradual one; must be a social and a moral process, working steadily in the mind and in the body of the community; but we contend, when new burdens have to be apportioned, when new revenues have to be procured, when the necessary upkeep of the State requires further taxes to be imposed—we contend that, in distributing the new burdens, a Government should have regard first of all to ability to pay and, secondly, that they should have regard to some extent, and so far as is practicable, to the means and the process by which different forms of wealth have been acquired; and that they should make a sensible difference between wealth which is the fruit of productive enterprise and industry or of individual skill, and wealth which represents the capture by individuals of socially created values. We say that ought to be taken into consideration. We are taking it into consideration now by the difference we have made in the income-tax between earned and unearned incomes, by the difference we make between the taxation which is imposed upon a fortune which a man makes himself and the fortune which he obtains from a relative or a stranger. We are taking it into consideration in our tax on mining royalties, in our licence duties and in our taxes on the unearned increment in land. The State, we contend, has a special claim upon the monopoly value of the liquor licence, which the State itself has created, and which the State itself maintains from year to year by its sole authority. If that claim has not previously been made good, that is only because the liquor interest have had the power, by using one branch of the Legislature, to keep the nation out of its rights. All the more reason to make our claim good now.

Again we say that the unearned increment in land is reaped in proportion to the disservice done to the community, is a mere toll levied upon the community, is an actual burden and imposition upon them, and an appropriation by an individual, under existing law, no doubt, of socially created wealth. For the principle of a special charge being levied on this class of wealth we can cite economic authority as high us Adam Smith, and political authority as respectable as Lord Rosebery; and for its application we need not merely cite authority, but we can point to the successful practice of great civilised neighbouring States.

Is it really the contention of the Conservative Party that the State is bound to view all processes of wealth-getting with an equal eye, provided they do not come under the criminal codes? Is that their contention? Are we really to be bound to impose the same burden upon the hardly won income of the professional man and the extraordinary profits of the land monopolist? Are we really to recognise the liquor licence which the State created, which the law says is for one year only—as if it were as much the brewers' or the publicans' property *for ever* as the coat on his back? No; it is absurd. Of the waste and sorrow and ruin which are caused by the liquor traffic, of the injury to national health and national wealth which follows from it, which attends its ill-omened footsteps, I say nothing more in my argument this afternoon. The State is entitled to reclaim its own, and they shall at least render unto Cæsar the things which are Cæsar's.

The money must be found, and we hold that Parliament, in imposing the inevitable taxes, is entitled not only to lay a heavier proportionate burden upon the rich than on the poor, but also to lay a special burden upon certain forms of wealth which are clearly social in their origin, and have not at any point been derived from a useful or productive process on the part of their possessors. But it may be said, "Your plans include other expenditure besides the Navy and Old-age Pensions. What about Insurance, Labour Exchanges, and economic development?" Those objects, at least, it may be urged are not inevitable or indispensable. It is quite true that the taxation which we seek to impose this year, and which is sufficient, and only sufficient for the needs of this year, will yield more abundant revenues in future years, and if at the same time a reduction in the expenditure on armaments becomes possible, we shall have substantial revenues at our disposal. That is perfectly true, but is that a reason for condemning the Budget? When we see on every hand great nations which cannot pay their way, which have to borrow merely to carry on from year to year, when we see how sterile and unproductive all the dodges and devices of their protective tariffs have become, when we remember how often we have ourselves been told that under Free Trade no more revenue could be got, is it not a welcome change for our country, and for our Free Trade policy, to find our opponents complaining of the expansive nature of a Free Trade revenue? I don't wonder that Tory Protectionists have passed a resolution at Birmingham declaring that the Budget will indefinitely postpone—that was the phrase—the scheme of Tariff Reform.

And upon what objects and policies do we propose to spend the extra revenue which this Budget will unquestionably yield in future years? People talk vaguely of the stability of society, of the strength of the Empire, of the permanence of a Christian civilisation. On what foundation do they seek to build? There is only one foundation—a healthy family life for all. If large classes of the population live under conditions which make it difficult if not impossible for them to keep a home together in decent comfort, if the children are habitually underfed, if the housewife is habitually over-strained, if the bread-winner is under-employed or under-paid, if all are unprotected and uninsured against the common hazards of modern industrial life, if sickness, accident, infirmity, or old age, or unchecked intemperance, or any other curse or affliction, break up the home, as they break up thousands of homes, and scatter the family, as they scatter thousands of families in our land, it is not merely the waste of earning-power or the dispersal of a few poor sticks of furniture, it is the stamina, the virtue, safety, and honour of the British race that are being squandered.

Now the object of every single constructive proposal to which the revenues raised by this Budget will be devoted, not less than the object of the distribution of the taxes which make up the Budget, is to buttress and fortify the homes of the people. That is our aim; to that task we have bent our backs; and in that labour we shall not be daunted by the machine-made abuse of partisans or by the nervous clamour of selfish riches. Whatever power may be given to us shall be used for this object. It is for you to say whether power will be given us to prevail.

But they say, "This uncertainty about the Budget is causing unemployment; you are aggravating the evils you seek to remedy." The Budget has not increased unemployment. Unemployment is severe in the country this year, but it is less severe this year than it was last, and it is less severe since the Budget was introduced than before it was introduced. The proportion of trade unionists reported to be unemployed in the Board of Trade returns at the end of September was 7.4 per cent., and that is lower than any month since May 1908, and it compares very favourably with September of last year, when the proportion was not 7.4, but 9.3 per cent.

I can well believe that the uncertainty as to whether the House of Lords will, in a desperate attempt to escape their fair share of public burdens, plunge the country into revolution and its finances into chaos—I can well believe that that uncertainty is bad for trade and employment, and is hampering the revival which is beginning all over the country. I do not doubt that all this talk of the rejection of the Budget is injurious to business, to credit, and to enterprise; but who is to blame for that? When did we ever hear of a Budget being rejected by the Lords before? When did we ever hear of a leader of the House of Lords proposing, like Lord Lansdowne, to decide whether he would tear up the British Constitution after consultation with the leaders of the drink trade? The uncertainty is not due to our action, but to their threats. Our action has been regular, constitutional, and necessary. Their threats are violent, unprecedented, and outrageous. Let them cease their threats. Let one of their leaders—let Mr. Balfour, for instance, say this year what he said last year, in the month of October, at Dumfries. Let him say, "It is the House of Commons and not the House of Lords which settles uncontrolled our financial system." Let him repeat these words, and all uncertainty about the Budget will be over.

I am amazed and I am amused when I read in the newspapers the silly and fantastic rumours which obtain credence, or at any rate currency, from day to day. One day we are told that it is the intention of the Government to seek a dissolution of Parliament before the Budget reaches the House of Lords—in other words, to kill the child to save its life. The next day we are told the Government have decided to have a referendum—that is to say, they will ask everybody in the country to send them a postcard to say whether they would like the Budget to become law or not. Another day we are told that the Government are contemplating a bargain with the House of Lords to alter the Budget to please them, or that we should make a bargain with them that if they pass the Budget we should seek a dissolution in January. Why should we make a bargain with the House of Lords? Every one of those rumours is more silly, more idiotic, than the other. I wish our Conservative friends would face the facts of the situation. "Things are what they are, and their consequences will be what they will be." The House of Lords has no scrap of right to interfere in finance. If they do, they violate the Constitution, they shatter the finances, and they create an administrative breakdown the outcome of which no man can foresee. If such a situation should occur a Liberal Government can look only to the people. We count on you, and we shall come to you. If you sustain us we shall take effectual steps to prevent such a deadlock ever occurring again. That is the whole policy of his Majesty's Government—blunt, sober, obvious, and unflinching.

THE CONSTITUTIONAL MENACE

NATIONAL LIBERAL CLUB, *OCTOBER 9, 1909*

(Originally published in *The Times*)

I have never been able to rank myself among those who believe that the Budget will be rejected by the House of Lords. It is not that I take an exaggerated view of the respect which that body would bear to the constitutional tradition upon which alone they depend. It is not that I underrate at all the feelings of personal resentment and of class-prejudice with which they regard, naturally, many of the provisions of the Budget. But I have a difficulty in believing that the responsible statesmen by whom they are led, and by whom we think they are controlled, would not hesitate as patriotic men before they plunged the finances of the country into what would be a largely irremediable confusion. And still more I find it difficult to believe that Party leaders, anxious no doubt for office on the most secure terms and at the shortest notice, would voluntarily run unusual risks in order to be able to fight a decisive battle upon exceptionally unfavourable ground. In common with most of us who are here to-night, I hold that the rejection of the Budget by the House of Lords would be a constitutional outrage. I do not think we are entitled at this stage to assume that such an outrage will be committed. We cannot credit such intentions, even though we read them every day brutally and blatantly affirmed by a powerful Party Press. We do not credit such intentions. We are, however, bound to be fully prepared against all contingencies. The necessary precautions must be taken. The fighting machine must undergo all those preliminary processes necessary for a rapid and efficient mobilisation. And the ground on which a great battle might take place, the theatre of war, must be scanned beforehand with military foresight. And that is being done.

But those who lightly estimate the crisis which will follow the rejection of the Budget by the House of Lords must be either strangely unimaginative or else they must be strangely ignorant of British history and of the British Constitution. The control of finance by the representative Assembly is the keystone of all that constitutional fabric upon which and within which all of us here have dwelt safely and peacefully throughout our lives. It is by the application of the power of the purse, and by the application of the power of the purse almost alone, that we have moved forward, slowly and prosaically, no doubt, during the last two hundred years, but without any violent overturn such as has rent the life and history of almost every other considerable country, from a kind of mediæval oligarchy to a vast modern democratic State based on the suffrages of six million or seven million electors, loyal to the Crown, and clothed with all the stately forms of the venerable English monarchy. Finance has been the keystone. Take finance away from the House of Commons, take the complete control of financial business away from the representative Assembly, and our whole system of government, be it good, bad, or indifferent, will crumble to pieces like a house of cards.

The rejection of the Budget by the House of Lords would not merely be a question of stopping a money Bill or of knocking out a few taxes obnoxious to particular classes; the rejection of the Budget by the House of Lords would mean the claim of the House of Lords—that is, the claim of a non-elective and unrepresentative Chamber—to make and to unmake Governments; and a recognition of that claim by the country would unquestionably mean that the House of Lords would become the main source and origin of all political power under the Crown. Now that is a great quarrel; that is a quarrel on which we had hoped, on which we had been taught, that the sword had been sheathed victoriously for ever. And that is the issue that is before us now. We do not intend to soften it in any way. The responsibility for the consequences must rest with the aggressor who first violates the constitutional tradition of our land.

The Budget is through Committee. We have had not merely an exhaustive but an exhausting discussion. I am told by ingenious calculators in the newspapers that over six hundred hours, from some of which I confess I have been absent, of debate have been accorded to the Committee stage. No guillotine closure has been applied. Full, free, unfettered debate has been accorded—has been accorded with a patience and with a generosity unprecedented in Parliamentary annals, and which in effect has left a minority not merely satisfied in all the conditions of reasonable debate, but unable even on grounds of the most meticulous partisanship to complain that the fullest opportunity has not been accorded to them. In all this long process of six hundred hours and upwards we have shown ourselves willing to make concessions. They are boasting to-day that they, forsooth, are in part the authors of the Budget. Every effort has been made to meet honest and outspoken difference; every effort has been made to gather for this Budget—the people's Budget, as they know full well it is—the greatest measure of support not only among the labouring classes, but among all classes in our vast and complicated community.

It has been a terrible strain. Lord Rosebery the other day at Glasgow paid his tribute to the gallant band who had fought in opposition to the Budget. Had he no word for his old friends? Had he no word for those who were once proud to follow him, and who now use in regard to him only the language of regret? Had he no word for that other gallant band, twice as numerous, often three times as numerous, as the Tory Opposition, who have sat through all these months—fine speakers silent through self-suppression for the cause, wealthy men sitting up to unreasonable hours to pass taxes by which they are mulcted as much as any Tory? Men who have gone on even at the cost of their lives—had he no word for them? We to-night gathered together here in the National Liberal Club have a word and a cheer for the private members of the Liberal Party in the House of Commons who have fought this battle through with unequalled loyalty and firmness, and who have shown a development of Parliamentary power to carry a great measure which I venture to say has no counterpart in the Parliamentary history of this country.

Well, that long process of debate, of argument, of concession, of compromise, of conciliation will very soon come to an end. When the Budget leaves the House of Commons the time of discussion, so far as we are concerned, will have come to an end. It will leave the House of Commons in a final form, and no amendment by the House of Lords will be entertained by us. I have heard it often said, and I have read it more often still, that there are some members of the Cabinet who want to see the Budget rejected, and I have even been shocked to find myself mentioned as one of these Machiavellian intriguers. To those who say we want to see the Budget rejected I reply, That is not true. As Party men we cannot be blind to the great tactical advantages which such an event would confer upon us. We cannot pretend that our feelings in such an event would be feelings of melancholy; but we have our work to do. Politics is not a game. It is an earnest business. We have our work to do. We have large, complex schemes of social organisation and financial reform on which we have consumed our efforts, and which we desire to see, at the shortest possible date, brought to conception and maturity. We do not want to see the finances of the country plunged into inextricable confusion, and hideous loss inflicted on the mass of the people and the taxpayers. For my part, I say without hesitation I do not at all wish to see British politics enter upon a violent, storm-shaken, and revolutionary phase. I am glad, at any rate, if they are to enter upon that phase, it shall be on the responsibility of others.

Our intentions are straightforward. We seek no conflict; we fear no conflict. We shall make no overtures to the House of Lords; we shall accept no compromise. We are not called upon to offer them any dignified means of escape from a situation into which they have been betrayed by the recklessness of some of their supporters. They have no right whatever to interfere in financial business directly or indirectly at any time. That is all we have to say, and for the rest we have a powerful organisation, we have a united Party, we have a resolute Prime Minister, we have a splendid cause.

I do not think we need at this stage speculate upon the result of a battle which has not yet been, and which may never be at this juncture fought. I have seen enough of the ups and downs of real war to know how foolish forecasts of that character often are. But when an army has been brought into the field in the best condition, in the largest possible numbers, in a spirit of the highest enthusiasm, at the most favourable season, and on the best possible ground—then I think, when our army has been brought into that situation, we can afford to await the supreme arbitrament with a cool and serene composure; and this mood of composure and of calmness may ripen into a kind of joyous and warlike heartiness, if we can also feel that the cause for which we are fighting is broadly and grandly a true and righteous cause.

Error, of course, there is always in all human affairs—error of conception, error of statement, error of manner, error of weakness, error of partisanship. We do not deny that, but strip both the great political Parties which to-day present themselves before the people of Britain, strip them of their error, strip them of that admixture of error which cloys and clogs all human action, divest them of the trappings of combat in which they are apparelled, let them be nakedly and faithfully revealed. If that were done, cannot we feel soberly and assuredly convinced that, on the main contested issues of the day, upon the need of social organisation, upon the relations between the two Houses of Parliament, upon the regulation and control of the liquor traffic, upon a national settlement with Ireland as we have made with Africa, upon Free Trade, upon the land—upon all of them separately, still more upon all of them together, if we ask ourselves in our most silent and reflective mood alone—cannot we feel a sober conviction that, on the whole, we hold the larger truth?

www.ingramcontent.com/pod-product-compliance
Lightning Source LLC
Chambersburg PA
CBHW031511040426
42445CB00009B/181